JOB ONE 2.0

Understanding the Next Generation of Student Affairs Professionals

---

SECOND EDITION

Edited by

Peter M. Magolda and Jill Ellen Carnaghi

University Press of America,® Inc.
Lanham · Boulder · New York · Toronto · Plymouth, UK

Dedication

To Our Parents

In memory of Charlie and Ann Magolda

In honor of Ang and Jeannine Carnaghi

Our first educators, coaches, and role models

—Peter and Jill

Contents

Unit III

Acknowledgements

Job One 2.0: Understanding the Next Generation of New Professionals in Student Affairs is possible because of the encouragement and enthusiasm of many individuals. Chief among them are the new professionals, in particular the ten individuals—Craig Berger, Shamika Johnson, Carrie Miller, Sarah O'Connell, Molly Pierson, Kimberly Rutledge, DuJuan Smith, David Stanfield, Sarah Steward, and Shiloh Venable—who trusted us enough to say, *"Yes, this sounds interesting"* and signed on to share their professional journeys in very personal ways. Their narratives make unique scholarly contributions to the profession.

We also are indebted to the contributors *of Job One: Experiences of New Professionals in Student Affairs* (Magolda & Carnaghi, 2004): Rozana Carducci, Kathleen Gardner, Molly Reas Hall, Diana Jaramillo, Christana Johnson, Stephanie Kurtzman, Deborah McCarthy, Kevin Piskadlo, Will Simpkins, and Craig Woodsmall. We were thrilled to learn that over eight years later all remain in student affairs, serving students and their campuses in increasingly significant and far-reaching ways. Nine of the ten were able to contribute to *Job One 2.0*, and we greatly appreciate their willingness to interpret new professionals' stories and support them as well as the collegians they serve.

Special thanks to Jen-chien Yu for her Internet information literacy talents; the outstanding resources contained in the appendix would not be possible if not for her efforts. Katie Shoemaker wrote discussion questions for each of the ten new professional chapters. Katie's efforts helped us achieve our aim of continuing the conversations that the new professionals initiated. Celia Ellison copyedited the entire manuscript, which enhanced it exponentially. Susan Gubelman provided final publication assistance. Finally we are indebted to Sarah O'Connell, who wrote the questions at the conclusion of the three cross-case analysis chapters and served as our extraordinary editorial associate throughout this project.

A theme that permeates nearly all of the new professionals' stories is the importance of colleagues who provided ongoing personal and professional support. Our colleagues at Washington University in St. Louis, Miami University, and ACPA–College Student Educators International made contributions too numerous to mention. In particular, we thank ACPA's Denise Collins, Vernon Wall, and Gregory Roberts for their encouragement to undertake this project. We also honor the memory of Donna Bourassa, who shepherded the publication of *Job One*. Had it not been for Donna's leadership in 2000, neither *Job One* nor *Job One 2.0* would exist.

Jill is most appreciative of the support of students, student leaders, staff and faculty, and, in particular, Sandy Graham. These folks continually keep her thinking and focused on providing the best possible experience for the undergraduate student population at Washington U. and beyond. On the home front, thank you Paul, Sarah, and Michael for your love and support "to do my best." And selfishly with Sarah and Michael headed to college all too soon, she wants the best and brightest student affairs educators to guide and support each on the next leg of their journeys.

Miami University's School of Education, Health, and Society granted Peter a sabbatical to allow him time to devote his energy to this scholarly project. Peter recognizes and appreciates the support of his faculty colleagues in the Student Affairs in Higher Education program, who assumed many of his responsibilities during his absence. Special and heartfelt thanks to Marcia Baxter Magolda for her gracious and unvarnished feedback as well as her unswerving personal and professional support.

Over the past three decades, our interactions with hundreds of graduate students and new professionals in student affairs have provided us insights and information we simply could not have gained if left to our own devices. We thank these colleagues and look forward to opportunities to continue learning with and from them.

—*Jill Ellen Carnaghi and Peter Magolda*

Preface

Peter M. Magolda and Jill Ellen Carnaghi

Why Job One 2.0: Understanding the Next Generation of New Student Affairs Professionals?

"Thanks, but no thanks," was our initial reply to ACPA–College Student Educators International's invitation to co-edit a follow-up book to our *Job One: Experiences of New Professionals in Student Affairs* text. It had been eleven years since we originally proposed the project and nine years since ACPA and University Press of America co-published it. *Job One* was a pleasant and hazy memory, one that we never expected to disturb or revisit.

Despite our tepid and kneejerk reaction to the invitation, it spawned two perplexing questions. "Are the experiences of new professionals in 2012 qualitatively different from the experiences of the previous generation of new professionals?" And, "Are these differences sufficiently distinct to warrant a new book focused on this next generation of student affairs educators?" After pondering these questions and consulting with numerous colleagues, our response was a resounding "yes" to both questions. Thus, we changed our minds and accepted the invitation.

Job One: A Look Back

For readers unfamiliar with *Job One* (Magolda & Carnaghi, 2004), our intent was to enrich understanding about the experiences of new professionals by soliciting input from an unlikely source: new professionals. Richardson (1975) stated, "There is nothing as sterile as a college where the process of growth and change is confined to the students" (p. 306). *Job One* showcased new professionals talking about their meaningful and, at times, messy development. We posited that if new professionals understand themselves, they would be more likely to understand and address students' needs, countering Richardson's assertion that the growth of collegians often eclipses the development of individuals who serve these students.

Our original book contained nine stories by ten new professionals (including one co-authored essay) about their first job searches and full-time work experiences within student affairs. Collectively, these narratives described new professionals' joys and anxieties as they formulated their professional identities, managed stress, satisfied supervisors' expectations, mediated cultural conflicts, and remained true to their own values. The stories highlighted new professionals' (a) rites of passage from graduate school to the world of work (Kuk & Cuyjet, 2009); (b) job search strategies (Paterson & Coffey, 2009); (c) socialization experiences (Rosser & Javinar, 2009); (d) varied work roles (e.g., educator, integrator, conflict mediator, disciplinarian, administrator, ethicist, and advocate); (e) pathways to success (Hamrick & Hemphill, 2009); and (f) reconciliation strategies that bridged the gap between their personal and professional beliefs and job expectations (Toma, Clark, & Jacobs, 1998). Six veteran educators (i.e., three senior student affairs administrators and three student affairs preparation program faculty members) wrote three companion chapters synthesizing and theoretically interpreting the new professionals' stories. We wrote the preface and a concluding chapter, which included an overview of the book, modest recommendations, and implications for practice.

Job One contributors included possibilities to ponder rather than "ready-to-implement" prescriptions for the book's four primary audiences: (a) graduate students preparing for the transition from graduate school to work; (b) new professionals immersed in their first jobs; (c) student affairs practitioners (e.g., supervisors and mentors of new professionals); and (d) faculty who teach in student affairs preparation graduate programs. Positive feedback during the past decade coalesced around the thickly described stories. Readers reported an enriched understanding about the complexities, paradoxes, contradictions, and intellectual and emotional struggles associated with new professionals and their hunt for job one. A book about new professionals written by new professionals filled a scholarly void by augmenting existing published works about new professionals in student affairs, mostly written by senior student affairs officers or graduate preparation faculty (Amey & Reesor, 2002, 2009; Barr, 1990; Coleman & Johnson, 1990; Cooper, Chernow, Miller, Kulic, & Saunders, 1999; S. Ellis, 2009; Trimble, Allen, & Vidoni, 1991; Tull, Hirt, & Saunders, 2009).

Job One 2.0: A Look Ahead

In *Job One 2.0: Understanding the Next Generation of Student Affairs Professionals,* we target the same four audiences and again invited new professionals to tell their stories. Several of these millennial-generation authors (Freeman & Taylor, 2009) revisit perennial issues that the Generation X new professionals discussed in *Job One* (Magolda & Carnaghi, 2004), such as graduate school success strategies (Freeman & Taylor, 2009), job satisfaction (Bender, 1980), socialization (Collins, 2009), supervision (Janosik, Creamer, Hirt, Winston,

Saunders, & Cooper, 2003), professional networking (Reesor, Bagunu, & Hazley, 2009), professional development (Carpenter & Miller, 1980), professional identity (Young, 1985), and home–work tensions (Blanchard, 2009). Yet several *Job One 2.0* new professional contributors introduce and discuss contemporary and previously unexplored issues, such as international student affairs opportunities (Kruger & Dungy, 1999; Ludeman & Strange, 2009), the importance of institutional type (Hirt, 2009), and the intersection of faith and student affairs (Magolda, 2010).

Although the format of this book (i.e., narrative chapters written by new professionals and interpretive chapters written by veteran professionals) resembles the organization of *Job One* (Magolda & Carnaghi, 2004), noteworthy differences exist. Obviously, we identified ten new professionals to recount stories about their first jobs in student affairs. These narratives resemble the experiences that Tull et al. (2009) discussed:

> The roads these new staff members have traveled to gain entry to the profession are varied. Certainly many have followed the traditional route—active involvement as undergraduates led them to master's programs in higher education and student affairs administration. There are other career paths, however. For instance, newly minted alumni who served as senior resident assistants or campus ambassadors as undergraduates often are hired as hall directors or admission counselors. Likewise, some new hires completed graduate degrees in other fields (e.g., psychology, sociology, communication) but were employed in assistantships and student affairs offices. They became enamored of the profession and elected to pursue postgraduate employment in the post-secondary sector. (p. ix)

We followed Tull et al.'s (2009) advice and highlighted diverse pathways into the profession by purposefully selecting new professionals whose life stories and journeys into student affairs are unique and whose stories highlight generational differences (e.g., questioning authority and the desire for instant gratification) between *Job One* and *Job One 2.0* contributors.

As we assembled a new cadre of new professionals with whom to collaborate, we wondered, "What ever happened to the ten new professional authors in *Job One*?" We remained in close contact with some of these contributors; we lost track of others' whereabouts. Our detective work unearthed a surprising discovery. Nearly a decade later, every original new professional contributor still worked in higher education. This revelation differs from Tull et al.'s (2009) research findings that estimate "departure from the student affairs profession range from 20% to 40%, most of which takes place with the first six years of the career" (p. x). This anomaly prompted us to invite them to contribute to *Job One 2.0* as veteran contributors. To our delight, all but one was able to accept our invitation.

Molly Reas Hall wrote the opening chapter, and Diana Jaramillo and Rozana Carducci are co-authors of the concluding chapter. Kevin Piskadlo and Christana Johnson co-authored the first cross-case analysis chapter; Craig Woodsmall and Kathleen Gardner collaborated on Unit II's cross-case analysis;

Will Simpkins authored the final unit's analysis chapter. In the appendix, Stephanie Kurtzman and Jen-chien Yu (a university librarian and new contributor) compiled online job search resources for new professionals. Sarah O'Connell and Katie Shoemaker are new professionals and new contributors, and they generated the discussion questions that appear throughout the book.

Although reuniting with several contributors from *Job One* is nostalgic and working with the new contributors for *Job One 2.0* highly satisfying, it was the many changes and upheavals in the academy over the past decade—changes that have fundamentally altered the work life of new professionals in student affairs—that finally influenced us to undertake this new project. Understanding these trends is a prerequisite to appreciating the stories and analyses that follow.

The Changing Nature of Student Affairs Work in Higher Education

Reflecting upon the past decade, it is safe to conclude that some aspects in higher education remain unchanged. Colleges and universities in general and student affairs in particular aspire to serve the public good, generate and disseminate knowledge both inside and outside the classroom, support student learning (leading to professional and personal growth), encourage students to identify and follow their passions and purposes in life, help students become ethical citizen-leaders, and facilitate collegians' interactions with individuals different from themselves.

Despite these longstanding and familiar aspirations, higher education—especially during the past eleven years—has experienced unprecedented and ubiquitous change (Housewright & Schonfeld, 2008) that has complicated new professionals' efforts to optimally support collegians.

First, an unstable world economy has resulted in diminished external support for higher education (e.g., state funding, alumni/ae giving). A byproduct of a struggling economy is the downsizing and consolidation of student affairs units. In 2013, student affairs educators have fewer career opportunities, which exacerbate already stressful job searches, especially for new professionals. Once on the job, these new professionals assume auxiliary work assignments to compensate for fewer staff. Securing employment in a bleak job market is a not-so-optimal way to begin a career, although a reality.

Second, skyrocketing tuition as well as campus scandals (fueled by social media's instantaneous capacity to disseminate information to the masses) has shaken the public's confidence in higher education, a confidence that steadily continues to erode. Rising operational costs and dwindling fiscal resources also have increased oversight (e.g., hyper-monitoring) of universities by state and federal legislators as well as boards of trustees. A popular "solution" is for colleges and universities to act more like corporations (Schrecker, 2010; White & Hauck, 2000) and less like educational organizations. Adopting and adapting corporate ideals—quality, efficiency, customer service, downsizing, entrepreneurship, corporate sponsorship, outsourcing, and branding—is commonplace within the academy. Although intrusive oversight coupled with efforts to "corporatize" universities seems far removed from the entry-level student affairs staff, it is not. Increasingly staff members, such as academic advisors, document each interaction with advisees to demonstrate their centrality to the mission of the university; the overemphasis on quantity, at the expense of quality interactions, is dangerous. Likewise, senior residence hall staff members overemphasize service by satisfying "the customer" at all costs (i.e., give the residents what they want) rather than focusing on learning and educating residents by both supporting and challenging them. Corporate ideas are a potent influence on new professionals' responsibilities and subtly influence how they interact with students.

Third, the information revolution has dramatically altered the work lives of student affairs educators, especially new professionals. For example, digital technologies such as Twitter, YouTube, and Facebook (Burgess & Green, 2009; Perez-Latre, Portilla, & Blanco, 2011) have changed the ways student organization advisors communicate with members (Junco & Chickering, 2010). Social media (Connolly, 2011; Martinez Alemán, 2011) provides individuals the freedom to independently access, create, re-create, and disseminate information. Prospective students no longer rely exclusively on admission counselors and campus view books to gain information about a college or university. Social media allows prospective students to communicate with each other and gain access to a multitude of perspectives before selecting a college (Magolda & Platt, 2009). Also, these technologies dramatically alter the work responsibilities of entry-level educators (Freeman & Taylor, 2009).

Finally, the demographics of higher education have dramatically changed over the past decade, and this trend will continue in the future. For example, the influx of international students attending American universities and vice-versa has diversified many historically homogeneous campuses and illuminated cultural differences, complicating new professionals' communication and mediation responsibilities (McIntire & Willer, 1992). Learning Center specialist jobs have changed because of these demographic shifts. For example, support for students for whom English is their second language is more commonplace on American campuses than traditional study-skills workshops (Sawir, Marginson, Forbes-Mewett, Nyland, & Ramia, 2012). University international student programs and study abroad staff positions continue to expand (despite university-wide downsizing efforts). These trends also have led to the creation of student affairs positions outside the United States (Hacker & Dreifus, 2010).

Job One 2.0 stories implicitly and explicitly discuss the impact of the economy, the influence of outside forces on student affairs, technology, and shifting demographics on their job searches and job duties, revealing unique, inescapable, contemporary, and contested issues—topics worthy of consideration, dialogue, and action.

The Power of Stories

The most distinct aspect of *Job One 2.0* is the emphasis on storytelling. In our view, there is no better way of enriching readers' understanding of what is happening than by telling stories (Whyte, 1943). "Stories are fundamental to the way we learn and to the way we communicate. They are the most efficient way of storing, retrieving, and conveying information. Because hearing a story requires active participation by the listener, stories are the most profoundly social form of human interaction and communication—Terrance Cargiulo" (as cited by Woods, 2011, p. 1).

Storytelling is part of the professional lives of all student affairs educators, especially new professionals. It is common for a new professional returning from a job interview to share stories about the campus visit. Likewise, student affairs preparation faculty use stories (e.g., case studies) to educate graduate students about the complexities, paradoxes, contradictions, and intellectual and emotional struggles and complexities of finding a job in higher education. Narratives teach and foster learning, making them a springboard for action. Recounting, listening, and analyzing stories illuminate problems, possibilities, and solutions. Witherell and Noddings (1991) argued that

> we live and grow in interpretive, or meaning-making, communities; that stories help us find our place in the world; and that caring, respectful dialogue among all engaged in educational settings—students, teachers, administrators—serves as the crucible for our coming to understand ourselves, others, and the possibilities life holds for us. (p. 10)

C. Ellis and Bochner (2000) documented the benefit of the narrative inquiry process for both authors and their audiences.

> The stories we write put us into conversation with ourselves as well as with our readers. In conversations with ourselves, we expose our vulnerabilities, conflicts, choices, and values. We take measure of our uncertainties, our mixed emotions, and the multiple layers of our experience. Our accounts seek to express the complexities and difficulties of coping and feeling resolved, showing how we changed over time as we struggled to make sense of our experience. Often our accounts of ourselves are unflattering and imperfect, but human and believable. (p. 748)

Each chapter in the book contains memorable, thought-provoking, and humanizing stories that provide opportunities for readers to learn about the authors, the profession, and themselves. Molly Reas Hall provides us with a conceptual overview and map of potential lenses with which to read and reflect upon the new professional contributors' (NPC) stories: the importance of relationships, fit, competence and confidence; generational differences that become all too apparent for us as editors and those not of the NPCs' generation; and great advice to accept (or at least recognize) and learn from one's imperfections.

Unit I focuses on the job search process. In Chapter 2, DuJuan Smith shares his story of how being "the only one" as well as a first-generation college student and transfer student shaped not only his college experience but also his decision-making and entrée into student affairs. The importance of relationships, mentors, and coaching cannot be overemphasized in describing DuJuan's success. Persistence, patience, and passion characterize Craig Berger's seemingly long and arduous path to his first job. His knowledge of self and ability to reflect even when feeling the pressure to take a job are what got him to find the right "fit" for him and his aspirations. He stays focused and uses any and all resources appropriately. In Chapter 4, Molly Pierson is all about relationships—both personal and professional—and how she picked herself up and moved on when the realities of job one did not meet her expectations. Molly reassesses and redefines her own needs and expectations within the context of a dual career partnership. Unit I concludes with Kevin Piskadlo and Christana Johnson discussing common and interrelated themes among the three new professionals. All three NPCs also persist and grow through adversity, especially when all does not quite go their way. They quickly develop alternative plans and ways of framing their challenges. With optimism, they confront harsh realities and trust their instincts, colleagues, and supervisors.

Unit II centers on new professionals' early days in their jobs and the changes that accompany job one: new places, new cultures, new colleagues, new professional identities. In Chapter 6, David Stanfield finds himself in Doha, Qatar. David immerses himself in this new environment. His ability to reflect on the differences from day one on the job serves him well. Sarah Steward in Chapter 7 may have stayed a bit closer to home than David but deciding on her job one provokes as much reflection and decision-making before accepting a job offer at a Buddhist-inspired institution. She looks inward and faces her assumptions about the kind of institution she wants to work in and determines institutional fit for herself. Sarah comes to her job one with the formal education to be successful, yet her delivery of her knowledge takes on very different processes as she learns about the students' and alumni's and alumnae's ways of being in the world. Sarah becomes a learner as well as an educator in her new position. In Chapter 8, Kim Rutledge takes significant risks when accepting a temporary student affairs job on the west coast—sight unseen, and where she knows no one who could assist with basic needs of finding housing, getting around the city, or developing friendships. Believing in herself, Kim finds housing and establishes support networks. When one means to an end does not work, try, try again; that is exactly Carrie Miller's story as she describes in Chapter 9. After some false starts and feeling like she is not building professional relationships, Carrie realizes her style and approach do not mesh with her new work environment and makes appropriate adjustments. Carrie finds some of her greatest satisfaction through integrating relationships with students, course work, and applying theory to practice. In the concluding chapter of this unit (Chapter 10), Kathleen Gardner and Craig Woodsmall illuminate the common themes that transcend David's, Sarah's, Kim's, and Carrie's stories: facing one's fears, taking risks, being vulnerable and resilient, and learning healthy coping skills. Kathleen and

Craig focus on resiliency and resilient people, insights that benefit all of us, not just those embarking on a job search.

Unit III's focus is on identity. Shamika Johnson (Chapter 11) discusses her dilemma to stay at her alma mater for job one or look beyond being geographically bound. She also attempts to come to some sort of resolution regarding her identity as a professional African American woman. Shamika identifies several lessons learned: how to think about a past incident of racism as she considers institutional fit, how to make the shift from graduate student to new professional at the same institution, and how to find appropriate support systems—all the while remaining true to herself. In Chapter 12, Matt Kwiatkowski examines another aspect of one's identity resulting in much soul searching (no pun intended) regarding his religion and his priority to work at a faith-based institution as he is tired of leading a segmented or dichotomous life. Matt finds his religious identity during his undergraduate years; in graduate school, Christianity comes to define him as well as causes him conflict with his inner beliefs and what he is experiencing. Graduate school gives him the time to clearly define himself and clarify his beliefs. He knows his job one must be at a place where he can live and work as a whole person and professional. In Chapter 13, Shiloh Venable shares her stops and starts with career and law school prior to landing in student affairs. Shiloh's passion for her undergraduate co-curricular activities leads her to a place of knowing she wants to be a change agent for good. During graduate school is when Shiloh's personal and professional selves come together and she identifies as a queer woman. Shiloh takes advantage of the many learning experiences to come to grips with who she is as an individual as well as a student affairs educator. In the concluding chapter of Unit III, Will Simpkins discusses the similarities of Shamika's, Matt's, and Shiloh's questions for an appreciation and acknowledgement of an integrated self. Will highlights and goes into some detail regarding how one's personal identities cannot be overlooked (at least for very long) as one takes on his or her professional role and responsibilities. The energy and time to lead "two lives" is exhausting. The tough economy does not make it any easier for these new professionals to find their job ones while attempting to manage their multiple identities and life roles while striving to attain some semblance of balance. Shamika, Matt, and Shiloh have the courage to identify the impact of their personal identities, articulating the importance of who they are and acknowledging the importance of these factors in their career decision making and subsequent job satisfaction.

In the final chapter, Rozana Carducci and Diana Jaramillo present a cross-case analysis of seminal ideas that transcend the various chapters. They use the theoretical concept of self-authorship to interpret new professionals' job one experiences, highlighting examples that promote self-authorship. They conclude with recommendations for student affairs faculty, graduate students, new professionals, and supervisors/mentors. At the conclusion of Chapters 2 through 14, Katie Shoemaker and Sarah O'Connell pose thoughtful and provocative discussion questions for both new professionals and supporters of new professionals. We hope that readers will discuss these questions and generate additional questions. In the Appendix, Stephanie Kurtzman and Jen-chien Yu compile a comprehensive and practical list of essential resources and recommendations for new professionals. The on-line resources support new professionals as they research job possibilities, interview on campus, negotiate job offers, move, and settle in to a new home and job. Stephanie and Jen also include helpful suggestions to ensure a smoother transition from graduate school to job one. The breath, depth, and practicality of these resources are remarkable.

Kirby (1984) noted, "Leaving the security of graduate school and entering the job market can be a tense and very anxious time for some. It can also be an exciting and challenging time, as the recent graduate seeks that very important first position" (p. 24). Barr (1990) affirmed these ideas and added the following.

> Acceptance of a first professional position in student affairs brings with it many questions, concerns, and emotions. Among the questions are those related to competence, achievement, relationships with new colleagues, satisfaction, and enjoyment. Each professional new to student affairs encounters a range of problems and concerns about the future. The process of transition and change brings with it both doubt and anxiety. (p. 17)

Job One 2.0 provides insights and possibilities about the transition from graduate school to the world of student affairs, while resisting the urge to offer smug, cliché-like, and glib "answers" to the many complex questions (noted by Kirby and Barr) that this transition evokes for graduate students, new professionals, graduate preparation faculty, and supervisors/mentors.

Quaye (2005), in his chapter entitled "Let Us Speak: Including Student Voices in the Public Good of Higher Education," made clear the value of listening to students' perspectives and experiences to fulfill higher education's public good. This book adopted Quaye's advice, letting new professionals speak and encouraging readers to listen to their voices, especially those voices that "remain often unheard, deserve space, recognition and merit" (p. 295). Listening to and analyzing stories will lead to a well-prepared and highly satisfied next generation of student affairs educators, because new professionals' unique contributions to higher education in general and student affairs in particular cannot be overstated.

REFERENCES

Amey, M. J., & Reesor, L. M. (Eds.). (2002). *Beginning your journey: A guide for new professionals in student affairs* (rev. ed.). Washington, DC: National Association of Student Personnel Administrators.

Amey, M., & Reesor, L. M. (Eds.). (2009). *Beginning your journey: A guide for new professionals in student affairs* (3rd ed.). Washington, DC: National Association of Student Personnel Administrators.

Barr, M. J. (1990). Making the transition to a professional role. In D. D. Coleman & J. E. Johnson (Eds.), *The new professional: A resource guide for new student affairs professionals and their supervisors* (pp. 17-29). Washington, DC: National Association of Student Personnel Administrators.

Bender, B. E. (1980). Job satisfaction in student affairs. *NASPA Journal, 18*(2), 2-9.

Blanchard, J. (2009). Reconciling life and work for the new student affairs professional. In M. Amey & L. M. Reesor (Eds.), *Beginning your journey: A guide for new professionals in student affairs* (3rd ed.; pp. 133-145). Washington, DC: National Association of Student Personnel Administrators.

Burgess, J., & Green, J. (2009). *YouTube: Online video and participatory culture*. Cambridge, UK: Polity.

Carpenter, D. S., & Miller, T. K. (1980). An analysis of professional development in student affairs. *NASPA Journal, 19*(1), 2-11.

Coleman, D. D., & Johnson, J. E. (1990). *The new professional: A resource guide for new student affairs professionals and their supervisors*. Washington, DC: National Association of Student Personnel Administrators.

Collins, D. (2009). The socialization process for new professionals entering student affairs work. In A. Tull, J. B. Hirt, & S. A. Saunders (Eds.), *Becoming socialized in student affairs administration: A guide for new professionals and their supervisors* (pp. 3-27). Sterling, VA: Stylus.

Connolly, M. R. (2011). Social networking and student learning: Friends without benefits. In P. Magolda & M. B. Baxter Magolda (Eds.), *Contested issues in student affairs: Diverse perspectives and respectful dialogue* (pp. 122-134). Sterling, VA: Stylus.

Cooper, D. L., Chernow, E., Miller, T. K., Kulic, K., & Saunders, S. A. (1999). Professional development advice from past presidents of ACPA and NASPA. *Journal of College Student Development, 40,* 396-404.

Ellis, C., & Bochner, A. P. (2000). Autoethnography, personal narrative, reflexivity: Researcher as subject. In N. K. Denzin & Y. S. Lincoln (Eds.), *Handbook of qualitative research* (2nd ed.; pp. 733-768). Thousand Oaks, CA: Sage.

Ellis, S. (2009). Words of wisdom. In M. Amey & L. M. Reesor (Eds.), *Beginning your journey: A guide for new professionals in student affairs* (3rd ed.; pp. 207-221). Washington, DC: National Association of Student Personnel Administrators.

Freeman, J., & Taylor, C. (2009). Changing student characteristics and socialization. In A. Tull, J. B. Hirt, & S. A. Saunders (Eds.), *Becoming socialized in student affairs administration: A guide for new professionals and their supervisors* (pp. 67-85). Sterling, VA: Stylus.

Hacker, A., & Dreifus, C. (2010, September 20). The trouble with going global. *Newsweek,* 54-57.

Hamrick, F., & Hemphill, B. O. (2009). Pathways to success in student affairs. In M. Amey & L. M. Reesor (Eds.), *Beginning your journey: A guide for new professionals in student affairs* (3rd ed.; pp. 147-171). Washington, DC: National Association of Student Personnel Administrators.

Hirt, J. B. (2009). The influence of institutional type on socialization. In A. Tull, J. B. Hirt, & S. A. Saunders (Eds.), *Becoming socialized in student affairs administration: A guide for new professionals and their supervisors* (pp. 45-66). Sterling, VA: Stylus.

Housewright, R., & Schonfeld, R. (2008). *Ithaka's 2006 studies of key stake-holders in the digital transformation of higher education.* Retrieved from http://eresearchlibrary.wordpress.com/2009/02/22/ithaka's-2006-studies-of-key-stakeholders-in-the-digital-transformation-in-higher-education/

Janosik, S. M., Creamer, D. G., Hirt, J. B., Winston, R. B., Saunders, S. A., & Cooper, D. L. (Eds.). (2003). *Supervising new professionals in student affairs: A guide for practitioners.* New York, NY: Brunner-Routledge.

Junco, R., & Chickering, A. W. (2010). Civil discourse in the age of social media. *About Campus, 15*(4), 12-18.

Kirby, A. F. (1984). The new professional. In A. F. Kirby & D. Woodard (Eds.), *Career perspectives in student affairs.* Columbus, OH: National Association of Student Personnel Administrators.

Kruger, K. W., & Dungy, G. (1999). Opportunities for international travel and professional exchange for student affairs professionals. In Dalton, J. C. (Ed.), *Beyond borders: How international developments are changing student affairs practice. New Directions for Student Services No. 86* (pp. 23-31). San Francisco, CA: Jossey-Bass.

Kuk, L., & Cuyjet, M. (2009). Graduate preparation programs. In A. Tull, J. B. Hirt, & S. A. Saunders (Eds.), *Becoming socialized in student affairs administration: A guide for new professionals and their supervisors* (pp. 89-108). Sterling, VA: Stylus.

Ludeman, R. B., & Strange, C. C. (2009). Basic principles, values, and beliefs that support an effective student affairs and services programme in higher education. In R. B. Ludeman, K. J. Osfield, E. I. Hidalgo, & H. S. Wang (Eds.), *Student affairs and services in higher education: Global foundations, issues and best practices* (pp. 4-9). Paris, France: United Nations Educational, Scientific, and Cultural Organization.

Magolda, P. M. (2010). An unholy alliance: Rethinking collaboration involving student affairs and faith-based student organizations. *Journal of College & Character, 11*(4), 1-5.

Magolda, P. M., & Carnaghi, J. E. (Eds.). (2004). *Job one: Experiences of new professionals in student affairs.* Lanham, MD: University Press of America/American College Personnel Association.

Magolda, P., & Platt, G. J. (2009). Untangling Web 2.0's influence on student learning. *About Campus, 14*(3), 10-16.

Martinez Alemán, A. M. (2011). Social media and learning: A profile. In P. Magolda & M. B. Baxter Magolda (Eds.), *Contested issues in student affairs: Diverse perspectives and respectful dialogue* (pp. 135-140). Sterling, VA: Stylus.

McIntire, D., & Willer, P. (1992). *Working with international students and scholars on American campuses.* Washington, DC: National Association of Student Personnel Administrators.

Paterson, B. G., & Coffey, C. (2009). Managing the first job search. In M. Amey & L. M. Reesor (Eds.), *Beginning your journey: A guide for new professionals in student affairs* (3rd ed.; pp. 185-206). Washington, DC: National Association of Student Personnel Administrators.

Perez-Latre, F. J., Portilla, I., & Blanco, C. S. (2011). Social networks, media and audiences: A literature review. *Comunicacion y Sociedad, 24*(1), 63-74.

Quaye, S. J. (2005). Let us speak: Including students' voices in the public good of higher education. In A. J. Kezar, T. C. Chambers, & J. C. Burkhardt (Eds.), *Higher education for the public good* (pp. 293-307). San Francisco, CA: Jossey-Bass.

Reesor, L. M., Bagunu, G., & Hazley, M. (2009). Making professional connections. In M. Amey & L. M. Reesor (Eds.), *Beginning your journey: A guide for new professionals in student affairs* (3rd ed.; pp. 109-131). Washington, DC: National Association of Student Personnel Administrators.

Richardson, R. C. (1975). Staff development. *Journal of College Student Personnel, 46,* 303-311.

Rosser, V. J., & Javinar, J. M. (2009). Quality of work life. In A. Tull, J. B. Hirt, & S. A. Saunders (Eds.), *Becoming socialized in student affairs administration: A guide for new professionals and their supervisors* (pp. 28-42). Sterling, VA: Stylus.

Sawir, E., Marginson, S., Forbes-Mewett, H., Nyland, C., & Ramia, G. (2012). International student security and English language proficiency. *Journal of Studies in International Education, 16,* 434-454. doi: 10.1177/1028315311435418

Schrecker, E. (2010). *The lost soul of higher education: Corporatization, the assault on academic freedom, and the end of the American university.* New York, NY: New Press.

Toma, J. D., Clark, C., & Jacobs, B. (1998). Reconciling the professional and the personal for the new student affairs professional. In M. Amey & L. M. Reesor (Eds.), *Beginning your journey: A guide for new professionals in student affairs* (pp. 67-85). Washington, DC: National Association of Student Personnel Administrators.

Trimble, R., Allen, D. R., & Vidoni, D. O. (1991). Student personnel administration: Is it for you? *NASPA Journal, 28*(2), 156-162.

Tull, A., Hirt, J. B., & Saunders, S. A. (Eds.). (2009). *Becoming socialized in student affairs administration: A guide for new professionals and their supervisors.* Sterling, VA: Stylus.

White, G. D., & Hauck, F. C. (Eds.). (2000). *Campus, inc.: Corporate power in the ivory tower*. Amherst, NY: Prometheus Books.

Whyte, W. F. (1943). *Street corner society: The social structure of an Italian slum*. Chicago, IL: University of Chicago Press.

Witherell, C., & Noddings, N. (Eds.). (1991). *Stories lives tell: Narrative and dialogue in education*. New York, NY: Teachers College Press.

Woods, R. (2011). *The value of storytelling*. Retrieved from http://www.distinct.ac.uk/resources/resourceindex/alignmentdocs/5.8.5-storytelling-bn-v2.pdf

Young, R. B. (1985). Impressions of the development of professional identity: From program to practice. *NASPA Journal, 23*(2), 50-60.

CHAPTER 1

Job One 2.0: The Next Generation

MOLLY REAS HALL

The journey from graduate student to full-time professional in student affairs is an exhilarating, scary, rewarding, and challenging rite of passage. The ten new professional contributors (NPCs) whose narratives form the heart of *Job One 2.0: Understanding the Next Generation of Student Affairs Professionals* work in a wide variety of functional areas on college campuses across the United States and beyond and provide firsthand accounts of new professionals' successes and struggles. Although each author discusses issues unique to his or her personal experience, collectively the narratives suggest that new professionals in student affairs share many common experiences. While securing and starting job one, new professionals engage in self-reflection, take risks, search for an ideal career fit (both from a functional area and an institutional perspective), forge and negotiate relationships, establish professional competencies, and ultimately remain true to their values and beliefs (even when friends, family members, and colleagues offer different perspectives). The NPCs provide insights into these and other issues and reveal how new professionals make meaning of their work.

Despite a growing body of literature aimed at new professionals in student affairs (e.g., Amey & Reesor, 2009; Magolda & Baxter Magolda, 2011; Tull, Hirt, & Saunders, 2009), few empirical studies focus on the experiences of new professionals as they search for and start their first jobs. Even less common are scholarly works written by new professionals for new professionals. *Job One 2.0* fills these voids by blending empirical research about new professionals in student affairs with new professionals' narratives.

Renn and Hodges's (2007) qualitative study of the experiences of new professionals in student affairs during their first year on the job identified three common themes: "the importance of relationships, institutional and professional fit, and issues of competence and confidence" (p. 367). Although several *Job One 2.0* NPCs discuss events from a longer time span than their first year of full-time employment, these authors discuss and affirm the importance of each of Renn and Hodges's themes—relationships, fit, and competence and confidence—as well as offer new insights. In the remainder of this chapter, I briefly introduce the Renn and Hodges themes, present additional NPC themes, and link these ideas to contemporary student affairs scholarship and my own career trajectory with the goal of providing a conceptual roadmap for the book.

THE IMPORTANCE OF RELATIONSHIPS

A primary concern for the NPCs in *Job One 2.0* was establishing and managing relationships. While taking risks such as accepting a temporary position or limiting one's job search to meet the needs of a partner, several NPCs explicitly describe the support they received from family members, friends, partners, mentors, supervisors, and colleagues. Just as student affairs educators provide their students with an appropriate blend of challenge and support to foster growth, NPCs acknowledged that they, too, need to be both challenged and supported to successfully launch their careers and mature as professionals.

In Chapter 4, Molly Pierson discusses challenge and support as well as the importance of her personal and professional relationships. She writes, "My relationship with my partner Josh made me feel centered and comfortable with myself. The relationships that I forged during graduate school and during my on-campus interview process gave me the support needed to succeed in a not-so-ideal work environment" (p. 32). However, colleagues and friends also challenged some NPCs, creating dissonance. These stories illuminate authors' notions of challenge and support and how achieving this balance is sometimes easier said than done. In Chapter 11, Shamika Johnson shares that she "had to determine how to balance the growth I wanted to receive with the comfort I needed to thrive" (p. 121). The experiences of the NPCs raise questions for readers such as "What kinds of relationships do new professionals need?" and "What kinds of relationships are you willing to establish with new professionals?"

THE IMPORTANCE OF FIT

NPCs richly describe the strategies that helped them identify jobs that aligned with their values. Fit between new professionals and their new positions from both a departmental and an institutional perspective is of paramount importance and a pervasive theme throughout the NPC narratives. For new professionals, developing a strong internal voice (i.e., self-authorship) is an essential prerequisite for clarifying one's values. Self-authorship (Boes, Baxter Magolda, & Buckley, 2010), which involves the integration of one's epistemological, intrapersonal, and interpersonal dimensions, is "characterized by internally generating and coordinating one's beliefs, values, and internal loyalties, rather than depending on external values, beliefs, and interpersonal loyalties" (p. 4). Baxter Magolda's (2010) longitudinal study of twenty-something collegians revealed these individuals' struggles to extract themselves "from external influence to move toward self-authorship" (p. 27). *Job One 2.0* NPCs reveal similar struggles while describing diverse journeys toward self-authorship. In Chapter 7, Sarah Steward offers a concrete example that illuminates the elusive idea of self-authorship and its interrelationship with fit.

> I admit there is risk in every decision we make, but what I was unwilling to risk were my authenticity and integrity. . . . I was being called to a little, Buddhist-inspired institution that was doing great and wonderful things. I had discovered my mission fit. I could no longer deny that my professional and spiritual curiosity as well as my intuition and passions were the true compasses I must follow, so I stepped into the unknown, accepted my new role as the career services coordinator at Naropa University, and headed west. (p. 74)

It took Sarah over three years to understand that as an educator, she had to be the epicenter of her own learning and undergo personal and professional transformation to meet students as her fullest self. Craig Berger (Chapter 3) also documents his journey to find an appropriate degree of fit and move toward self-authorship in his narrative. He writes,

> There were times during my search when idealism drove my activity, as I believed there was a perfect job that would value who I was while also being in a civic engagement office and within my desired geographic area. After a few months of finding nothing while watching several classmates quickly secure jobs, I questioned this assumption. I responded by moving too far in the other direction, eventually concluding that any position would do and that I could exert enough control in any new environment to tailor it to my preferences. Although this approach led me to apply for more jobs and resulted in more invitations to interview, I realized that taking such an approach was foolhardy and naïve. These offices and institutions were complex, political organizations, and there were going to be dynamics that I could not just ignore or change. Coming to this understanding restrained me from investing myself too much in positions that had little to no connection to who I was or what I wanted to do with my life and my career. I was seeking a meaningful job and a position that was simply good enough for me. (p. 27)

Shamika Johnson (Chapter 11) points out the power of external influences and the challenges associated with staying true to her internal voice. "Sometimes it is hard to stay true to myself because I am pressured by those around me to change or fit in, but standing my ground in the midst of the pressure has benefitted me greatly. When I am free to truly be who I am in a work environment, I know I have found a fit" (p. 126). Shamika asserts, "Defining who I am and what's important to me were essential to my success in my first full-time position in student affairs" (p. 123). Kim Rutledge (Chapter 8) also writes on this theme, stating "I was determined that once I graduated I would secure work that fulfilled me, no matter how difficult the task" (p. 82).

Even when there was intense pressure to secure a job, or friends and family members had other ideas about the best course of action to take, the NPCs ultimately realized that they needed an appropriate sense of fit between themselves and their new positions in order to be successful and feel fulfilled. By remaining determined, exercising patience, and demonstrating a willingness to compromise on aspects of job one that were not "must haves," the NPCs achieved success in securing meaningful employment. Their stories raise questions such as "How can reflection aimed at accessing one's inner voice be cultivated?" "How does one learn to recognize and trust one's inner voice?" and "How can new professionals devise strategies to identify work that aligns with these principles?"

THE IMPORTANCE OF COMPETENCE AND CONFIDENCE

"Regardless of the process, what appeared to be important was that they [new professionals in student affairs] used their work experience as a laboratory in which consistently to examine and improve themselves as professionals" (Renn & Jessup-Anger, 2008, p. 327). New professionals aspire to be competent and confident. The NPCs expressed a keen interest in their professional development and proactively sought learning opportunities, especially when they did not feel that colleagues were sufficiently addressing their needs in this area. DuJuan Smith (Chapter 2) expresses this strong interest in professional development in sharing that he "found ways to create professional development opportunities around me by pursuing conferences, trainings, and webinars. Anything that would help me become more polished in my position, I did it" (p. 20). Several NPCs reveal that collegians were an unexpected source of professional development. Carrie Miller (Chapter 9) shares that as a residential life coordinator, "I found the most success in building my relationship within the community when I spent more time listening and learning about their community than talking. The more I started to listen, the more I learned and found a rather unexpected source of both professional and personal development" (p. 96).

Reflection and risk-taking were two important activities that bolstered competence and confidence. Whether reflection was a solitary or a collaborative exercise, it helped new professionals establish their internal voices and set a desirable course for the future. Shiloh Venable (Chapter 13) writes, "The ability to reflect on my past experiences was the key to determining a course that has led to more happiness than I could have expected" (p. 140). Matt Kwiatkowski (Chapter 12) summarizes a key belief held by the group of NPCs in writing that "although taking risks can be a scary and unsettling process in the moment, they are absolutely necessary to personal and professional growth" (p. 136). Whether relocating across the country, moving to a different country, or staying at the same institution after graduate school, each NPC took risks that initially created anxiety and stress but ultimately led to rewards.

Mentoring enhanced new professionals' competence and confidence. Renn and Jessup-Anger's (2008) study of 90 new student affairs professionals during their first year of full-time employment found that the biggest challenges participants faced centered on their professional identities and navigating cultural adjustments. The experiences shared by the *Job One 2.0* NPCs affirm these challenges. Renn and Jessup-Anger suggested that new professionals may be able to make a smoother transition to full-time employment in student affairs by seeking to learn from their experiences, viewing setbacks as learning opportunities, and utilizing guidance from mentors and supervisors.

Several NPCs sought the support of colleagues to grow as professionals. David Stanfield (Chapter 6) arguably faced the largest cultural transition as he began work at Carnegie Mellon University's international branch campus in Qatar. David invested a great deal of time and energy in understanding both his new environment and the diverse group of people within it. He notes that a key factor in his successful transition was "regular reflective conversations with my supervisor about culture and the implications for our work" (p. 64).

New professionals also recognized that in order to be effective student affairs educators, they needed to maximize their own potentials. Matt Kwiatkowski discusses the importance of tending to his own needs in Chapter 12. He writes,

> I espoused the idea of tending to the needs of the whole student, yet I continued to treat aspects of my life as discrete and mutually exclusive entities. How do I de-compartmentalize my life? How can I understand students if I cannot understand myself? . . . This [job one] experience, combined with my college and graduate school experiences, has made me a more holistic person, one who feels comfortable with the various dimensions of his identity, sharing those areas, and encouraging that development in others. (pp. 129, 136)

For new professionals, gaining competence and confidence—which involves reflection, risk-taking, mentorship, and learning to author one's life— takes time and energy. This process of developing competence and confidence is made even more challenging by the near-universal desire to achieve "both a satisfying work life as well as a satisfying personal life" (p. 89), as noted by Kim Rutledge in Chapter 8. Nearly every NPC addresses this tension, raising questions such as "Is balance possible?" and "What are barriers to achieving balance?"

THE IMPORTANCE OF GENERATIONAL DIFFERENCES

Many values explicitly and implicitly expressed by the NPCs (e.g., work–life balance) are values typically associated with the Millennial Generation (i.e., individuals born between 1981 and 1996). Although the narratives and analysis chapters in *Job One 2.0* highlight issues such as relationships, fit, and competence and confidence, the authors also remind readers that these issues do not exist in a vacuum. Understanding the impact of generational influences on new professionals is essential.

Several NPC stories illuminate the nine Millennial intrinsic values defined by Espinoza, Ukleja, and Rusch (2010). They include work-life balance, reward, self-expression, attention, achievement, informality, simplicity, multitasking, and meaning. *Job One 2.0* readers will find Millennial Generation norms discussed throughout the NPC chapters.

Because Millennials tend to have different expectations for supervision than members of previous generations, these differences can create challenges in the workplace. At times, Baby Boomer (born 1946–1964) and Generation X (born 1965–1980) managers struggle to connect with and successfully supervise and mentor Millennial employees. Understanding generational values can help new professionals, seasoned professionals, mentors, and graduate preparation faculty members understand and work toward better relationships, fit, and increased competence and confidence.

Millennials tend to

> have high expectations of their employers, and they want to provide direct and fair input to their managers. They want managers to be involved in their professional development. . . . They seek out creative challenges and view peers as vast resources from whom to gain knowledge. They want to be recognized and valued the first day on the job. (Espinoza et al., 2010, p. 10)

Millennials expect that supervisors will take a personal interest in them and act as their advocates. Many NPCs convey these same expectations in their narratives, perhaps most poignantly by DuJuan Smith (Chapter 2) in his positive assessment of his supervisor and co-workers.

> A key part of my success in my first professional student affairs job was having a great supervisor and supporting team of coworkers. My supervisor . . . recognized I was new to the field but valued my past experiences and perspectives. He regularly treated me as if I knew what I was doing; he allowed me the time and space to learn the position, the job responsibilities, and the culture of the institution. . . . We processed my strengths and strategized on ways I could improve my areas of opportunity. . . . The foundation of our relationship was honesty. It was always important to receive growth-focused feedback, even if it was a message I did not want to hear. (pp. 18-19)

In return, Millennials provide their workplaces with "energy, fresh perspective[s] and ideas, technological expertise, honest opinions and feedback, and high productivity" (Espinoza et al., 2010, p. 55). In the words of a recent report on the Millennial Generation published by the Pew Research Center (2010), today's new professionals are "confident, connected, and open to change." Many *Job One 2.0* NPCs embody these attributes. The vast majority of the NPCs describe opportunities they seized to improve work processes and increase efficiency, enhance transparency, and benefit students and co-workers. These NPCs worked hard, readily offered their opinions (even when they were not solicited), proposed changes and implemented improvements approved by supervisors, and shared their energy and passion with their students and colleagues.

However, as in Carrie Miller's experience (Chapter 9), common Millennial traits such as the need to make one's mark in the workplace and to know why decisions are made are frequently misunderstood by supervisors. Although Carrie does not mention the age or generation of her supervisor, her narrative reveals a common disconnect between Millennial employees and non-Millennial supervisors. Rather than viewing the source of some common Millennial traits as a profound desire to make a difference, supervisors of Millennials can misperceive supervisees' actions in the workplace as arrogance or challenging authority. Carrie writes,

> Before student staff training began, I wanted to compile all of the policies and procedures in a single written document. As a result, I had to ask numerous questions to gather background information on how things had worked or not worked before my arrival. During this investigation, I rarely felt like I said the "right" thing. At my core, I simply wanted to understand how things worked. Asking *why* questions allows me to understand not only the mechanics of a process but also how it influences those involved. I felt compelled to understand how and why [Ohio Wesleyan University] developed its policies, procedures, and traditions. I mostly posed my questions to my supervisor and the other [residential life coordinators]; conversations with my supervisor never seemed to go well. My questions, and even more so my suggestions to change the . . . procedures, flustered her. (p. 93)

Given Millennials' interest in professional development and building strong relationships with their supervisors, synergistic supervision may be an ideal approach for today's new professionals. Synergistic supervision integrates meeting the needs of the organization with the professional development needs of individual staff members. Winston and Creamer (1997) described synergistic supervision:

> An important characteristic of synergistic supervision is that it has a dual focus on accomplishment of the organization's goals and on support of staff in accomplishment of their personal and professional development goals. Furthermore it is based on joint effort, requires two-way communication, focuses on competencies, and is growth oriented, goal based, systematic and ongoing, and holistic. (pp. 42-43)

Because one of the primary factors associated with new professionals leaving student affairs is the lack of quality supervision in their careers, the effective supervision of new professionals is critical to the stability and continuity of student affairs as well as to individual employees and managers (Creamer & Winston, 2002, as cited in Tull, 2006). These issues raise questions for the reader such as "How do your values align with values of colleagues from other generations?" "What would synergistic supervision look like in your work setting?" and "What actions do you take when generations collide?"

The Importance of Accepting and Learning from Imperfections

The NPCs offer honest and unvarnished stories about their imperfect lives working in imperfect colleges and universities, revealing valuable lessons learned while navigating the job search process and job one. In sharing their experiences—the highs and the lows, the good and the bad—they directly and indirectly offer valuable insights for graduate students, new professionals, supervisors of new professionals, and graduate program faculty, reminding readers that it is not just senior student affairs practitioners and faculty members who have wisdom to share. NPCs know that a professional position is a fit when they can be their authentic selves and when faithfulness to one's values and beliefs is not compromised. They recognize that securing job one requires hard work, both in determining what one really wants and then in making those desires a reality. They also recognize that they cannot always get what they want. Shamika Johnson (Chapter 11) champions this sentiment in writing, "I recognized that I may not always get everything I want in a job. I had to accept the reality that no job is perfect" (p. 123). Just as no individual student affairs educator is perfect, no supervisor, job, or institution is perfect. In the words of a former student affairs professional association president, "All people and organizations are flawed" (as quoted by Cooper, Chernow, Miller, Kulic, & Saunders, 1999, p. 399). Making the best of a situation is generally a wise course of action. This is important advice echoed by Molly Pierson (Chapter 4). She writes,

> Despite the frustration of being so focused on administration and office management, there were many things I came to love about my work—mostly relationships with colleagues and supervisees. I was quickly getting to know other academic advisors on campus and developing a sense of collaboration. I was among a group of dedicated professionals who cared deeply about the students. I valued being in a professional community that shared my commitment to student growth and learning. (p. 36)

Looking back on my own job one experience, my now thirty-something self would like to tell my twenty-something self to "relax." Job one is just one stage (albeit an important stage) in an individual's professional journey. As a graduate student in student affairs in the late 1990s, members of my academic cohort often referred to the two years spent in the program as a journey. Graduate school was a time of tremendous growth for me; when I graduated in 1999, it was satisfying to believe that my journey of self-discovery was mostly complete and I had "arrived" as a bona fide student affairs professional. Little did I know that my journey was just beginning. I believe that if the four intended audiences of *Job One 2.0* (i.e., graduate students, new professionals, supervisors of new professionals, and graduate preparation faculty) were to view students' time in graduate school as one step in an individual's lifelong professional journey rather than a journey in itself, it would help new professionals successfully navigate challenges unique to job one. If job one does not turn out to be all that a new professional hoped it would be, that is okay. One's first job in student affairs is just one step in a lifelong professional journey; it is not a final destination. Although job one is a time to contribute and show what one can do, it is also a time to continue to learn and grow. It certainly was for me.

When I accepted my first job after graduate school, 1 had no way of knowing where I would be 13 years and five jobs later. Like many others, many of my career decisions have not simply involved me, but my partner. When we met, my partner was beginning a doctoral program. I moved from the Midwest to New England to join him, then to the west coast after he completed his Ph.D. and accepted a postdoctoral position, and then to the east coast as he began a tenure-track faculty position. Rather than derailing my career, my many moves have provided opportunities to work in functional areas that I never would have considered and to take on new challenges. Having so many different jobs helped me to discover where I fit best professionally, ultimately leading me to where I am now as a doctoral student pursuing a career in assessment and evaluation. It has all been part of my professional journey. Although some jobs and experiences were definitely more enjoyable and enriching than others, I gained valuable knowledge and experience at each stop along the way. Viewing things as "it's all part of the journey" 13 years ago would have saved me quite a bit of frustration during my first couple of jobs as well as a considerable amount of angst about what my future would hold.

Perhaps most importantly, job one is a time of growth. Viewing job one in this light would help graduate students in student affairs master's programs and new professionals as well as supervisors of new professionals and graduate program faculty. Viewing job one as a time of growth would remind supervisors that new professionals have much to offer and much should be expected of them and that supervisors also have a responsibility to develop competence and confidence in the next generation of student affairs professionals. Because most new professionals look to supervisors for guidance and support, supervisors play a very influential role (for better or worse) in the socialization of new professionals. Student affairs graduate program faculty are in an ideal position to communicate to students (and to remind new professionals with whom they keep in contact) that the journey students begin in graduate school does not end but continues as part of an individual's lifelong professional journey.

REFERENCES

Amey, M. J., & Reesor, L. M. (Eds.). (2009). *Beginning your journey: A guide for new professionals in student affairs* (3rd ed.). Washington, DC: National Association of Student Personnel Administrators.

Baxter Magolda, M. B. (2010). The interweaving of epistemological, intrapersonal, and interpersonal development in the evolution of self-authorship. In M. B. Baxter Magolda, E. G. Creamer, & P. S. Meszaros (Eds.), *Development and assessment of self-authorship: Exploring the concept across cultures* (pp. 25-43). Sterling, VA: Stylus.

Boes, L. M., Baxter Magolda, M. B., & Buckley, J. A. (2010). Foundational assumptions and constructive-developmental theory: Self-authorship narratives. In M. B. Baxter Magolda, E. G. Creamer, & P. S. Meszaros (Eds.), *Development and assessment of self-authorship: Exploring the concept across cultures* (pp. 3-23). Sterling, VA: Stylus.

Cooper, D. L., Chernow, E., Miller, T. K., Kulic, K., & Saunders, S. A. (1999). Professional development advice from past presidents of ACPA and NASPA. *Journal of College Student Development, 40,* 396-404.

Espinoza, C., Ukleja, M., & Rusch, C. (2010). *Managing the millennials: Discover the core competencies for managing today's workforce.* Hoboken, NJ: John Wiley & Sons.

Magolda, P. M., & Baxter Magolda, M. B. (Eds.). (2011). *Contested issues in student affairs: Diverse perspectives and respectful dialogue.* Sterling, VA: Stylus.

Pew Research Center. (2010). *Millennials: A portrait of generation next. Confident. Connected. Open to change.* Washington, DC: Author.

Renn, K. A., & Hodges, J. P. (2007). The first year on the job: Experiences of new professionals in student affairs. *Journal of Student Affairs Research and Practice, 44,* 604-628.

Renn, K. A., & Jessup-Anger, E. R. (2008). Preparing new professionals: Lessons for graduate preparation programs from the national study of new professionals in student affairs. *Journal of College Student Development, 49,* 319-335.

Tull, A. (2006). Synergistic supervision, job satisfaction, and intention to turnover of new professionals in student affairs. *Journal of College Student Development, 47,* 465-480.

Tull, A., Hirt, J. B., & Saunders, S. A. (Eds.). (2009). *Becoming socialized in student affairs administration: A guide for new professionals and their supervisors.* Sterling, VA: Stylus.

Winston, R. B., & Creamer, D. G. (1997). *Improving staffing practices in student affairs.* San Francisco, CA: Jossey-Bass.

UNIT I

CHAPTER 2

I Am Not Jamal*

DuJuan Smith

I entered the classroom and scanned the room to find a seat. I preferred to sit somewhere in the middle, not too close to the professor and not too far away from the door. As my peers began to file into the classroom, I noticed I was the only African American student. This is an occurrence with which I am familiar, as I am typically the "only one" in my classes. About five minutes after the official start of class, the professor introduced herself and began the first day of class ritual. I expected the instructor to take attendance, review the syllabus, facilitate class introductions, and allocate time at the end for questions. As my professor began calling names for attendance, I waited patiently knowing it would take some time to get to me. Somewhere in the middle of roll call, I heard the professor call out the name "Jamal." Preoccupied reviewing the syllabus, I did not notice what was happening around me. After I heard Jamal's name called the third time, I looked up from my syllabus to find the professor and entire class looking at me. I chuckled to ease the awkward moment, but eyes of the entire class continued to burn expectantly at me. Finally, it hit me—the class thinks I am Jamal. I was both confused and insulted by the assumption that I, the

---

* The name Jamal is a pseudonym.

only Black man in the room, must be named Jamal. The tension finally broke when I stated plainly, "I am not Jamal."

I grew up with someone named Jamal. We were both the product of single-parent homes, raised in a housing development on the south side of Chicago. Our view of the world did not extend beyond our neighborhood. Despite our limited perspectives, we both dreamed big and often talked about what it would be like to become successful one day. When you grow up in a neighborhood like ours, you are initially unaware that you are different. Plenty of love, yet painted with a backdrop of heartache and violence, characterized the colorful environment where I spent my formative years. By the age of three, my father committed murder and was lost to the prison system. I would not see him again until I was 22 years old. By the age of five, I had already felt the sharp pain of losing someone you love to meaningless violence. By age seven, I had a gun pulled on me while going to the corner store and had been shot at while playing outside near the playground with my friends. At age nine, I received an invitation to join a gang, which I declined. By the age of 12, I knew what drug and alcohol addiction looked like. Unfortunately in my neighborhood, these were everyday occurrences.

Jamal and I endured these hardships together; however, I was fortunate enough to have a strong-willed mother who refused to give her children to the streets. My mother ran a strict household, one I did not understand or appreciate until I was much older. Education was mandatory. My mother saw education as one way I could expand my horizons. Punishments in my household involved the daily newspaper and pop quizzes. My mother mandated that I know key information from random sections of the newspaper. She even established an agreement with all of my teachers that if her signature was not on my homework, they were to reject it. This meant my work had to first meet her approval; her signature ensured perfection. Jamal did not have the same strong support system at home. Although my mother loved Jamal as if he was one of her own, life was not the same for him.

Jamal and I grew up in what some may call the "ghetto" or the "hood." Our neighborhood was not perfect, but it was home. In the midst of the chaos, we were a community—rich in love and support. Growing up there taught me to be resilient and empathetic to the struggles of others. It was the first place I truly understood the concept, "bad choices do not equate to bad people." However, I remember feeling ashamed of where I lived. I hated feeling "different" from everyone outside of my geographical environment. I would never allow my friends to drop me off at my home. It had to be at the bus station five blocks away. My neighborhood wanted to celebrate my success in school by featuring me in a newsletter and I refused. I wanted to feel normal—the kind of normal I saw on television. I remember being in awe of Bill Cosby's popular sitcom, *The Cosby Show*. It was difficult to see a successful African American family seem so perfect. It seemed unfair and unreal because it did not resemble my reality; however, it gave me something to aspire to in the future. I began to focus my energy on becoming successful.

By high school, Jamal began to hang with the wrong crowds. He was angry at the world. Slowly but surely, he became angry with me. By his senior year of high school, Jamal had multiple encounters with the police and regularly sold drugs. Although I never agreed with his life choices, I understood why he felt this was the only way. In his mind, this was the only path for people who grow up where we lived. The only people who I knew of who made it out of my community were those drafted into the NBA. I knew I had to see where education would take me or suffer the same fate as Jamal and others like him. Searching for the right college overwhelmed me. I did not know where to begin or where to look. My high school guidance counselor was an excellent resource. He understood that the college-search process intimidated me, and he provided the necessary support in guiding me to appropriate resources. My knowledge of college was limited to what I saw on television. There was one show in particular that Bill Cosby produced, entitled *A Different World*. The show followed the college lives of multiple characters at a historically Black institution. With this being my primary point of reference, I limited my college search to only historically Black institutions. From college fairs to on-campus visits, I immersed myself in the selection and application process. In the end, I decided to attend Howard University, a prestigious Black institution rich in culture, history, and education. After revealing my top choice to my mother, she was equally excited about this decision.

As we continued to research Howard University, however, the cost of attending the institution became a huge concern. We did not have a college savings fund. I applied for some scholarships, but these still fell short of covering my freshman-year expenses. I had to accept the harsh reality that attending Howard would not be possible for me. I was devastated; throughout my entire education, I believed that if I worked hard and got good grades, I could go anywhere for college. My hard work did not translate into attending my first choice school. Shortly after this letdown, I received an acceptance letter from Tennessee State University (TSU). The financial aid packet was more reasonable, and I received an academic scholarship. With my finances in place, I headed to TSU.

As a first-generation college student, college was a scary place. It was a brand new environment with people from a variety of backgrounds in one location for the same purpose: to get a degree. I struggled to find anyone at home I could talk with about my experiences. Overall, being at TSU was an overwhelming experience; it was the first time I was away from home, I didn't know anyone at the university, and I struggled to maintain connections with my friends from home in the face of so much newness. By the end of the first year, however, I found that I enjoyed my classes, benefitted from the cultural experiences, and grew as a person. Despite these positive changes, I ultimately decided to return to Illinois for school. I chose Northern Illinois University (NIU). It was an hour away from Chicago, which would give me moderate independence while still allowing me the opportunity to return home if I needed to get back. I found resources at NIU to help me to become engaged in the Huskie community. I developed relationships with my peers and NIU staff that made the campus truly a home away from home. Through my involvement in student organizations, I began to recognize my unique talents and gifts. Using my newfound leadership skills, I worked my way up the ranks of the student government association. In my senior year, I met with the Vice President of Student Affairs, Dr. Brian Hemphill, who introduced me to the world of student affairs. He told me I could continue doing what I was doing in undergrad for the rest of my life. Along with this verbal encouragement, he sent me to my first NASPA conference and connected me with a staff member at NIU, who became my mentor under the NASPA undergraduate fellows program (NUFP). NUFP, formerly known as the Minority Undergraduate Fellows Program, educates and exposes undergraduate students interested in student affairs to the various career paths they can pursue in higher education.

When the time came to apply to graduate school, I fluctuated between two paths: student affairs in higher education or clinical mental health counseling. I had always felt a pull towards pursuing counseling. As sociology major, I became fascinated with how we interact with both the people around us and with our environment. The classes I took provided me with invaluable intellectual insights into the world where I grew up. It was in these classroom settings that I was exposed to and began to better understand the perspectives of those with experiences different from my own. Furthermore, it was one of the first times in my life that I felt that so many of my peers misunderstood my identity and upbringing. I found other people's perspectives on urban communities and the people who come from those environments to be greatly inaccurate. It was from this sense of being misunderstood that I began my exploration into my identity during my undergraduate years. From study abroad to my involvement in student organizations, I learned to define myself for myself. NIU was the place where I became the person I was destined to be. As a result of all this self-discovery and change, I saw counseling as the opportunity to help others understand events in their lives.

I spoke with various mentors about my struggle to decide whether to pursue a higher education degree or a counseling degree. They all responded with the same advice: student affairs will take you further. Although I respected their perspectives, the advice did not resonate in my heart. Finally, one of my most trusted mentors gave me a piece of sage and simple advice. He told me, "Choose the path that feels right for you. No matter what you choose to study for your master's degree, if student affairs is where you belong, that is where you will end up. On the bright side, choosing counseling will only enhance your brand and it sets you apart from others in student affairs." Heeding these words of wisdom, I selected counseling. I pursued and obtained my Master of Science in Education in clinical mental health counseling from NIU while maintaining my professional ties to student affairs through NASPA and co-curricular activities on campus. It was a decision with which many of my peers vehemently disagreed. They argued that I was missing out on "higher education." As I endured backlash for choosing a path that felt right to me, I once again realized, "I am not Jamal."

To me, this expression, "I am not Jamal," conveyed that everyone has the right to be his or her own person. I understood there was a "suggested" yellow brick road for those aspiring to work in student affairs, but in my life I had seldom followed the traditional path. I learned early the importance of finding my own voice and defining my own path. One of my mentors always said, "Run your own race." I interpreted this statement to mean do not use the career moves of your peers or colleagues as a measuring stick for determining your success and self-worth. This aphorism served me well in my first professional position in student affairs. My interests and passion motivated my career choice. I knew and stood by what was ideal for me and not what might be ideal or right for others. As an undergraduate, I felt a natural inclination to join student government, and I remained active within student government until my graduation. While I found student government to be the driving force behind my interest in student affairs, some of my peers served as resident/community advisors within their residence halls as a means to get involved in higher education leadership. I never considered working within residence life as a student—at the time, that was not my interest or passion. One path was not better than the other; each of us found our way to this field based on our unique interests and experiences.

My first professional job in student affairs was at Moraine Valley Community College in Palos Hills, Illinois, as the Coordinator of Judicial Affairs. I must admit, if someone had told me I would work in judicial affairs when I was an undergraduate, I would have laughed. I understood the functions of the office and fundamentally agreed with its purpose; however, I never thought I would come to be so passionate about this work. I learned a valuable lesson from this surprising experience: be open to possibilities. I chose judicial affairs because I naturally handle high conflict situations well. I attribute my calm demeanor in high conflict situations due to the environment in which I grew up; there was always conflict going on around me—and sometimes involving me—so I had to learn to calmly figure out solutions. As the oldest son, if I allowed our high conflict neighborhood to break my spirit then it might have affected my siblings' abilities to carry on as well. I also taught myself how to set boundaries and not allow things to affect me. If something destructive happened in my neighborhood, I learned early not to take those issues back to school with me so that I could accomplish what I needed to accomplish.

I chose the community college setting to gain a better perspective on how they operated and how to best serve their unique student population. Community colleges are quickly becoming home for many more students than ever before in higher education and they particularly attract students in transition. Students' transitions may include earning trade certifications, transferring to four-year institutions, training for specialty careers, preparing for GED completion, and changing careers. The most difficult aspect of working within a community college setting as a judicial officer is the open enrollment, which means the college accepts anyone from the community who wants to attend. For many students, this is their first exposure to college. Some students use it as a means to figure out what they want to do next. The community college setting provides support and confidence to students as they prepare for the next step in their lives or academic journeys. For staff members, the community college where I worked specialized in supporting professional development and continued learning opportunities. Each semester the college hosted "college learning days" when students were not required to attend classes, but faculty and staff spent the entire day engaged in learning about new trends in the field and best practices, celebrating our successes, and strategizing ways to strengthen our areas of opportunity.

In retrospect, judicial affairs was the perfect marriage of my higher education experiences and my counseling background. My counseling training provided me the technique and experience in individual and group therapy sessions, opportunities to work with community agencies, and extensive training in working from the *Diagnostic and Statistical Manual of Mental Health Disorders*, diagnosing clients, and developing treatment plans. I infused these skills into my judicial meetings and referred students to appropriate resources on campus. In this work context, I created processes that embodied the standard adjudication process while adding a much-needed component: a humanistic perspective. The concept of shifting the paradigm from working with "bad people" to working with good people who happen to make bad decisions was one that intrigued me. This way of interacting with students aligned with my values; I believe in the uniqueness of every situation and every person involved. Again, my upbringing plays a large part in how I formed this philosophy. I know why Jamal made the choices he made and often wonder how different his life would have been if he were engaged in a system more concerned with helping him instead of punishing him. I wonder if a police officer or neighborhood agency had referred him to counseling or a program focused on providing at-risk teens with life skills and employment training, could those resources have changed or influenced his perspective on life?

What I recognized early in my career is that judicial affairs educators have a rare opportunity to engage students during a potentially life-changing time: when a bad decision has been made. I coined the phrase "sanctions equal goal setting," meaning that educators can use the judicial process to get troubled students on the right path by connecting them with campus resources and personal development opportunities. This approach embraces sanctioning as action planning. Student conduct can often feel like the dark side of student development; however, every dark night has the potential to become a bright day.

LESSONS LEARNED FROM JOB ONE

A key part of my success in my first professional student affairs job was having a great supervisor and supporting team of coworkers. My supervisor, Chet Shaw, recognized I was new to the field but valued my past experiences and perspectives. He regularly treated me as if I knew what I was doing; he allowed me the time and space to learn the position, the job responsibilities, and the culture of the institution. I learned the importance of never just doing the job but doing the job well—simply put, leaving a lasting impression through the work and things I leave behind even after I have left the position. Any place I work should be better as I prepare to leave it. We processed my strengths and strategized on ways I could improve my areas of opportunity. During my conversations with Chet, he helped me understand issues and politics on every level of the community college. It became my standard to evaluate any case or problem by identifying all of the critical players and assessing the multiple layers involved. The foundation of our relationship was honesty. It was always important to receive growth-focused feedback, even if it was a message I did not want to hear.

I learned the importance of self-care as well. In a highly intense role like mine, it was critical to establish necessary boundaries to prevent burnout. For me, the drive home was my relaxation time. I listened to music that calmed me or made phone calls to people I had been meaning to contact. When I arrived at home, the first thing I did was change my clothes. It helped me to make the transition from one part of the day to the next. I rarely discussed work outside of the job. When asked about it, I kept my responses brief and expended as little energy as possible. Engaging in high-level crises or emotion-filled situations requires a lot of energy from me. Discussing these situations and events outside of work was the equivalent of reliving those moments and reconnecting to those feelings. Not discussing work became a strategy for me to preserve my energy on what was most important: resolving the case and referring all parties to the appropriate resources. The beauty for me was my role required strict confidentiality, meaning I could not discuss cases. Although I had my work email linked to my phone and occasionally checked for messages, I never addressed nonemergency emails when I was not at work. Most of this sounds simple, yet I was surprised how these small acts preserved my sanity.

It is essential for me to have a life outside of work. A healthy social life filled with leisure activities with family and friends is necessary. The job will always be there, and I will have plenty of time to excel at it when the time is appropriate. Having a support system that exists outside of work benefitted me by providing opportunities to establish different kinds of goals among people who hold me accountable to them. This helps to keep my life balanced. Time away from work allows me to appreciate what it is I do and why it is I do it. Whether it is planning an annual vacation trip or taking mental health days to rest, it is important to have something in place to help me regain my strength and focus.

Being proactive is essential. I never left anything to chance. Being proactive to me means understanding my job responsibilities and being able to predict or forecast projects or themes based on my experience and best-practice benchmarking. For example, complaints from faculty members about disruptive students were typically received via email without adequate detail for further action. In an effort to strengthen our reporting process, I developed an incident reporting form for faculty that outlined all of the necessary information we would need to proceed with the student referral. If I was not sure about something, I sought clarity. In addition, I was not afraid to initiate new projects. If my supervisor liked my proposals, we implemented them. If he did not like a particular proposal, we discussed ways to make it better. If there were things I wanted and needed to get from the position, I searched for them. I found ways to create professional development opportunities around me by pursuing conferences, trainings, and webinars. Anything that would help me become more polished in my position, I did it. I made it a part of my job description to report on current trends and best practices in the field.

To be successful in this field, I believe you must infuse yourself into your professional experience. This not only makes your work authentic, but it affects the students we engage within our everyday lives. Through my first professional experience, I made the transition from a first-generation college student to a first-generation student affairs practitioner. Like the first time I stepped foot on a college campus, this world was new to me. It can be intimidating at times because it continues to extend far beyond my comfort zone. It is not easy to share my experiences with others; however, I do it because my past reflects the present realities in some of our students' lives. I want to serve as an advocate and example for those who may be losing hope—for those, like Jamal, who find it difficult to believe we can transform our lives and circumstances. No matter where my career takes me, my focus will be on student development and transformation. Furthermore, no matter how far up I climb, I will not forget what it was like to be at the bottom. The most important lesson I learned throughout my journey is "I am not Jamal." I am DuJuan. I created my own path and was a trailblazer in my family and among my peers. Even if I looked at the journeys other people took or listened to perspectives given to me from mentors, I control my professional experience. I have to own this experience, because it will help to define what I am about and who I am in the profession. Exploring my personal and professional identities and finding my voice are the greatest assets I have acquired in the field. I have established my values and ideals, and I participate in projects that match my professional identity; however, I am not afraid to take a risk and try something outside of my comfort zone. If I do not affirm who I am, others will define me. My upbringing and my experiences affect this profession; all of our stories do. By us coming together, we are creating a diverse pool of thoughts and ideas that strengthen our ability to better serve our students. My first professional position in student affairs is my foundation, but it does not have to define me.

CHAPTER 2 DISCUSSION QUESTIONS

New Professionals

- How have your personal and professional experiences shaped your decision to become a student affairs professional? How is your journey similar to and different from that of your colleagues?
- How has your involvement in student affairs influenced your identity?
- How do you balance "running your own race" with "running someone else's race"?
- Have your mentors influenced you and your career choices? If so, how?

Supporters of New Professionals

- What are characteristics of a promising new professional?
- What are the characteristics and responsibilities of an ideal mentor?
- How can mentors encourage new professionals to make unique, self-inspired contributions to their work?
- If new professionals are not as self-motivated as DuJuan, are there strategies to help inspire this drive?

—*QUESTIONS PREPARED BY KATIE SHOEMAKER*

CHAPTER 3

Making the Most of the Long Job Search

CRAIG R. BERGER

After several months of writing cover letters, navigating online applications, scheduling phone interviews, and allowing my anticipation to rise, the last three possible universities dismissed me. After enduring the last of the phone calls, I sat at my parents' dining room table—my "office," as my family called it—and for the first time, I felt defeated. These last rejections hurt more than others because, for the first time in my search, I had no lingering prospects. My job search had come to a screeching halt.

Sitting there dejectedly that summer night in June 2011, I replayed the past several years in my head. "Why was this happening?" I wondered. My mentors and advisors from my former institution—Penn State Erie, The Behrend College (where I worked for three years in an entry-level residence life position between my undergraduate experience and my graduate program)—told me how well positioned I was. I would have highly coveted fulltime experience and a graduate degree upon re-entering the job market. Yet, as I reflected on the rejections I had received, I realized that the majority of my classmates were looking for jobs similar to my Penn State position, which was an entry-level position in residence life. I was interested in securing my first job post-graduate school in a service–learning, civic engagement, or leadership office, not a residence life department like so many of my peers. Although I recognized that the circumstances of each job search do not make for easy or fair comparisons to peers' searches, I felt increasing pressure to get a job sooner rather than later because of my previous experience and crystal-clear career aspirations.

Telling classmates, former colleagues, and mentors that I was living with my parents, who continued to support me into my mid-20s and while my bachelor's and master's degrees collected dust, was difficult and embarrassing. With each passing day, my self-imposed pressure intensified. Even my friends' and mentors' supportive responses (which I very much appreciated) led my overactive mind to wonder how others actually perceived my joblessness. Did they question my capacity to manage my job search? Did they think I was not working hard enough? Were they feigning optimism and encouragement while secretly thinking that I was a loser? With no opportunities on the proverbial horizon, I questioned the clarity of my career plans. Did I need to revise my plans in the face of this seemingly brutal job market?

During one phone call with the chair of a search committee, I learned that candidates possessing doctorates were also unsuccessful and unemployed. It was then that I recognized that my full-time work experience advantage alone was not going to land me a job. I was sleepwalking through my job search foolishly assuming that fate would intervene and save me. If my search was going to have a happy ending, I needed to examine more closely my sense of self and identity, paying particular attention to qualities that distinguish me from other candidates.

Additional job opportunities surfaced a few weeks after my search stalled. Two positions interested me. Both jobs were at the University of Maryland, Baltimore County (UMBC), which is a mid-sized honors university in Baltimore. The positions available were a leadership position and a position working with student government and civic engagement initiatives on campus. Using the wisdom I gained from my previous professional experience and learning about UMBC's culture and values through its presence in social media, I quickly concluded that the student government/civic engagement position was my top choice. Furthermore, I concluded that UMBC's collaborative and innovative campus environment was the place for me. While this prospect was promising, the reality of the situation continued to intrude on my positive thoughts. The summer was ending. Universities were posting fewer jobs, and most of my graduate school colleagues had begun work. Would I be the unemployed 1% of the graduate students from my academic program?

Luckily, I was not left pondering this thought for long. On back-to-back days, representatives from each search committee at UMBC contacted me expressing interest in scheduling phone interviews. Having reached the phone interview stage previously in my search, I remembered walking away from those experiences feeling tentative at best about my performance and, in one particular experience, dejected. Unanticipated questions, a poor phone connection, and my own nervousness flustered me. Recalling those unpleasant experiences, I prepared for each of these new phone interviews feverishly, recognizing the opportunities in front of me and resolving to make the most of them.

After speaking with both UMBC search committees over the phone, I realized I had improved my phone interview skills. While other phone interview experiences felt a bit more formal and hard to decipher how they were progressing, I noticed that I came away from the calls with UMBC feeling like I got to know specific, authentic people and not simply generic search committee members. I recognize that in any interview process the questions posed to the candidate implicitly communicate the skills and style of the institution and hiring office personnel. In both of these interviews, I felt the questions the search committee members asked hinted at an intensely collaborative and innovative work environment, a setting to which I was drawn. For the first time, I came away from both phone interviews pleased with the experience, in terms of the people I met and my comfort in answering their questions.

After a few days passed, I received a call from one of the search committee chairs notifying me that both committees were inviting me to visit UMBC's campus and interview for both positions. To make the process more convenient, both committees decided that I could interview for each position on the same day, especially because I would be meeting with many of the same people for each position. Meeting with two search committees, several administrators, and many students made for a long day, but I also had the opportunity to learn as much as I could about the responsibilities of the two positions and the institution's culture. I recalled feeling comfortable in nearly every conversation while also believing that there was more to learn from the people and from the environment. At the end of the day, I met with my eventual supervisor who asked me which position I thought would fit me better. I told him that I felt the civic engagement/student government position fit me the best as it drew on many of my passions and previous experiences. I waited a week before UMBC made an offer, and I accepted the position of Coordinator of Campus and Civic Engagement.

Although the last few weeks of the job search—filled with the excitement and anticipation of on-campus interviews and positive feedback—passed quickly, the majority of the process progressed at a snail's pace. Fortunately, the need to complete my graduate work distracted me from the job search until May. As I packed my belongings and moved into my parents' house following graduation, I found myself with even more time on my hands than I had expected. In those last weeks of May and throughout the month of June with my parents both working, I spent the weekdays alone with my laptop, constantly scouring the well-known student affairs and civic engagement job sites for appealing positions. This routine quickly wore on me. How was I going to sustain myself all summer by hitting the refresh button? Increasingly, I understood that I was not going to be able to completely eradicate the waiting game from the process. I recognized that although I could not control the speed of the hiring institutions and their representatives, I could spur myself to find more productive and fulfilling ways to pass the time. For the remainder of this essay, I will reflect on how I channeled my frustration with the job search into meaningful, productive tasks that not only focused me as a candidate but, once hired, enhanced my learning and professional development.

STAYING FOCUSED

In recalling my job search process, I realized that I never felt sorry for myself. There were times that made me question my plans more deeply than I had previously allowed myself to do, but even then I was re-tooling in the face of rejection and staying focused throughout the job search process. I believed that a large part of whether or not I found a job that fit my needs depended upon my initiative and performance; however, I recognized that I was blessed to have a strong family behind me, a privilege that not everyone experiences. Although I may have questioned the circumstances in which I was living under my parent's roof as a grown man, I never had to question that I had a place to live. Living with my parents and surrounded by childhood memories provided a rare opportunity to contemplate how much I had grown. I occasionally recalled my mom's aphorisms, amused that they still maintained relevance. "When you keep score, nobody wins" may have been coined in response to trivial matters like spelling tests or the brands of book bags, but as I was resisting the temptation to compare my job search with those of my peers, it reminded me to focus on what I could control. I also enjoyed the company and support of two good friends from high school, one of whom was conducting his own job search in higher education. Remembering the assets I did have—my family, my friends, professional mentors, and terrific professional and academic experiences—immunized me to any feeling of resignation and spurred me to keep moving forward.

MODELING PATIENCE

While I was energized and moving forward, I also knew that I had no choice but to exhibit patience. I was not going to land a job by exerting sheer will. As prospective institutions convened search committee meetings, communicated with mammoth candidate pools, and navigated fiscal calendars and other political realities, I needed to withstand the hours and days when the phone did not ring and no new messages were in my inbox. Early in the process, I felt this ongoing clash of clichés in my head. As "good things come to those who wait" battled with "carpe diem," I realized that I would need to reconcile the two. I eventually understood that seizing the day did not mean turning a boring or undesirable job into something glamorous in the interest of manufacturing progress. I also could not rely on a dream job randomly appearing. Instead, I needed to use the time institutions were providing me to create additional, calculated opportunities. Toward the end of my search, I embraced an active patience, reviewing attractive job descriptions for desired skills I had yet to hone (and developing those) and communicating with my professional contacts in hopes of discovering connections to prospective institutions. These activities kept me on my feet and strengthened me as a candidate throughout the job search.

REDISCOVERING THE PAST

I also spent my down time thinking about the meaningful events that led me to this critical juncture in my professional and personal life. In sorting through my belongings that summer, I rediscovered school projects from my high school and college days, application essays, and old resumes that spurred reflection about who I am and the experiences I considered to be the most fundamental and life-changing. Reading these documents helped me zoom out of the job-search process and re-contextualize what I was doing against the larger backdrop of my life. I could trace my interests over time, moving from history to music to education and my passion for politics and democracy that maintained a steady presence throughout all these changes. I recalled maintaining an interest in political consulting and the campaign management field until I recognized that the day-to-day job responsibilities accompanying this career (crafting negative campaign advertisements and strictly evaluating my work on whether or not the campaign won) did not match my more collaborative, optimistic values. I remembered how I arrived at wanting to work in the field of civic engagement in a higher education setting, working with idealistic students and recognizing the value in my ability to listen, be patient, motivate, and encourage critical thinking. I slowly compiled lessons and experiences, building a sturdier rationale for my career plans that used my talents and created positive change. Whether these experiences were jolting (such as when I was told by my undergraduate institution that I was not qualified to study in Washington, DC, for a semester) or eye-opening (such as when I led an alternative spring break trip as a residence life professional and realized I could blend politics with my work), they formed something unique that I could offer to employers. I was responsible for clearly conveying what this unique set of deliverable qualities was.

In all of these documents and projects from the past, I recognized that the majority involved listening and being able to place myself in others' shoes. I understood from my prior professional experiences that these were ideal skills within student affairs, especially in the civic engagement functional area I was looking to enter. I realized that I was going to need to talk more about my empathy and my listening skills, not only because I knew that's what was desired but because these were the most foundational pieces of my practice and my personality. Although I could have acknowledged to anyone when prompted that I was strong in these areas, it took serious reflection to realize that empathy and listening skills formed such a large part of my personal and professional identity.

PROCESSING THE RIDE

Continuing the theme of reflection, writing in a blog was another summer project that helped. Although looking backward and forward while surmising where I needed to go next helped, I felt a need to process my experience in the present. Knowing that I am an introvert who enjoys writing, I chose blogging as my outlet. The process of wrestling with my thoughts and making sense of them aided me in gaining perspective and making the job search more bearable. The day after my job search had all but fallen apart, blogging helped me the most. I sat down at my makeshift desk at the dining room table and started writing. That morning I started stream-of-consciousness typing. Ideas flowed from my mind, through my fingers, and filled the once-empty textbox on my computer screen. Starting with the line, "I'm not sure if I was naïve or what," I laid bare my frustrations, acknowledging that I significantly restricted my search, both in identifying civic engagement as my desired student affairs functional area and looking exclusively for job opportunities within several hours of my family. This blog post helped me get back on track, as it led me to identify for the first time how I was going to need to adjust my strategy and my tactics. I understand that blogging is not for everyone, yet having an outlet through which I could process the roller coaster nature of the job search significantly aided my well-being.

RESETTING EXPECTATIONS

This reflective work assisted me in maintaining a healthy perspective on what I was actually hunting. I equipped myself to approach available positions in a balanced way through avoiding feeling sorry for myself, identifying who I am and what skills and experiences I would carry into a job, and ably processing the twists and turns of the job search. There were times during my search when idealism drove my activity, as I believed there was a perfect job that would value who I was while also being in a civic engagement office and within my desired geographic area. After a few months of finding nothing and watching several classmates quickly secure jobs, I questioned this assumption. I responded by moving too far in the other direction, eventually concluding that any position would do and that I could exert enough control in any new environment to tailor it to my preferences. Although this approach led me to apply for more jobs and resulted in more invitations to interview, I realized that taking such an approach was foolhardy and naïve. These offices and institutions were complex, political organizations, and there were going to be dynamics that I could not just ignore or change. Coming to this understanding restrained me from investing myself too much in positions that had little to no connection to who I was or what I wanted to do with my life and my career. I was seeking a meaningful job and a position that was simply good enough for me.

MAKING THE MOST OF SOCIAL MEDIA

The last task on which I focused during my down time was enhancing my use of social media in the job search. When I began preparing for my phone interviews with UMBC, I remember reading a blog named "Co-Create UMBC," created by a member of the Office of Student Life in 2007. Many universities used traditional websites populated with mostly static content to educate job candidates, but I noticed this site—full of personalized perspectives on UMBC news, events, history, and culture—and immediately realized that I had stumbled upon a goldmine. In a series of posts called "Real People Profiles," the blogger introduced various campus community members to readers, not only introducing them in their on-campus roles but also emphasizing the unique aspects of their personalities. I also read about campus traditions, like the campus bonfire that occurs as a part of each fall homecoming celebration (and was first organized only a few years earlier based on a student's suggestion), as well as a community journal tucked beneath a bench in the campus rock garden. Most importantly, I recognized the office's values, like collaboration, innovation, and diversity—all integral parts of the UMBC community. By the time I arrived on campus for my interviews, reading four years' worth of blog posts made me feel like I had already been there and met many staff and students.

In exposing me to notable community members, critical events in the life of the university, and the ideologies at work on campus, "Co-Create UMBC" helped me see that the office's actions and values followed closely those same values the university espoused. For me, this blog spoke volumes about UMBC's institutional culture and the environment in which I would be working. I recognize that there are many colleges and university administrators who would consider employees writing about their day-to-day experiences for students to be dangerous territory, too risky to allow. Yet with "Co-Create UMBC," I realized that not only were many different UMBC community members commenting on the blogger's posts, but these posts were fed into an online campus portal named "MyUMBC," an electronic campus hub containing information on student-planned campus events, student discussion boards, and feeds from many different UMBC websites. Thus, the site posted everything the blogger wrote for the entire campus to see, and anyone possessing a MyUMBC account could "paw" (or "like") a post, and if inclined, offer feedback for the whole UMBC community to view. This open approach to social media suggested that the institution trusts its employees, views them as people capable of possessing opinions, and values a robust exchange of ideas.

CONCLUDING THE LONG, HOT SUMMER

My summer of unemployment began without much promise. Having graduated from my master's program with no serious leads for any jobs, not much time passed before I realized how difficult the next several weeks or months would be. Noting that I had a choice between pessimistically disengaging from the process or productively using this spare time, I worked on these six areas (staying focused, modeling patience, rediscovering the past, processing the ride, resetting expectations, and making the most of social media), to strengthen my candidacy while enduring the long process.

As I sit in my office at UMBC about six months removed from experiencing the low point in my job search, I recognize that working on these six areas not only improved my candidacy but also prepared me to succeed in my job. Advising all aspects of the student government is my largest responsibility at

UMBC. With this comes a duty to foster an empowering atmosphere for students: an environment that encourages young adults to explore their passions and interests, examine where they have come from, and understand where they wish to go and that assists them in developing tools and resources to make that leap. I find that I can easily relate to students in their occasional struggles with the intimidating nature of putting their work, their passion, and themselves on the line with no apparent guaranteed outcome. I remember initially shying away from fully investing myself in the job search for fear of coming away with nothing. As the summer progressed, I realized I needed to apply myself fully if I was going to be successful, and I eventually discovered that I had the power and stamina to do this. Recalling the process of refocusing my job search allows me to empathize with student leaders as they discover their own power and learn how to work with others to make change. The process of initiating change is long and messy. It can be both frustrating and exhilarating. There is no promise of success, yet taking the risk of going through the journey developed and strengthened me.

Not only do I see the links from my job search work to my current responsibilities at UMBC but I also realize the work I did over the summer has paid off. A few weeks after being hired, several students approached the student body president regarding offensive posts on the MyUMBC online discussion board. These topics, which I thought about significantly in my preparation for my UMBC interview, played a large role in working with students to resolve the matter.

In reflecting on my work at UMBC, I recognize that each of my current responsibilities represents a piece of each of my past experiences that I loved, making it easier for me to be authentic in my work. Student government formed the core of my undergraduate identity while at Allegheny College, something by which everyone knew me. I also participated in a leadership retreat, the Collegiate Leadership Conference, at Allegheny allowing me to develop authentic relationships with other students, administrators, and staff on campus and heavily influencing my decision to enter the field of student affairs. Interestingly, I have already served as a facilitator for our own leadership retreat within the first few months on the job, again leading to strong relationships with members of the UMBC community I had not previously met. Finally, I find that working with students in my current position involves a significant number of one-on-one conversations, getting to know students on an individual basis and examining with them what they wish to change on campus and how to create a strategy. Similarly, serving as a resident director in graduate school for a living–learning community with a self-governance theme involved many intentional one-on-one conversations with students. Observing similarities between my previous experiences and aspects of my new job at UMBC are not surprising, given that I felt comfortable enough to apply for the job in the first place. However, as I reflect on these months in my new position, my love for my work stems from the differing aspects of my passions and philosophy that are sprinkled throughout my job duties, my professional environment, and the institution. The work I did this summer made these aspects easier to see.

I currently find myself in a place where the possibilities energize me: possible relationships, possible educational moments, and possible life-altering events. I embrace every opportunity to learn as much as I can about the students, my colleagues, the institution, the duties and responsibilities of my job, and the city of Baltimore. As of now, I have found the best possible fit for me. I also recognize I did the groundwork needed to be hired and to experience on-the-job success. I am fortunate to find myself in such a positive situation. I have everything I could possibly want in this position, and I am aware that this kind of ideal setting is rarely the outcome of a first job search. While the pressures of the job search have receded and each day demonstrates how terrific the outcome has been, I find myself confronting other questions as I contemplate the future. Is it possible to secure two dream jobs in one's professional career? Have I peaked too early? Although I know that I will have quite a bit of time to ponder the answers to these questions in the upcoming years, I also recognize that making the most of this long job search taught me that there is always something on the horizon for which I can prepare.

CHAPTER 3 DISCUSSION QUESTIONS

New Professionals

- What personal and professional insights about yourself will influence your next job search?
- What are your aspirations for your next job search? What steps are you taking to attain these aspirations?
- Which of your professional and personal experiences energize you?

Supporters of New Professionals

- How can you support (e.g., staying positive, keeping motivated, encouraging reflection) new professionals during their job searches?
- How can you help new professionals like Craig create realistic expectations when it comes to the job search, particularly when they compare themselves to others?
- Typically, new professionals lack patience during their job searches. How can you help new professionals balance getting a job with getting the "right" job?

—*QUESTIONS PREPARED BY KATIE SHOEMAKER*

CHAPTER 4

Self-Defining Relationships and Redefining Expectations

MOLLY PIERSON

I used to fear that a close intimate relationship would lead my personal life to dictate my professional career. However, through my commitment to my partner and willingness to embark on a co-navigated job search journey, I have come to understand that the relationship I feared would keep me from achieving my personal aspirations actually fueled my passions and continues to provide me purpose in my career. Managing relationships and personal expectations defined my first job as the Honors Program Coordinator at Saint Louis University and contributed to my sense of personal growth there.

My graduate school experience is where my personal relationship and professional aspirations first collided. I developed a passion for student conduct and conflict resolution and, certainly noteworthy, committed to the love of my life. By graduation in May 2009, I was on the verge of moving to St. Louis and getting married but was still unemployed. Fortunately, two weeks later, a potential employer called. It was not my dream job in residential life (i.e., the ideal stepping-stone to a career in student conduct); instead, this job prospect was an academic program management position (i.e., a not-so-ideal stepping stone to my career pursuits). Intrigued, uncertain, and anxious to wrap up the job search process, I accepted the Honors Program Coordinator position.

Throughout this stressful job search ordeal, I gradually defined what mattered to me—my relationships. My relationship with my partner Josh made me feel centered and comfortable with myself. The relationships that I forged during graduate school and during my on-campus interview process gave me the support needed to succeed in a not-so-ideal work environment. Once I began working, the importance of relationships also became a centerpiece of my professional identity.

GRADUATE SCHOOL AND STARTING TO DEFINE VALUES IN THE PROFESSION

In retrospect, my relationship with my mentor—the Vice President of Student Affairs and our advisor for student government at my alma mater, Washburn University—influenced my choice to pursue a career in student affairs. Denise Ottinger helped me focus my interests and encouraged me to apply to the Higher Education and Student Affairs (HESA) department at Bowling Green State University. My trust in her guidance led to a string of quick decisions. Within a short span during my senior year, I changed my career aspirations from working in the medical field to higher education, took the Graduate Record Exam, and applied to the Bowling Green State University's College Student Personnel program. The HESA faculty accepted me into the program; two weeks following graduation from Washburn University, I moved to Bowling Green, Ohio.

During my graduate studies, I had a series of self-defining moments and, most importantly, self-defining relationships. I spent my first graduate school summer with a small cohort of students who, like me, had assistantships at small colleges in Northwest Ohio. We enrolled in a student development theory seminar during the summer term. We quickly created a strong bond, and my new colleagues not only provided advice and support during the seminar but throughout my two years as a graduate student. To this day, I rely on and value those relationships. The student development theory seminar introduced me to relevant topics of great interest to me. I explored how relationships affect student growth and self-identity. I discovered that through conflict and relationship dissonance, individuals can learn about themselves in meaningful ways. Relationships were helping me form a better sense of my personal identity, and I began to understand why, as described by the student development theories I was learning.

I spent my first year in graduate school as a hall director at a small Catholic college in Michigan, Sienna Heights University. A unique aspect of this small community was the strong relationships among individuals across the entire campus. I supervised a small staff of resident advisors (RAs) and was the only live-in professional staff member. I encountered numerous crises, including a student death and a fight on the same night. I remember sitting in the room with a campus police officer who informed two students about the death of their friend. I will never forget that conversation and my reactions and feelings. It was during this tragedy that I felt my true purpose being fulfilled—forging meaning-ful relationships with students. I value helping students make sense of an issue they are struggling to understand and providing them comfort and support. Henceforth, I have never shied away from telling a student something difficult or addressing an issue or concern directly. I recognize the importance of human interactions, and I knew that I could be there for them and provide the appropri-ate balance of challenge and support. Our community at Sienna demonstrated a genuine sense of solidarity; a support network stretched across academic affairs and student affairs. I understood the value of human scale organizations and human relationships. Again, these relationships gave me the strength needed to make it through the good and not-so-good times.

My assistantship during my second year of graduate school was in the HE-SA office. I assisted in recruiting and admitting the next cohort of graduate stu-dents. I lived in a sorority house and served as a mentor for the residents. Living with a small group of women and helping them with even the smallest concerns solidified my purpose of being there for students. As a HESA intern, I had many interactions with faculty, but most importantly, I had the opportunity to wel-come and serve as a resource for the new graduate students. The one-on-one contact and conversations with colleagues every day not only helped me learn the value of having professional colleagues but also gave me a sense of support-ing my peers. In addition, these experiences helped me better understand my passion for and interest in mentoring. They also helped me develop my values regarding relationships and provided me opportunities to apply my classroom knowledge to practice (and vice versa).

It was the time spent in my practicum at the University of Michigan that gave me clear direction and the tools I needed to be an intentional, effective con-flict mediator and community builder. I took part in helping student affairs pro-fessionals and students rebuild communities when relationships were most vul-nerable: when students engaged in behaviors that were adverse to community standards and affected their peers negatively. I started to think more complexly about relationships and how each student conflict situation was different given the context and the individuals involved. I had never before considered how approaching conflict from a purely relational level could lead to greater benefits and growth. I thought back to my strongest relationships and realized that when I successfully worked through a tough situation with someone my relationship with that person was deepened. I also learned a lot about myself.

Weekly for three semesters, I implemented a residence-based conduct pro-cess that used restorative justice as an influence. Restorative justice is a conflict resolution model. The program focused on the harms and needs of the communi-ty and the responsibility of the person who caused those harms to make repairs. Restorative practices require students who violate a policy or community stand-ard to participate in a community circle where they sit with those they negative-ly influenced and collectively forge a resolution. For the first time, I saw the student development theory I learned in the classroom actually apply to students. Students became aware of multiple perspectives, considered the thoughts and feelings of others, and usually became more responsible individuals. I used my seminar assignments to better understand how the restorative practice process can help students develop and grow. I connected it to Kohlberg's (1976) theory of moral development, Kolb's (1984) theory of experiential learning, and Baxter Magolda's (2009) theory of self-authorship. I presented the insights I gained from blending theory with practice at two national conferences. This work was and still is a passion of mine with the root being the tremendous opportunities for moral growth and self-reflection it provides students.

My shared interest in this particular area also generated two important relationships. My supervisor at the University of Michigan taught me what it meant to have a good supervisor: someone who exposes you to new ideas, supports you in your creativity, and encourages you to grow as a professional. I also grew closer to a colleague who was writing his dissertation on restorative practices. We often traveled to Ann Arbor together to attend community circles, and he pushed me to think more critically about my interest in and knowledge about conflict resolution. I learned the value of sharing an interest with colleagues and feeling a network of support in the work being done for students. Conversations with these two colleagues created an opportunity for me to learn more about my area of passion although it was not a part of my direct job responsibilities.

I realized that my career interests were narrowing quickly. Yet a question persisted—could my more focused career aspirations dovetail with my relationship with Josh? Trying to secure a job while Josh simultaneously applied to law schools was stressful to say the least. Uncertainty reigned. I turned down what I thought was an ideal first job because of Josh. My original fear of personal relationships keeping me from career interests really set in, and I tried my best to apply confidently and positively for jobs only in St. Louis that appeared to be mutually compatible for both Josh and me.

THE JOB SEARCH

I really wanted to work in residential life where I could work one-on-one with students and apply what I had learned about restorative practices to student conduct. I envisioned attending professional conferences, interviewing with a few schools, getting two or three on-campus interviews, and then selecting my ideal job. Unfortunately, the process was far more complex and turbulent. I attended a major conference, and I interviewed with a few schools in or near St. Louis. However, I did not get the hoped for on-campus interviews for the two residential life jobs open in the St. Louis area. I quickly realized that working in residential life was not going to be an option for me. Plan B: I applied for everything and anything that would allow me to work on a college campus in student affairs. I applied for admissions, advising, and administrative positions—some sure bets and some long shots. To my surprise, three weeks before our wedding, I received invitations to interview for two separate positions at Saint Louis University. I found myself overwhelmed with the joy of making a commitment to someone I deeply cared for and feeling relieved that I might just get a job.

During a thirty-minute phone interview, an interviewer posed what I thought sounded like an odd question: "What do you think about Scrabble?" Being a big Scrabble fan, I gushed about my love for the game. Laughter exploded on the other end of the phone. I, too, laughed when I learned that the question was about travel, not Scrabble. I made a lasting impression! Laughter can sometimes be the best way to start a relationship and reveal your humanness and vulnerabilities, and in this case, it was. I had an on-campus interview and met with the director, the current coordinator, and a few students. Twenty minutes after the interview concluded, I was the new Honors Program Coordinator. Because of my conversations during the interviews, it was clear that my soon-to-be supervisor valued me and vice versa. I personally connected with my future colleagues. Admittedly, I put trust in my personal relationships and put my passion for restorative justice and student conduct on hold.

FIRST DAYS ON THE JOB

The first day on the job had its usual issues and one that unexpectedly left my new spouse taking the bus and light rail home from downtown St. Louis. As I finalized last-minute details on the car ride to campus (we shared one car), I realized that the human resources session was on the medical campus that was more than a walk from my new office. Long story short, I had to keep the car, and my partner was stuck taking public transportation home. On day one, I realized how critical Josh's support would be for the year to come.

During my first days on the job I started to develop some good relationships. I quickly bonded with another young woman, a campus minister. She, too, had moved to St. Louis to be with her partner. Our lunches really helped me keep life in perspective and value the strength a shared experience can bring. This relationship quickly put to rest one of my big concerns about taking the job—the fear that being in a small department would leave me isolated and without the support a larger department (as in the residential life experience) usually provides.

It quickly became evident that department staff members were overworked, and the director had many responsibilities beyond our department initiatives. We worked additional hours because we cared about supporting one another and, most importantly, supporting students. Fortunately, my supervisor was an inspiring person and helped me believe that I had what it took to move the department in a positive direction. She is the one who helped me translate my student affairs expertise to this unique academic environment. She infused more service-learning and campus involvement expectations into the honors curriculum that encouraged me. She encouraged me to be creative and bring my knowledge to life in the work we were doing. Although I had freedom, I was seeking a supervisor who could provide more guidance and feedback on the work I was doing. I valued our friendship and relationship but knew I would need more to be a better professional in the future.

BEING THE STUDENT AFFAIRS EXPERT

I was the only one in my office with a background in higher education. Translating what I learned in graduate school to a language that made sense and spoke to other professionals in the office regularly challenged and frustrated me. I corresponded with department administrators about course listings. Most of these individuals wanted to make sure class information was accurate. Seldom did we talk about the many good conversations I had with students about classes or campus life. I struggled with my job responsibilities. I was an office manager who administered policies and procedures. When students visited the office, I only saw them in passing and instead helped graduate student staff give guidance to students. Establishing and maintaining interpersonal relationships with honor students seemed secondary to my managerial roles.

I primarily corresponded with academic departments in coordinating honors classes, reviewed honors applications, created reports and proposals for additional departmental support, and was the advisor for the honors student association. I talked to the occasional upset parent and was the first to troubleshoot any issue that came our way. I was focusing on relationships and corresponding more with those outside of the student population than with students, something I had foreseen doing later in my career but not in my first job.

Despite the frustration of being so focused on administration and office management, there were many things I came to love about my work—mostly relationships with colleagues and supervisees. I was quickly getting to know other academic advisors on campus and developing a sense of collaboration. I was among a group of dedicated professionals who cared deeply about the students. I valued being in a professional community that shared my commitment to student growth and learning. I involved myself in advising committees. I represented our department and made efforts to extend better support to campus partners.

The days I liked most were the ones where I had the opportunity to brainstorm with colleagues and talk about how to support students' development through their advising experiences. The advisors at Saint Louis University believed the advising experience for students was more than just picking classes. These professionals strove to support the students holistically and played critical roles in making sure they achieved their final goals of learning and graduating. These colleagues provided me the strength and guidance to be successful in my newfound area of student services. I discovered the value of the advisor–student relationship and developed a deeper respect for academic advising. Through my friendships with advising colleagues, I learned that the advisor–student relationship was more intricate and complex than I once thought. Advisors serve many roles for students depending on students' needs, and this support system is critical for student success.

I worked in a department where I could make changes for the betterment of students without worrying about too much red tape. This was different from what I expected. With colleagues, I was able to create and implement systems to encourage student learning outside the classroom as such systems did not previously exist. We not only encouraged honors students to excel and be challenged in their studies, we also provided them opportunities to grow as individuals. My role was to make sure the initiatives kept moving forward and that we communicated this with other departments. I took pride in the work I was doing for students mostly indirectly, but at times, directly. Being there for students in all capacities was paramount for me.

Again, most of my work for students was indirect. This altered the way I envisioned student–student affairs educator relationships. It was not one-on-one interactions but instead consisted mostly of advocating for students. One instance in particular will never leave me. As part of my supervisor's responsibilities, she also oversaw a scholarship program for students committed to the ideals and values of Martin Luther King, Jr. There were some proposed changes to the allocation of this scholarship program. I sat in meetings taking notes and started to crunch my own numbers. There were a handful of us who realized that although advocates argued that the change would benefit students given their financial aid packages, in the end they would receive less money. My supervisor graciously heard my concerns and with her support I, along with a few on the committee, took a stand against the change. I could not sit there knowing that students who needed the scholarships would be harmed. Sending an email here and there, taking meticulous notes, asking for other thoughts, I helped ensure that the scholarship allocation formula remained intact. I let my passion for helping students go beyond my direct duties. These actions helped me find my purpose again of being there for students when they needed it most. My support was not based on forming conventional student affairs interpersonal relationships with students.

One of the most rewarding experiences for me was helping one of the honors students apply for the Truman Scholarship. I knew she was a strong candidate. I read over her essays and policy proposal. I fine-tuned her personal statement and offered critical feedback while affirming her sense of confidence. I conducted mock interviews. I drove four hours to attend a session on the Truman Scholarship to collect any information that would benefit her. I watched as she gained confidence in herself and transformed into the woman she was meant to be. She became a Truman Scholar, and she helped me realize again my passion to help students become who they want to be.

QUESTIONING FIT AND CREATING OPPORTUNITIES

Despite all the positives of my position, I wondered how I would become an educator down the road if I seldom had the opportunity to spend quality time with students. My abilities and strengths during graduate school came to life whenever I worked with students in crisis. Except for the occasional students who appeared at the office door crying because they really needed to drop a course, crisis management was the exception not the rule in my world of work. I questioned whether time spent in this way was best for my career.

During my graduate studies when the semester ended, I changed my daily routines without the students on campus. I enjoyed this student-free time and used it to refresh and work on unfinished projects. However, in my current job, I realized that most of my work would remain constant over break. Once the students left, including our two graduate students, I was the only one in our office. In the solitude of the office over winter break, I became more committed to figuring out what the next year would entail.

I remember sitting in my windowless office with my feet resting on our heater as I contemplated the questions, "Am I where I am supposed to be?" "Am I providing the services students truly need?" Suddenly smelling the burning of rubber, I quickly pulled my feet off the heater, and seeing the burn mark on one of my shoes, laughed to myself. It was time for me to stop sitting around waiting for something to change and time to take the initiative toward finding a place where my professional passions and personal relationships were both fulfilled.

As the spring semester began, I became deeply committed to making the best of my current situation while simultaneously exploring the possibility of finding a job more suited to my interests and talents. I remained convinced it was possible to do both. Considering other job opportunities did not mean that I had to quit building on the progress I had made the previous semester. I finished my administrative responsibilities more quickly so I could dedicate more hours to advising students (e.g., advising the honors student group). I petitioned, with the support of my supervisor, to teach an entry honors seminar focused on my area of interest: conflict resolution and restorative practices. I involved myself with advising RAs for the honors living–learning community, fulfilling my love for working in residential life. Over time, I realized that a job in residential life is what would make me happy. Subsequently, I applied for hall director positions at my current institution and at a nearby university.

A huge challenge of leaving any job, especially after one year, is deciding when to tell your supervisor. Since I chose to apply for a job internally at the university, I immediately told her about my intentions instead of waiting to learn if I was a finalist. She sensed I had something serious to discuss, because I was a little insistent about scheduling a meeting with her. Moreover, since our working relationship was great, it seldom required sit-down conversations. It was this strong working relationship that made it easier to tell her about my interest in and intention to apply for other jobs. Concurrently, I wanted her to remain confident that I would continue to do a good job regardless of the outcome of my job quest.

It was a hard conversation. I was deeply committed to the honors students, but I had to be honest. My supervisor accepted the news calmly but with disappointment, given that with most first jobs, there is the expectation of staying two or three years. She offered me more opportunities that aligned with my career aspirations including teaching a course and the potential of becoming an assistant director in the next year or two. However, I could not deny my relationship voids. I wanted more student interaction, an opportunity to put my passion into practice, and a network of student affairs colleagues with whom I would work on a daily basis. I assured her of my commitment to the program whether or not I got another job the following year, and I committed to keeping her posted on my advancement in each process.

Knowing that I had done everything I could for myself gave me a sense of clarity. I recommitted to my job and worked less selfishly, realizing what I was building might never be seen by my eyes, but I could make a difference for the students and the staff that followed. This was an important lesson to learn early in my career. I did not take myself too seriously. I remained proud of my accomplishments but realized that what matters was the impact I had on others— most importantly, students. Being committed did not mean I needed to stay in a job that was the wrong fit for me. Instead, it was about ensuring that my decisions continued to make a difference for the students.

LEAVING WITH COMPASSION AND TAKING LESSONS WITH ME

I did not let the idea that I might not be in my current job the following year stop me from pursuing initiatives for the betterment of our program. I thought of the things that frustrated me most and thought about how I could make it easier for the next person. I streamlined processes that consumed much of my time to allow for more time with students. I focused on strengthening our office relations with campus partners to establish a strong foundation for the next honors staff.

I also worked with an information technology specialist to streamline our honors curriculum audits. With our growing number of honors students, the handwritten updates our two graduate student staff regularly made overwhelmed them. Before the year concluded, we had a process in place that just needed some tweaking. I also petitioned for more student workers to help answer phones and complete administrative tasks that otherwise took away from the time in my position that could be dedicated to developing and implementing new initiatives and improving old processes. By the end of the semester, we had more than doubled the number of student worker hours. I learned a valuable lesson from the job: perseverance and focusing on what is good for the department gave me a strong sense of purpose and accomplishment.

Soon I was offered and I accepted a job in residential life at an institution that would allow me to display my passion for restorative practices. Although I was ready to leave Saint Louis University for my dream job, I was not ready to leave those with whom I had worked. Encouraged by my supervisor, I took an active role in finding my replacement. I knew there was someone out there who would do my job better. I spent the majority of my last days helping train new graduate students, delegating responsibilities to the experienced student workers, and creating transition materials for the new program coordinator. Leaving a job does not have to mean broken relationships. Instead, by leaving with compassion, I felt I had re-established how important those I worked with were to me, and I recommitted myself to students by leaving the place better than I found it. The guilt of leaving those I had grown close to quickly vanished as I realized that my choice to leave could be an opportunity for the department as well as myself.

I was fortunate that I fulfilled my commitment to ensuring an even better future for our department. We found a qualified candidate, a seasoned professional with interests that aligned with the office's mission. I departed knowing that the work I had done mattered and that the person who came after me would only serve students better. I was able to leave my first job with a sense of peace. The honors program was on to bigger and better things, and I was on my way to fulfilling my life's passion in my ideal job as a much better person.

SELF-DEFINING RELATIONSHIPS REDEFINED MY CAREER EXPECTATIONS

One year later, my relationships at home as well as in the work place redefined how I saw myself as a professional. My trust in my relationship with my partner grew tremendously, especially during the times I was most unhappy in my job. Being happy and satisfied with my life outside of work made me a more positive and effective professional. Supportive colleagues continuously remind me that although the work was not what I was most passionate about, we still made a difference in the lives of students. By working in an area outside of my interest, I became a more well-rounded professional and more committed to my area of interest. I was able to leave my first job feeling satisfied, renewed, and ready to pursue my passion; most importantly, I am confident that the relationships I develop will continue to be one of the greatest contributors to my sense of professional fulfillment.

REFERENCES

Baxter Magolda, M. B. (2009). *Authoring your life: Developing an internal voice to meet life's challenges.* Sterling, VA: Stylus.

Kohlberg, L. (1976). Moral stages and moralization: The cognitive-developmental approach. In T. Lickona (Ed.), *Moral development and behavior: Theory, research, and social issues* (pp. 31-53). New York, NY: Holt.

Kolb, D. A. (1984). *Experiential learning: Experience as the source of learning and development.* Upper Saddle River, NJ: Prentice-Hall.

CHAPTER 4 DISCUSSION QUESTIONS

New Professionals

- How often do you take time to reflect on the past and present? What conditions support this reflection?
- How do personal and professional relationships influence the work you do and decisions you make?
- How do you know it is time to move on professionally and seek a new job, similar to Molly?
- How do you reconcile supervisor-supervisee differences?
- How do you manage career interests and personal life?

Supporters of New Professionals

- How do you help new professionals develop and manage relationships with colleagues as a new working professional?
- What challenges do new professionals face as they move from graduate student to professional staff?
- How can you maintain relationships with former supervisees or students as they expand their professional networks?
- What strategies do you employ to support new professionals as they make transitions to the work place?

—QUESTIONS PREPARED BY KATIE SHOEMAKER

CHAPTER 5

Identity and the Job One Experience

KEVIN PISKADLO AND CHRISTANA JOHNSON

The transition from graduate student to new student affairs professional is both exciting and anxiety provoking. The reflections by DuJuan Smith, Craig Berger, and Molly Pierson offer keen insights about this transition for graduate students, new professionals, and seasoned professionals who mentor new professionals. These three storytellers are honest and authentic, exposing the common thoughts and feelings (both positive and negative) of new professionals at a pivotal time in their lives. Negotiating the unpredictable nexus between their past roles and identities and their new and emerging ones, DuJuan, Craig, and Molly have recounted personal and familiar stories. Most readers will easily relate to the hopes, dreams, opportunities, uncertainties, struggles, lessons learned, and new beginnings that these authors reveal.

We will discuss four common and interrelated themes that transcend the three aforementioned narratives: how the authors (a) demonstrate a strong sense of self and the need to be true to one's identity, (b) reveal how to manage experiences that do not align with expectations or aspirations (c) highlight the critical role that fit plays in the successful transition from graduate student to new professional, and (d) remind readers about the importance of support networks and supervisors. We situate the authors' stories and our themes within various interpersonal, intrapersonal, identity, and cognitive development theories. Finally, we describe how the authors' stories and our theoretical interpretations relate to our everyday practices as mid-level professionals in student affairs.

DEMONSTRATING A STRONG SENSE OF SELF AND THE NEED TO BE TRUE TO ONE'S SELF AND IDENTITY

One prevalent theme in the three narratives is the importance of having a secure sense of self, a state when an individual is able to identify, describe, and defend a system of beliefs that creates what Baxter Magolda (2001) referred to as one's internal foundation. Repeatedly, the authors' strong internal foundations served them well as they developed personally and professionally. From their experiences as undergraduate students to their postgraduate roles as emerging leaders in student affairs, each of the three storytellers explicitly discussed life decisions. DuJuan bucked the advice of mentors and friends when selecting a graduate school academic program. Craig debated whether to take any old job or be patient and wait for his dream job. Molly had to decide when it was time for her to seek other employment opportunities, when conventional wisdom would suggest she stay put. Their decisions were both sound and easy when each enacted his or her espoused values consistent with strong internal foundations and the ability to reflect critically on the congruence between emerging evidence and sense of self.

DuJuan's, Craig's, and Molly's knowledge of and emphasis on the self illustrates several identity development theories. DuJuan's self-described identity development aligns with Cross's revised nigrescence theory, which centers on the process of becoming Black (Cross & Fhagen-Smith, 2005). This theory describes Black identity development as involving four stages: pre-encounter, encounter, immersion-emersion, and internalization (Cross & Fhagen-Smith, 2005). Two components of Cross's revised model are evident in DuJuan's story. First, DuJuan shared his socialization into Black culture as he recounted his childhood and adolescent years on the Chicago streets—streets that claimed the lives of many of his childhood friends. These experiences align with Stage 1, pre-encounter, where a person can either be alienated from other African-Americans, demonstrating an internalization of racism and self-hate, or strongly attached to other African-Americans, where there is little internalization of racism and positive self-concepts result (Cross & Fhagen-Smith, 2005). Despite neighborhood violence and troubled friends, DuJuan resisted the urge to alienate himself from others from his community. Instead, he displayed a strong attachment to other African Americans, specifically to his mother as she mandated that he obtain a meaningful education.

The second component of Cross's revised model, internalization, is evident in DuJuan's story. He implicitly discussed the importance of race and culture, high self-esteem, and ego development. Yet, there are also three subcategories further describing development. A nationalist, bicultural, or multicultural perspective can be adopted. Evidence of this can be found when DuJuan distinguished himself from another, presumably Black, student to his professor and classmates on the first day of class. At first, to defuse the tension in the classroom, he tried to casually dismiss the racial assumptions they had all made: because of his skin color he must be Jamal. Eventually, he had to state bluntly, "I am not Jamal." His frustration that he had to make this distinction for those in the classroom indicates a high level of racial and cultural salience and either a bicultural or multicultural perspective (Cross & Fhagen-Smith, 2005). After all, Black people do not all look alike and, as DuJuan stated, "everyone has the right to be his or her own person" (p. 17). Through these challenges and opportunities, DuJuan more fully defined himself. His experiences, and the skills and knowledge that developed as a result, helped him to navigate his graduate school selection process.

Identifying and selecting a graduate school is a challenging ordeal for most candidates. This process was particularly complicated for DuJuan. He experienced a developmental crisis as he weighed the pros and cons of two different and competing fields of study. Although many of his mentors and friends lobbied for him to enroll in a more traditional student affairs graduate program, DuJuan selected a less-conventional counseling program. Ultimately he concluded that counseling better aligned with his values. Experiencing and reflecting on this critical decision point was vital to his development: "I learned early the importance of finding my own voice and defining my own path" (p. 17).

Craig discussed the importance of being true to oneself, especially when facing the challenges of a prolonged and painful job search. Temporary unemployment is an increasingly common experience for individuals with earned master's degrees due to economic uncertainty and an anemic job market.

Craig's story mirrors a learning process common to many adults seeking employment. Outside of formal learning that occurs in classrooms, Merriam, Caffarella, and Baumgartner (2007) described two types of adult learning: non-formal and informal. Non-formal education occurs outside of formal learning arenas and includes three sub-categories: self-directed learning (i.e., intentional and conscious), incidental learning (i.e., unintentional and occurring as a side-effect of doing something else), and socialization or tacit learning (i.e., not intentional or conscious and being realized upon reflection; Marsick & Watkins, 1990).

Informal learning—rooted in everyday experiences—best describes Craig's learning while unemployed. Many adults, like Craig, do not realize that their activities are also learning opportunities, even though this is the most common form of learning for adults (Merriam et al., 2007). The result of Craig's incidental, informal learning was his ability to remain true to himself. With his degree in hand, he unexpectedly returned to his childhood home. Although this was admittedly disappointing and mildly embarrassing, Craig took advantage of this down time to thoughtfully reflect upon himself and his identity. Surrounded by artifacts of his childhood, he easily identified and reflected upon his own developmental path. All around him were images of his past—reminders of the values he embraced as a child and refined as an adult after purposeful and honest reflection. Craig took stock of his current life and identified and critically reflected upon values most important to him. He identified how values such as collaboration and empathy interacted with his commitment to social justice in a way that not only made up his internal foundation but also were consistent with the civic engagement functional area he was seeking to join.

Social media played an important role in Craig's process of reflection and discovery. Over time, he successfully stayed focused, modeled patience, rediscovered the past, processed the ride, reset expectations, and made the most of social media.

Craig's ongoing blog documented his job search process, which necessitated that he not only reflect on his identity and experiences but also write and publish them. This deliberate and public process helped him manage his job search experience and the inevitable emotions that emerged in the course of a protracted search. As he described it, "This reflective work assisted me in maintaining a healthy perspective on what I was actually hunting. I equipped myself to approach available positions in a balanced way through avoiding feeling sorry for myself, identifying who I am and what skills and experiences I would carry into a job" (p. 27).

Through reflection, Craig energized and motivated himself, resulting in a renewed search for a position that most closely aligned with his values and career aspirations. Craig's internal foundation served as an important and valuable guide. Even after finding an ideal work setting and successfully securing his dream job, he applied the lessons he learned from his job search to his new job responsibilities.

Molly also connected with and refined her internal foundation during her job search experiences, although qualitatively different from those of DuJuan and Craig. Student affairs mentors, graduate school classmates, and exposure to student development theory during her graduate studies helped Molly first identify and then define her sense of self and create her internal foundation. This process, she wrote, led to the discovery that human relationships played an important role in both her personal and professional lives. As she described it, "relationships were helping me form a better sense of my personal identity, and I began to understand why, as described by the student development theories I was learning" (p. 32) These critically important relationships influenced all facets of her life, helping her in her work with students and in managing the inevitable ups and downs of her life. Relationships helped Molly contextualize her experiences in her first position, a role that she excelled in but that did not satisfy her talents and interests.

The importance of relationships for Molly is an example of Josselson's (1996) theory of psychosocial identity development. Josselson's longitudinal study of women's development from college through their early forties provides insight into the most prominent issues evident in Molly's story. Described as guardians, pathmakers, searchers, and drifters, Josselson's research concluded that women often fall into one of these four patterns.

Molly provided evidence of being congruent with pathmakers, a status exemplified by a willingness to commit to new challenges (Luyckx, Schwartz, Goossens, Beyers, & Missotten, 2011). Pathmakers often expressed dissatisfaction with career choices following college and would often make the changes necessary to find work that was more consistent with their identities (Evans, Forney, Guido, Patton, & Renn, 2010). When she realized that her administrative honors program position was inconsistent with her identity and values, Molly took action. She sought employment positions in residence life, an area of higher education more congruent with her identity and internal foundation.

Although each of the experiences described by the authors is unique, the development of strong internal foundations allowed each of them to identify fundamental values and make decisions based on these values. All of these new professionals situated themselves in graduate preparation programs and professional positions that provided synergies between who they are personally and their professional actions.

This theme reveals the importance of taking the time to be reflective and to do the hard work of formulating and articulating values. Clarifying values is a process that should be woven into the fabric of graduate curricula and part of the job search process. For example, interviewers of new professionals should be transparent about the values and philosophies that guide their work and their department, allowing prospective employees a chance to conduct a cultural audit to determine levels of congruence during the interview process. When new employees arrive, supervisors should commit to formal and informal professional development opportunities to continue these discussions with new professionals and, when appropriate, align work functions to take advantage of the many beneficial outcomes of matching work tasks with the person.

MANAGING EXPERIENCES THAT DO NOT ALIGN WITH EXPECTATIONS

For DuJuan, Craig, and Molly, *excitement* best describes their feelings upon entering the student affairs profession. Bolstered by the knowledge and skills they gained during their graduate studies and graduate work experiences, these new professionals were ready to find their dream jobs and excited to begin their careers. However, these new professionals began their job search processes with the idealized perceptions that there was one perfect job for each of them and that finding and securing those jobs would be easy. As such, when their job searches commenced, their unrealistic expectations did not align with their experiences. This was particularly evident with Craig and Molly.

With three years of work experience in residence life to go along with his new master's degree, Craig anticipated a quick and successful job search process, which did not happen. As his colleagues accepted job offers, he remained at his parents' home working around the clock to become gainfully employed: "There were times during my search when idealism drove my activity, as I believed there was a perfect job that would value who I was while also being in a civic engagement office and within my desired geographic area." (p. 27). Molly too, experienced some friction between her job search expectations and her reality. Although she applied for residence life positions that matched her professional interests, she only searched for positions in close proximity to her partner. This geographical restriction complicated her search process.

Impatient with unemployment, initially Craig and Molly treated the job search as if it were taking place in a vacuum, acknowledging that they were qualified and well prepared yet not paying sufficient attention to larger environmental contexts. Finding a student affairs position is often a difficult task that requires patience and perseverance, and both new professionals sought employment at a time when the United States economy was struggling and colleges and universities across the country were slow to fill job vacancies. Further complicating their searches was the fact that job seekers greatly outnumbered the positions available.

The incongruence between expectations and experiences for these two new professionals continued even after they settled into their new positions. For example, accepting an administrative position outside of student affairs presented Molly with several challenges. As the only staff member in her office with a student affairs degree, Molly experienced culture shock. The background and philosophical culture that she embraced as a graduate of her higher education and student affairs program (e.g., cultivating supportive professional environments and taking the time to develop and maintain meaningful relationships with students) clashed with the cultural norms of her colleagues. Her job responsibilities and espoused values were incompatible. "I was an office manager who administered policies and procedures" (p. 36), she wrote, not the student affairs educator she aspired to be.

Molly's lack of connection with her co-workers and her work context differed greatly from DuJuan, who credited his supervisor and co-workers with supporting his professional development. Current research on the experiences of new student affairs professionals indicates that satisfying and supportive peer relationships are an important part of the socialization of new professionals and often play a role in the persistence of new professionals to stay in the field (Renn & Hodges, 2007; Strayhorn, 2009).

For DuJuan, the conflict between his expectations and reality took place earlier in his life: lack of funds dashed his dream of attending Howard University as an undergraduate. Recognizing the absence of college funds, financial aid, and scholarships, DuJuan acknowledged how incredibly disappointing it was to give up his dream. "Throughout my entire education, I believed that if I worked hard and got good grades, I could go anywhere for college. My hard work did not translate into attending my first choice school" (p. 15).

Although DuJuan did not explicitly discuss his job search, he noted that he never imagined a career in judicial affairs, where he now works. His school and life experiences helped him reveal passions that he did not know existed as he was able to skillfully apply what he learned in his counseling program with the skills he honed growing up in an environment where high-conflict situations were a constant. His ability to successfully negotiate these settings allowed him to work with students in similar high-conflict environments as well as establish boundaries to keep work issues in the office and not take them home with him.

DuJuan encouraged readers to be open to the possibilities and to dream, realizing it is possible that expectations may not match one's reality. These challenging experiences, however, created the dissonance so crucial to the new professionals' ongoing personal and professional development and allowed them to shed their student identities in the process of creating their professional ones. In each of the examples above, the authors came away from these situations with knowledge and experiences that will serve them well in their personal and professional lives.

Understanding the Critical Role That Fit Plays in the Transition From Graduate School to Job One

Several empirical studies in student affairs validate the importance of fit between individuals and their environment (Renn & Hodges, 2007; Renn & Jessup-Anger, 2008). Holland (1997), whose person–environment theory is quite familiar to those in career services, concluded that factors such as beliefs, interests, and behaviors intermix to create a particular personality type.

Holland's research resulted in six different types for both individuals and environments (realistic, investigative, artistic, social, enterprising, and conventional), each type offering distinct interests and values (Evans et al., 2010). The degree to which a person matches with his or her environment can have an impact on the experience in the work place.

The level of congruence between personality type and environment is particularly important in these three stories. DuJuan's and Craig's job searches resulted in accepting job offers that aligned with their personality types. Positions in judicial affairs and civic engagement, respectively, allowed these new professionals to find a synergy between their professional philosophies and the work they were doing. As Craig explained, "My love for my work stems from the differing aspects of my passions and philosophy that are sprinkled throughout my job duties, my professional environment, and the institution" (p. 30).

Molly's experiences differed from those of DuJuan and Craig. Anxious to find a job yet prioritizing the need to live in St. Louis with her partner, Molly concluded that compromise was inevitable. After a couple of failed interviews for residence life positions, she "applied for everything and anything that would allow me to work on a college campus in student affairs" (p. 34). Only twenty minutes after the interview concluded for the honors program coordinator, she found herself employed in higher education.

Although Molly immersed herself into her new role and felt she ably served her department, the person–environment incongruence was obvious. She made many valuable contributions to her new department and was satisfied with many aspects of her work environment, but a chance encounter with her office heater not only left her with burn marks on her shoes but also provided the push that she needed. As she described, "it was time for me to stop sitting around waiting for something to change and time to take the initiative toward finding a place where my professional passions and personal relationships were both fulfilled" (p. 38). In her case, it was a search for greater student interactions and connections with more traditional student affairs co-workers.

Finding fit between who they are and their professional positions was extremely important for these authors and congruent with the findings of other studies that have explored the experiences of new professionals in student affairs (Renn & Hodges, 2007; Renn & Jessup-Anger, 2008). It is certainly an important consideration, because those that experience a stronger fit between personality and environment are more likely to have more satisfying experiences.

Uneasiness with their first positions in student affairs, as experienced by Molly and those who participated in a recent study by Renn and Hodges (2007), highlights the need for a more nuanced understanding of fit and the benefit of divorcing this concept from finding the perfect job. The perfect job concept sets up the new professionals for almost certain disappointment when they realize both that nearly all positions will have aspects that may not be consistent with their dreams and that the ideal job may not exist. Graduate students need to use their critical thinking skills when visiting campuses during job interviews and possess the ability to conduct mini-cultural audits to reveal institutional and office values. Being able to identify the subtle clues of an organization's culture, Bess and Dee (2008) stressed, "is important for understanding what the institution stands for and how and why its members behave in different ways" (p. 362).

COMPREHENDING THE IMPORTANCE OF SUPPORT NETWORKS AND SUPERVISORS

Craig, Molly, and DuJuan discussed the importance of support networks before and during their job searches as well as in their first student affairs positions. They also described constructive roles their initial supervisors played during their first jobs. Renn and Hodges (2007) conducted research on new student affairs professionals and their experiences during their first positions. Their participants identified three significant factors: the importance of relationships, institutional and professional fit, and issues of competence as new professionals.

Many of these stories mirror what other new professionals encounter in their relationships and support networks, including those co-constructed with supervisors. Although Renn and Hodges's (2007) research centers on respondents' first year as student affairs professionals, many of their findings apply to Molly's, DuJuan's, and Craig's undergraduate experiences, job search processes, and first jobs. Craig greatly benefited from the relationships he had with his support network (i.e., family, friends, cohort members, and mentors) during his extended job search. Although he worried about what they thought of him as they expressed reassurance and support, he realized how important they were as they "immunized [him] to any feeling of resignation and spurred [him] to keep moving forward" (p. 25).

DuJuan described a more extensive network of supporters, including his mother who insisted that he attend college, his high school guidance counselor who helped him navigate the college application process, and the vice president of student affairs at his undergraduate institution who helped him identify student affairs as a profession and connected him with a mentor through the NASPA Undergraduate Fellows Program. He also described another mentor who encouraged him to "choose the path that feels right for you" (p. 16) and pursue the master's degree most meaningful to him as opposed to acquiescing to others' expectations. Craig's and DuJuan's experiences with their support networks are consistent with one of Renn and Hodges's (2007) findings: support from mentors and family, among other connections, are "the most common source of positive [e.g., DuJuan's mother and mentors] and stressful [e.g., other higher education mentors] relationships" (p. 373).

DuJuan discussed his relationship with his first supervisor, someone who allowed him the freedom to learn and grow by analyzing his strengths and areas of opportunity. His supervisor also challenged him and gave "feedback, even if it was a message [he] did not want to hear" (p. 19). In this capacity, his supervisor acted as a mentor that, as Renn and Hodges (2007) pointed out, is not always the case.

Molly's experiences further support the importance of realizing that one's supervisor may not always be a mentor. Renn and Hodges's (2007) research indicates that good supervision often occurs in graduate assistantships because the capacity to be a mentor is built into the experience. In her first job, Molly was the only staff member with formal higher education training, and her supervisor had "many responsibilities beyond . . . department initiatives" (p. 35). Both of these factors may have contributed to why she did not have meaningful professional development. Having already experienced the powerful influence of a good supervisor during one of her graduate assistantships, this void in her job was obvious. Fortunately Molly's professional and personal network "gave [her] the strength needed to make it through the good and not-so-good times" (p. 35). Yet a lesson from Molly's experience is understanding that one's supervisor may not be a mentor, and it is up to the new professional to find her or his own mentors (Renn & Hodges, 2007).

CONCLUSION

Kevin's Insights

The process of reflecting upon my own experiences and journey into higher education for *Job One* (Magolda & Carnaghi, 2004) was easily one of the highlights of my then early career. The level of reflection and critical analysis required to tell my own story was extremely important to my personal and professional development. I hope this is the case for DuJuan, Craig, and Molly as well as the other new professionals who participated in this project. Rereading my own story as I prepared to co-author this chapter provided an important reminder of who I was then. The thoughts, feelings, and reflections of a new professional captured in print provide an interesting opportunity to compare where I have been and where I am now. Like Craig, who was able to look around his childhood home for reminders of the person he once was, the story I wrote then did very much the same thing for me.

As I reflect on my career, having an internal foundation is very important as I continue to grow and develop as a more-seasoned higher education educator. I remember quite well the concept and amount of reflection encouraged by my faculty during graduate school, wondering at the time why reflection was necessary. The importance of reflection has become apparent, not only in the stories told here but in the continuous reflection that I do in my work. My career in higher education and student affairs is more than a job; it is a calling. As such, doing the difficult work of better understanding who I am and what I believe has certainly made me a better person and a more effective educator and administrator. Knowing who I am and being able to articulate my values and beliefs create that internal foundation that Baxter Magolda (2001) described, acting as a compass that will always guide me in my work. Fortunately, the colleges and universities where I have worked, the decisions I have made and continue to make, and my work with students are generally consistent with my beliefs. With a deeper understanding of the values that are most meaningful to me and an appreciation of the importance of being able to audit an organization's culture, I have found myself working at institutions and with colleagues who share a commitment to those things I hold most critical. Certainly there have been times when there have been disconnects between these things, and the confidence of having an internal foundation has provided me the strength and motivation to address them.

Although the perfect job does not exist, there are those positions that fit better with my values and internal foundation than others. Experience has led me to become a better auditor of organizational culture, and a growing professional network has helped me navigate through various decisions in my career. The role and importance of these support networks for new professionals was quite clear in the authors' three stories, and I have benefited greatly from those who have been willing to help guide my career. My own growth and longevity in higher education and student affairs would not have been possible without the support and guidance of mentors who have helped me navigate higher education—offering advice, challenge, and support when necessary. Although their involvement with me has ebbed and flowed throughout my career, I have been fortunate to have my first mentor continue to be an invaluable resource. Jackie Elick was my residence life mentor at Miami University; since our first interaction, she has been an unwavering source of support and an important resource for me. Our professional relationship has evolved to become more collegial than when I was a graduate student. I still regularly contact her for consultations and to exchange ideas. This is a relationship that has played an immense role in my professional life. It is important that I contribute to the field by assuming this role with graduate students and new professionals as well.

One area where I have always sought advice is when I was deciding to explore other professional opportunities. It is often a difficult choice and I certainly experienced that when I left Notre Dame in the summer of 2003. The desire to be closer to family led me to seek positions on the east coast and my new role as Director of Academic Advising at Bentley University provided an opportunity not only to return to Boston but also to apply all that I learned in my first position to my new responsibilities. Although I thought I would spend only a few years there before finding another challenge, I found Bentley to be the ideal institution to continue my career. I was quickly charged with a growing list of tasks, was encouraged to start a doctoral program, and even began teaching a graduate course in the Higher Education in Student Affairs program at Salem State University. Simply put, the intervening years between *Job One* and *Job One 2.0* have been a time of great growth both personally and professionally.

My original chapter in *Job One* centered on the theme of crossroads and starting over again. Ironically, I find myself doing just that as I write this chapter. After nine years at Bentley, I have recently started a new position at Stonehill College, a small Catholic institution founded by the same Holy Cross order that founded Notre Dame. As I concluded my work at Bentley, I found myself experiencing a mix of excitement and anxiety, the same feelings as when I wrote the earlier chapter so many years ago. I recall the ending to my chapter, and it describes perfectly my current situation: "As I look forward to greater responsibilities, I am preparing to start all over—again" (Piskadlo, 2004, p. 25).

Christana's Insights

Reading the stories written by DuJuan, Craig, and Molly was a joy and an honor. I reminisced about my job one experience—especially my obsession with my own job search process. I hate to admit it, but it is so true! I looked back at my first job search and had a good laugh. I hope that I was not so transparent that the potential employers I interviewed with could tell all the trouble I took attending to the littlest detail, such as worrying about the type of resume paper I should use or creating the perfect telephone interview environment.

Then I quickly realized, as did DuJuan, Craig, and Molly, that institutional and professional fit was of paramount importance to me. I did not want to find any old job for the sake of securing employment, although being in the workforce was and is very important to me. Instead, I wanted to find a professional home where I could connect with student affairs colleagues and students and where I would have the opportunity to grow as a professional. DuJuan, Craig, and Molly articulated that much more clearly and eloquently than I did; however, these lessons are nearly universal to all student affairs professionals, not just the "newbies."

These stories remind me to stay connected and to maintain support networks and develop new ones as I transition to different positions. I lost connection with some of my colleagues from my master's program, and it remains a true regret. Maintaining those connections can help all of us stay grounded both personally and professionally. It definitely worked for Molly.

Balancing work and outside activities is essential. DuJuan offered useful strategies. His advice to change clothes after coming home from work is more than a symbolic gesture to create boundaries. Every student affairs professional has lived through times where there is an "all hands on deck" situation, and we come home completely exhausted and exhilarated. This is a familiar experience in our field; however, I have seen and experienced the negative repercussions of not respecting these boundaries. It does not have to be that way. We can stay true to ourselves, maintain appropriate boundaries between work and home, and stay connected to our support networks both at work and at home, all the while indulging our passion for student affairs. In fact, doing so has helped me learn how to stay rooted in the field.

Finally, I value the idea of finding a mentor. I admit, an immediate supervisor can seem like the logical choice; however, it is also necessary to realize that he or she may not fit the bill. DuJuan and I were very lucky that our supervisors were mentoring matches for us. Molly, unfortunately, not so much; it was her support networks, both personal and professional, that sustained her.

The lessons learned from reading DuJuan's, Craig's, and Molly's stories are important and relevant to almost any student affairs context. I have learned much from the essays, and I hope other readers do as well.

REFERENCES

Baxter Magolda, M. B. (2001). *Making their own way: Narratives for transforming higher education to promote self-development.* Sterling, VA: Stylus.

Bess, J. L., & Dee, J. R. (2008). *Understanding college and university organization: Theories for effective policy and practice.* Sterling, VA: Stylus

Cross, W. E., Jr., & Fhagen-Smith, P. (2005). Nigrescence and ego identity development: Accounting for differential Black identity patterns. In M. E. Wilson & L. E. Wolf-Wendel, (Eds.), *ASHE reader on college student development theory* (pp. 259-268). Boston, MA: Pearson. (Reprinted from *Counseling across cultures,* 4th ed., by P. B. Pedersen, J. G. Draguns, W. J. Lonner, & J. E. Trimble, Eds., 1996, Thousand Oaks, CA: Sage)

Evans, N. J., Forney, D. S., & Guido, F. M., Patton, L. D., & Renn, K. A. (2010). *Student development in college: Theory, research, and practice* (2nd ed.). San Francisco, CA: Jossey-Bass.

Holland, J. L. (1997). *Making vocational choices: A theory of vocational personalities and work environments.* Odessa, FL: Psychological Assessment Resources.

Josselson, R. E. (1996). *Revising herself: Pathways to identity development in women.* San Francisco, CA: Jossey-Bass.

Luyckx, K., Schwartz, S. J., Goossens, L., Beyers, W., & Missotten, L. (2011) Processes of personal identity formation and evaluation. In S. J. Schwartz, K. Luyckx, & V. L. Vignoles (Eds.), *Handbook of identity theory and research* (pp. 77-98). New York, NY: Springer.

Magolda, P. M., & Carnaghi, J. E. (Eds.). (2004). *Job one: Experiences of new professionals in student affairs.* Lanham, MD: University Press of America/ACPA.

Marsick, V. J., & Watkins, K. E. (1990). *Informal and incidental learning in the workplace.* New York, NY: Routledge.

Merriam, S. B., Caffarella, R. S., & Baumgartner, L. M. (2007). *Learning in adulthood: A comprehensive guide.* San Francisco, CA: Jossey-Bass.

Piskadlo, K. (2004). Starting over—again: The many crossroads of a new professional. In P. M. Magolda & J. E. Carnaghi (Eds.), *Job one: Experiences of new professionals in student affairs* (pp. 13-25). Lanham, MD: University Press of America/ACPA.

Renn, K. A., & Hodges, J. (2007). The first year on the job: Experiences of new professionals in student affairs. *Journal of Student Affairs Research and Practice, 44,* 604-628. doi: 10.2202/1949-6605.1800

Renn, K. A., & Jessup-Anger, E. R. (2008). Preparing new professionals: Lessons for graduate preparation programs from the national study of new professionals in student affairs. *Journal of College Student Development, 49,* 319-335.

Strayhorn, T. L. (2009). Staff peer relationships and the socialization process of new professionals: A quantitative investigation. *College Student Affairs Journal, 28*(1), 38-60.

UNIT I DISCUSSION QUESTIONS

- What do you know now that you did not know before reading stories written by DuJuan, Craig, and Molly?

New Professionals

- What expectations do you have as you enter your first job? Which of these expectations are non-negotiable and which are negotiable? How will you communicate these expectations during your job search?
- To what extent have you allowed the expectations or opinions of others (e.g., supervisors, faculty, other students) influence your path? As you begin your search and your first job, how will you ensure that you are cognizant of your expectations and how they may differ from others' expectations?
- How will you determine if the position, institution, supervisor and colleagues can assist you in meeting your expectations?
- How will you respond if a new job does not live up to your expectations?

Supporters of New Professionals

- What job search strategies have been particularly effective or unsettling for new professionals?
- What are your expectations of colleagues and new professionals?
- What memories from your first job search help you better understand the issues new professionals face?
- What are unique contemporary issues (e.g., social media, economy, demographics) that differ from those of past generations of new professionals?

—*QUESTIONS PREPARED BY SARAH O'CONNELL*

UNIT II

CHAPTER 6

Stranger in a Somewhat Strange Land

DAVID STANFIELD

As I began the job search process during my final year of graduate school, I fantasized about what it would be like to work overseas in student affairs. I applied for domestic positions while casually searching for international opportunities on the side. The lack of international job postings confirmed my suspicion that student affairs is primarily an American profession that does not exist in the same capacity abroad. After months of investigating international job vacancies with no luck, I had abandoned hope for an overseas adventure. However, late in the spring semester 2006 I had a breakthrough. At the recommendation of a mentor, I learned about Carnegie Mellon University's recently established international branch campus in Doha, Qatar. I thought to myself, "An American institution with a campus overseas—surely they must follow a model similar to the main campus?" My aspiration of pairing student affairs in an international context suddenly seemed possible.

A search on Carnegie Mellon's website revealed a student activities vacancy on the Qatar campus. Although the Middle East was certainly not my ideal locale due to initial apprehensions about safety and a potentially unwelcoming environment for Americans; after investigating the position further, I applied. The first step in my job search research was to locate Qatar on a map and scour various Internet sources to learn about this nation. I learned that Qatar is a small peninsular country sharing a southern border with Saudi Arabia and has a population around 1,000,000. Much of Qatar's economy centers on a thriving oil and gas industry. A government organization called the Qatar Foundation established several projects focused on enhancing educational opportunities, scientific research, and community development. The largest project, Education City, consists of six American branch campuses. Each institution offers different degrees in the areas they are most known for on their U.S. campuses. Carnegie Mellon in Qatar opened in 2004 offering business administration and computer science degree programs.

A few weeks later, much to my surprise, I received a phone interview. For the second phase in the process, I interviewed with administrators at Carnegie Mellon's main campus in Pittsburgh. This remote prospect of working in student affairs overseas was rapidly becoming a possibility. The invitation for a final interview in Qatar left little time for internal processing—I was on a plane within days. The lengthy 24-hour plane journey to Qatar was surreal; throughout the flight, my mind raced with questions. Am I really on my way to the Middle East? Will I be safe? What happens if I get a job offer? How will my family and friends react? I will never forget stepping off the airplane that night into an intense humidity that instantly made my skin feel wet—a not-so-gentle reminder that I was visiting a coastal desert city during the heat of summer.

During the four-day campus visit and interview, I concentrated on answering four questions. Could I envision myself living in Qatar? Were the job and institution good fits? How would this affect my relationships with friends and family back home? Would I be safe? The weeklong trip went by in a flash. I spent most of my visit meeting with staff, faculty, and students and attending a few campus events. A majority of the faculty and staff were expatriates, many from the United States. Some wanted to discuss my qualifications and fit for the position, and others spent time explaining the institutional ethos and life in Qatar. I appreciated their candor when explaining the joys and trials of living abroad. Overall, most faculty and staff enjoyed life in Qatar although it was not always easy. I sensed a collective enthusiasm as they described both the professional and personal aspects of their lives. The students were diverse in nationality and gender and conducted themselves much in the way I would expect American students to act in an interview. Their level of professionalism and ability to ask relevant and challenging questions impressed me. I also appreciated their willingness to teach me about their culture.

My excitement about the position, university, and country grew throughout the process, but I was careful to recognize that my enthusiasm could partially be a result of a strong desire to live and work abroad. I am adventurous at heart, so it was important not to let the exhilarating interview process overshadow potential shortfalls. The main drawback of living and working abroad appeared to be the separation from family and friends. It was already difficult to find time to visit loved ones when only living a short plane ride across the United States, so surely 7,000 miles and a $1,500 plane ticket would make those relationships even more difficult to maintain. As part of the benefits package, the university covered airfare for one round-trip ticket home per year along with generous time off, which helped alleviate some concerns.

Despite the American media's frequent portrayal of the Middle East as dangerous, safety and security varies greatly across the region. During my interview, I met with the staff member in charge of security and was pleasantly surprised to learn that Qatar managed to avoid the turmoil plaguing several other countries in the Middle East. In fact, I heard from multiple staff members that they felt safer living in Qatar than at home in Pittsburgh. Still, I recognized a sad reality in our modern age—safety could not be guaranteed anywhere in the world. After weighing the positive and negative aspects of this opportunity, I concluded that I would accept the job if offered. Several weeks later, what was an unrealistic dream became a reality when I received and accepted the offer. A month later, I started the same journey back to Qatar, but this time without a return ticket.

CONTEXT MATTERS

I intentionally arrived in Qatar almost two weeks before my scheduled first day of work. I wanted time to settle in, explore my new home, and interact with colleagues before the students arrived. In graduate school, I particularly enjoyed learning about college student cultures by applying an anthropological lens to exploring students' group identities and values. I approached my assimilation process like a class research project aimed at discovering a new culture. First, I spent time exploring my surroundings by identifying various artifacts and customs and attempting to interpret their meaning. I also sought to apply advice I heard repeatedly throughout graduate school: "Make the strange familiar and the familiar strange."

The initial artifacts I sought were familiar. Anyone who has traveled internationally understands the pervasive American influence on the world—our music, movies, clothes, and food are ever-present. With few exceptions, one expects to find a McDonald's in urban environments across the globe. In Qatar, I found the McDonald's—and the Chili's, Dunkin' Donuts, and Applebee's, among other eateries. Although some might be excited to discover a few of their familiar sites from home, I was disappointed. After all, I moved abroad in part for the adventure—to experience the new and different. Having my favorite sandwich available at the local Chili's hardly seemed adventurous. My new colleagues offered recommendations for which grocery stores to buy American items, which malls had American-style home items, and even how to apply for a special license required to purchase alcohol. It seemed like there were too many opportunities to recreate my previous life. I knew that surface-level observations often held deeper meanings and wondered what these familiar elements really said about Qatari society.

Concurrently, other elements of Qatar seemed remarkably different. In the first few weeks I recall the uniqueness of hearing the Muslim call to prayer five times a day throughout the city, driving through the crazy roundabouts, and observing the varieties of national garb. During the obligatory new-employee orientation, the human resources staff explained local customs, traditions, and expectations, revealing other less-obvious aspects of the culture that dramatically differed from my own. We learned that Qatar followed a conservative branch of Islam called Wahhabism. Outside of immediate family, Muslim men and women did not interact with each other until they were married, which also applied to non-Muslim foreigners interacting with Muslims of the opposite sex. Local Qataris dressed conservatively: Men wore white robes called thobes, and women wore black abayas and covered their hair. Expatriates were not expected to wear the national dress but did need to dress conservatively by covering their shoulders and knees. Another HR employee warned the audience that when greeting Muslims of the opposite sex one should wait for them to initiate a handshake, as they might not be comfortable with physical contact. I learned when meeting with students of the opposite sex I should ask if they prefer the office door open or closed. I considered what was familiar about these "strange" customs. Certain elements of this culture reminded me of my conservative Christian upbringing in Texas. During college, I recall church sermons advising students to avoid being alone with members of the opposite sex where rational judgment could easily succumb to unwholesome temptations.

The process I followed to learn about my new surroundings set an important foundation for my work with students. By exploring and attempting to understand the environment in which they lived, I began to recognize the various factors that influenced their daily lives and shaped their values. Reflecting back on my graduate school and internship experiences in the United States, I wondered why I did not follow a similar approach to familiarizing myself with the various "foreign" institutional environments I encountered. As an American working in my home country, I had mistakenly assumed that I understood all U.S. environments and how they influenced the institutions and students. Once I returned to the United States, I promised myself that I would strive to make the familiar strange. I would assume less and question more.

DEEPER REFLECTIONS ON CULTURE AND IDENTITY

After several weeks slowly making sense of my new surroundings through personal observation and coworker descriptions, it was finally time to start working. The student population at Carnegie Mellon in Qatar was predominantly from the Middle East and South Asia. One work responsibility was advising new student orientation, so the first students I met were orientation counselors. They introduced me to new aspects of identity. The greeting sequence in Qatar is as follows. First, introduce yourself. Second, establish country of origin. Qatar is overtly multicultural—Qatari nationals comprise about one-fourth of the population. The remaining 75 percent of residents come from all over the world, with a heavy concentration from the Middle East, North Africa, and South Asia. Five of the orientation counselors represented this diversity. Abdul (a pseudonym) was Indian and traveled to India frequently, although he was raised in the

Gulf. Mohammed was a proud Egyptian and moved to Qatar in high school. Yusuf was Palestinian, born in Qatar, and not permitted to travel to Palestine due to political restrictions. Hanoof was half Scottish, half Iraqi and had lived in Qatar since she was a teenager. Finally, Maryam was the only Qatari national, which meant that she had Qatari parents. My attempt to "understand the culture" just got more complicated.

Like Mohammed, most students took pride in their national identities, even if they had never lived in or visited their home countries. In graduate school, identity questions centered on race, gender, sexual orientation, and religion. I recall few instances discussing what it meant to be an American. The students at Carnegie Mellon in Qatar taught me that nationality is a central element of identity for many people in the world. They enjoyed the opportunity to teach the "new guy" about the individual aspects of their national identities, and I enjoyed listening. Immediately and continually, I realized how little I knew about the world.

Familiarizing myself with other nationalities also forced me to consider what it means to be an American. I reflected on the hidden privileges of my American identity: the freedom to openly express opinions without fear of reprisal, the ability to participate in electing government officials, and the ease of traveling to most foreign countries with an American passport. For most of my life, I treated these privileges as an entitlement. I continually reflected on which aspects of my own culture would not translate to other countries and which characteristics of foreign cultures Americans could benefit from understanding and perhaps adopting. In Qatar, it became clear that a benevolent monarchy was a political model well suited to their unique context and history. I questioned the pervasive American belief that all countries would benefit from becoming more democratic in nature. Moreover, I admired the strength and importance of familial relationships present in many students' cultures and wondered if America would benefit from focusing more on family and less on the individual.

Although I understood the importance of intercultural interaction from an intellectual perspective, firsthand experience helped me fully realize the benefits. I became a better professional and global citizen by learning about "the other" through cultural exchange. Many student affairs professionals and students in America seldom have the chance to work or study abroad, so I began considering alternatives for intentional exposure to new cultures. For students, one innovative example was a Carnegie Mellon course that facilitated dialogue between students on the Doha and Pittsburgh campuses. The jointly taught course explored concepts of privilege, responsibility, and community through a series of sociocultural issues, one of which was national identity. Through modern video conferencing technology, students in Qatar and the United States explored identity and culture together. Students reported that they learned a significant amount about themselves and others through this experience. I recalled the various short-term study and professional development trips exploring higher education abroad offered to graduate students and professionals. I wished I had paid more attention to those opportunities while in graduate school.

Another important aspect of the students' identities was religion. Although the Carnegie Mellon student population came from many diverse nations, a strong majority identified as Muslim. I enjoyed talking about my faith and was relieved to discover that many students felt the same way. In the beginning, I was nervous to share my personal beliefs because we came from different faith traditions. Unlike my experience with students in the United States, I found that students in Qatar integrated their faith into conversation comfortably and regularly. This encouraged me to share more openly; despite our religious differences, students appreciated that I was a person of faith. We discovered common ground in our shared belief in a higher power. I taught students about Christianity, and I learned a substantial amount about Islam from them. I wish that all Americans could spend a day with these students discussing Islam, as I am confident they would come away with a fresh perspective on an often-misunderstood faith. Furthermore, these interactions encouraged me to be intentional in helping American students explore their faith in the future. In graduate school, I shied away from discussing spiritual issues with undergraduate students unless we shared the same faith tradition. I worried such conversations would be contentious and counterproductive. I was concerned that students would perceive my interest in these topics as proselytizing. However, working in an environment at Carnegie Mellon in Qatar where students openly discussed and even encouraged conversations about religion, I began to understand what religious dialogue looked like at its best. My experience with students in Qatar helped me realize that the goal of interfaith dialogue is not to pick the "best" argument; rather, it's about identifying areas of shared understanding between faiths and maturing in one's own faith by understanding the faiths of others.

Faculty and staff perspectives on culture and identity provided another means to enhance mutual understanding. Discussions examining the local culture were a frequent occurrence among expatriate staff and faculty. I found most of these conversations a helpful piece of the interpretation puzzle leading to more thoughtful and complex interpretations. For instance, I benefited from regular reflective conversations with my supervisor about culture and the implications for our work. Although there was a vocal minority that tended to cast non-Western cultures in a negative light, most of the faculty and staff with whom I worked shared my desire to learn about other cultures and strove to refrain from casting negative judgment. In hindsight, I would more intentionally challenge the minority who exhibited a "my culture is better than yours" mentality.

ON THE JOB

Considering the cultural differences and unique student demographics, I wondered which aspects of my student affairs training and practice would be relevant. During graduate school, I did not recall discussing whether student development theory, leadership education, or organizational theory applied to international contexts. I realized that graduate school equipped me with the skills necessary to examine and understand my new environment and culture. Three key themes emerged as I applied these cultural insights and other aspects of my student affairs experience to my new job: the importance of analyzing underlying assumptions, the process of cultural adaptation, and the opportunity for innovation.

Underlying Assumptions

Anyone who has worked at a small institution understands the importance of having a generalist mindset. This was the case at Carnegie Mellon in Qatar where, as the director of student activities, I wore many hats, including the coordinator for the community standards process. The majority of cases I adjudicated were academic in nature resulting from cheating or plagiarism incidents. Similar to my experience in the United States, very few students openly admitted to committing a violation even though cheating and plagiarism violations are typically accompanied by hard evidence such as the Internet source from which students copied. I approached my student meetings much in the same way I did during my judicial affairs graduate assistantship in the United States: listening to students' interpretations of the story, explaining their rights and responsibilities, and offering advice to either appeal or accept responsibility based on the evidence and what I thought was in their best interest given the circumstances.

After meeting with several students to discuss academic integrity violations, I noticed a pattern of students who inadvertently plagiarized. At first I discounted my observation and attributed it to careless mistakes such as forgetting to use quotation marks or proper citation. However, one memorable plagiarism case helped me realize there might be more to the story. Maryam had obviously plagiarized part of her essay from an Internet source; however, it became clear that it was not due to malicious intent or carelessness. Her understanding of plagiarism differed from the university policy. I wondered if the concepts of plagiarism and cheating could differ among cultures.

Because of my meeting with Maryam, I reviewed transcripts from previous cases, and I discovered several similar misunderstandings. I had a sense that this discovery was important, so I approached my supervisor with these new insights. This marked the starting point of an important research project to understand communication focusing on cheating and plagiarism. With the institutional research staff from Doha and Pittsburgh, we conducted focus groups and individual interviews with faculty, staff, and students. We discovered that high school experiences heavily influenced students' beliefs about plagiarism. In high school, some students (especially in the Indian schools) learned that knowledge was generated jointly between people and should be openly shared across humanity. Instructors encouraged students to borrow freely from sources without citation.

This perspective clearly conflicts with the American conception that individuals develop and own ideas. Other students attended high schools that discussed plagiarism but had definitions covering only part of the Carnegie Mellon code. Through this research project, we also learned that many of the mostly

American faculty assumed that students already understood cheating and plagiarism and therefore spent minimal time discussing the intricacies during class. It was clear that faculty and staff should more carefully and fully explain these concepts to students to prevent future incidents. We implemented several new strategies to address the issues raised in the report, including a new workshop on academic integrity required for every first-year student. Additionally, we presented the results of the research project to faculty and encouraged them to discuss plagiarism and cheating in more depth and with more frequency. We never entertained the idea of altering the cheating and plagiarism policy; as an American institution promising an American education, it was important to uphold the same academic standards as our home campus.

This project revealed to me that, as an American, I had certain beliefs and underlying assumptions about cheating and plagiarism that I had not consciously identified. Before engaging in the research project, I also assumed students had certain baseline knowledge about cheating and plagiarism; this assumption was incorrect. This story serves as a reminder that as a student affairs educator, I held many unidentified and unexamined assumptions that guided my work. When working with a diverse student population, it was especially important to identify underlying assumptions and recognize how they affected my practice. Finally, I considered the degree to which international students studying in the United States understand the American outlook on cheating and plagiarism. I wondered if international students had special training on academic expectations and standards during their orientation programs.

Cultural Relevance

A primary aim of Carnegie Mellon in Qatar was to recreate the educational experience students receive on the home campus in Pittsburgh. However, I quickly learned that neither the curriculum nor the co-curriculum should be transferred with unexamined replication. When advising and designing programs, I considered the institutional ethos of the main campus alongside the unique cultural context and learner characteristics of students in Qatar. Discussing programming ideas with students helped determine if adaptation was necessary. These interactions saved me from many embarrassing mistakes. I once wanted to hold an off-campus retreat at a local hotel and learned from a student that the hotel I suggested had a reputation as a place where men brought their mistresses. Not a single Qatari female student would have attended that retreat.

In other instances, students proposed cultural adaptation. As the advisor for student government, I often helped guide this process. The most contentious issue occurred when the student government officially requested a women-only student lounge. Their rationale was to create a comfortable space for women students to remove their hijabs and relax outside the presence of men. Students felt strongly about the issue, so I helped them navigate the process by raising the implications and offering suggestions on their written proposal. From an institutional perspective, this issue was complex because various aspects of the university mission seemed to be in conflict. A foundational element of the institutional mission was the value of a coeducational experience. Conversely, we strove to respect local culture and create a comfortable learning environment for all students. Students, faculty, and staff discussed the student government's report at great length. The chief student affairs officer had the final say, and she ultimately decided not to support a women-only lounge due to the strong institutional belief in the benefits of maintaining a fully coeducational environment.

Although the decision disappointed many students, several benefits emerged from initiating the process. Personally, it encouraged me to reflect on how I supported students and how the institution could better communicate its mission and align it with student values. Another positive outcome was the establishment of a group called the Women's Initiative, which brought together students and staff to explore women's issues on campus and create a support structure to address gender-related topics on campus.

Innovation and Enthusiasm

Institutions in their infancy are an opportunity for innovation, and a majority of American international branch campuses are less than ten years old. Many U.S. institutions steeped in tradition and facing budget crises offer few opportunities to create new programs and modify existing ones, which can thwart young professionals' creativity and enthusiasm. I thrived on creativity and was thankful to find an institution and supervisor who welcomed new ideas and encouraged innovative approaches to student learning.

In my third year, my supervisor asked me to take on the additional responsibility of coordinating first-year co-curricular programs. I had the highly unusual opportunity to design a set of co-curricular programs from the ground up. The only program that currently existed specifically targeted for first-year students was new student orientation. To be successful the new programs would need to align with institutional values and be developmentally geared to first-year students. To design the core competencies and learning outcomes, I established a committee with wide representation from faculty and staff who worked with first-year students as well as several upper-class students. I knew this would make the process more complicated and take longer, but to generate the best possible outcomes, I understood it was essential to solicit diverse opinions and get buy-in from a variety of constituencies. Additionally, at a new institution faculty and staff have fewer commitments and are generally more excited to provide input that will help shape new initiatives. The result was a comprehensive and widely agreed-upon set of program goals and learning outcomes that helped guide the program creation process. My work experience in Qatar confirmed my preference for high-energy environments that encourage creativity and innovation. Although likely harder to find in the U.S., I will seek similar institutional environments where innovation and energy are evident in their mission or with a supervisor supportive of this style.

As my five-year journey in Qatar ended, I reflected on my original considerations when deciding to take the job. Could I see myself living in Qatar? Most days I loved living in Qatar. The good and the bad were all part of the experience, and I have a new perspective on the world as a result. Living abroad is an intense opportunity to learn about oneself and the other. Was the position and institution a good fit? Yes, my professional philosophy was directly in line with Carnegie Mellon's institutional values, and as a result, my work was exciting. Moreover, working in a generalist student affairs position exposed me to a wide variety of professional experiences I would not have had at a larger school. Was it safe? Of all the places I have lived and traveled, I cannot recall a place where I felt safer. Did I lose touch with friends and family? Yes, with a few, but I made many new friends in Qatar. Additionally, every year I had the opportunity to visit friends and family back home for extended periods due to a generous vacation package. As long as American higher education remains a gold standard and internationalization persists, student affairs will continue to emerge around the world. This begs the question, where in the world is my next assignment?

CHAPTER 6 DISCUSSION QUESTIONS

New Professionals

- What is your comfort level with risk-taking when seeking employment?
- What are some strategies for strengthening comfort with risk?
- How would you conduct a campus audit to learn about campus norms and compare them with your own values and interests?

Supporters of New Professionals

- What advice would you offer to mentees who seek employment abroad or in a different cultural context?
- How can you help new professionals appreciate their accomplishments even when they fall short of their aspired goals?
- What are distinctive characteristics of this generation of new professionals that distinguish them from past generations?
- What strategies do you employ for integrating reflection into supervision?

— *QUESTIONS PREPARED BY KATIE SHOEMAKER*

CHAPTER 7

The Possibility of Transformation

SARAH STEWARD

Before we begin the interview, we'd like to introduce you to one of our traditions at Naropa University: the bow. We bow to begin and to conclude our meetings, classes, events, and other gatherings. For the first part of the bow, we sit up straight with our hands on our thighs, and we try to gently let go of the thoughts and distractions that we might have. During the second part, we bring awareness and non-judgment to the present moment: the people surrounding us, the room we are in, ourselves and our emotions, etc. Finally, we bend at the waist to symbolize our commitment to being present with one another. This is simply an invitation, so feel free to join us only if you wish.[1]

As I processed this "invitation" during my first on-campus interview for a job after graduation from my master's program, my mind immediately raced to Interviewing 101. No matter the formality, you are always "on," and this bow did not seem optional. So I gathered up my courage and wiped my clammy hands on my thighs as I prepared for my first bow at Naropa University. At the time I had no idea this simple yet deeply meaningful tradition would become a part of my everyday interactions.

The day before my interview, I had flown into the Denver International Airport and taken the shuttle into Boulder, Colorado—home of Naropa University. A sense of place was a top priority when my partner and I discussed our relocation after completing my graduate studies, and receiving an invitation to interview for a career services coordinator position in a city nestled at the foot of the Rocky Mountains thrilled us. Little did I know at the time that this small, Buddhist-inspired institution that touts contemplative education as its foundation would transform me as a professional and, more importantly, as a person.

Learning Reconsidered: A Campus-Wide Focus on the Student Experience (Keeling, 2004), a guiding document for the student affairs profession, encourages higher education professionals to assume the role of transformative educators, meaning we should strive for a "holistic process of learning that places the student at the center of the learning experience" (p. 1). It has taken me over three years to begin to understand that as an educator I, too, must be willing to be the center of my own learning experience and be willing to undergo personal and professional transformation to truly meet students as my fullest self. To me, this is imperative to transformative education.

I write to share with you my process of entering job one and its profound impact on how I understand my work and myself. In this chapter I highlight key issues I faced as I determined my fit within the vastly diverse field of higher education. This process began by deconstructing the career myths I held about what makes the "perfect first job" after completing my graduate studies, listening to my own internal values and beliefs to fully commit to an institution that was nontraditional but was a mission fit for me, and embracing my vulnerability by opening myself to new ways of knowing and being.

As a career counselor, aspects of my story resemble the elements of career development that many of the students and alumni/ae with whom I work experience. Students and alumni/ae address barriers, discover career fits, and delve into the adventures of learning more about their professional identities along the way. In telling my story, I also explore how my understanding of career development not only allows me to reflect on my personal experience but also has changed the way I approach my work with students and alumni/ae who choose to study at a non-traditional higher education institution.

DECONSTRUCTING CAREER MYTHS AND DISCOVERING MISSION FIT

During the final semester of my graduate program, my partner and I discussed where we hoped to move after I completed my degree. We decided to head west toward the mountains after spending two years in a small, Midwest town. We were particularly drawn to Colorado, because it offered easy access to outdoor activities and was an equal distance from my home state and his (North Dakota and Iowa) where our families still reside. With these two priorities in the forefront, I embarked on my search for job one, beginning in February 2008.

One of the first job openings I discovered was at Naropa University for the career services coordinator position. I was drawn to the university's website as it described its student body as artists and environmentalists and writers and caregivers and activists and eclectics. It was both a graduate and undergraduate institution with a little over 1000 students who studied environmental leadership, Indo-Tibetan Buddhism, peace studies, transpersonal counseling psychology, writing and poetics, as well as many other interesting degree programs. I was fascinated that it was a fairly young institution founded by Chögyam Trungpa Rinpoche, a Tibetan Buddhist teacher and lineage holder who brought Buddhist teachings to the United States in the 1970s, and it was once home to people like Allen Ginsberg and still is home to the poet Anne Waldman. It began as a graduate institute before offering four-year undergraduate degrees in the early 2000s. Additionally, it had only become an accredited institution in 1986. Yet, it was Naropa's mission statement that captivated me.

> Inspired by the rich intellectual and experiential traditions of East and West, Naropa University is North America's leading institution of contemplative education.
>
> Naropa recognizes the inherent goodness and wisdom of each human being. It educates the whole person, cultivating academic excellence and contemplative insight in order to infuse knowledge with wisdom. The university nurtures in its students a lifelong joy in learning, a critical intellect, the sense of purpose that accompanies compassionate service to the world, and the openness and equanimity that arise from authentic insight and self-understanding. Ultimately, Naropa students explore the inner resources needed to engage courageously with a complex and challenging world, to help transform that world through skill and compassion, and to attain deeper levels of happiness and meaning in their lives.
>
> Drawing on the vital insights of the world's wisdom traditions, the university is simultaneously Buddhist-inspired, ecumenical and nonsectarian. Naropa values ethnic and cultural differences for their essential role in education. It embraces the richness of human diversity with the aim of fostering a more just and equitable society and an expanded awareness of our common humanity.
>
> A Naropa education—reflecting the interplay of discipline and delight—prepares its graduates both to meet the world as it is and to change it for the better. (http://www.naropa.edu/about-naropa/mission-statement.php)

I was enlivened and curious about the unique offerings, rich history, and contemplative educational focus of Naropa (Coburn, 2011). I found the position of career services coordinator inspiring. What would it be like to work with students and alumni/ae who chose Naropa as their place of study? I knew I had stumbled upon a rare gem, so I applied. However, my excitement began to wane as a month passed and then two.

In the meantime, I applied to a few other job vacancies, one of which was a career counselor position working with engineering students at a public university in Colorado. It was a stable position and the possibility of working with engineering students interested me. Nonetheless, it did not evoke the same initial intrigue and enthusiasm that Naropa did. In late April, I participated in phone interviews for both this position and, finally, the one at Naropa. Due to the timing of the two different interview processes, my decision came down to accepting Naropa's offer for the career services coordinator position or accepting an on-campus interview for the engineering career counselor role at the public university.

As a student affairs professional who works with people involved in career decision-making processes, I have come to understand we all hold various ideas or myths around career that we inherit from our family members, friends, mentors, and colleagues; our professional fields and industries; our cultural identities and groups; and our society. I intentionally use the word *myth* for the messages we hold around careers because they can be so strong that they blind us to see other possibilities, or they force us to exclude other possibilities. Unless we acknowledge them for their exclusive nature and deconstruct them, they can adversely influence our decision-making processes. The tricky part about career myths is they appear rational, but in reality they fail to take into account our true passions and intuitive senses. Although I hold this belief about career myths, I was no exception to the phenomenon. As my final semester drew to a close and my career decision loomed over me, the career myths I was carrying about what makes an ideal first job after graduation surfaced. These internal and external voices were loud and clear and fiercely competed to drown out my initial enthusiasm about and intuitive connection to Naropa University.

For instance, some of the ideas I held about the engineering career counselor position were that it was a safe choice and a good job choice. The institution was reputable, and I would be working on a team of seasoned career professionals. Other messages I was weighing were (a) I had never heard of Naropa University (and neither had any of my colleagues) and (b) the concept of contemplative education, although intriguing, was foreign to me. I wondered if I would be able to find work after Naropa since not many peers seemed to know about this institution. In other words, I wondered if I would be limiting my career possibilities by accepting a position at a nontraditional institution. Additionally, I had self-doubt. What made me think I had "enough" experience to be the only career professional at an institution? I was just graduating; beyond the practical experiences I gained while in graduate school, I only had one year of full-time professional experience between my undergraduate and graduate studies.

Beyond these career myths, the one that was most difficult for me came from my family. Naropa University was a Buddhist-inspired institution, and my upbringing included attending Christian church functions twice a week, teaching Sunday school and summer Bible school, and going to church camp every summer. I vividly remember telling my mother about the decision I had to make. After our initial conversation, she called me back to express her ultimate fear. She was afraid that if I chose to work at Naropa, I was going to become a Buddhist. Sound the condemnation bells!

Little did she know—or maybe wanted to admit—that I had been on a path of some kind of spiritual and religious exploration ever since I had left home for college. I was by no means an expert on world religions, but the concept of how people make meaning of their lives through spiritual understanding and religious practices intrigued me. I had critically examined the historical implications of the Bible during my first semester as an undergraduate student, which turned my belief system on its head. The devout traditions and rituals I witnessed when studying and traveling in predominantly Muslim countries humbled me. And my favorite courses during my final year as an undergraduate were my Buddhism class where we examined various traditions and my month-long, intensive yoga class where we practiced and explored the rich, deep history of this contemplative practice.

Yet after contemplating my mother's fear and the other myths, doubt and confusion reigned, and I felt misaligned. Myths often hold elements of truth for how we identify our beliefs; otherwise, we would not hold them. So, as I pondered my decision, I had to ask myself, "Did I truly believe all of this? What decision is best for me, regardless of what my colleagues or family members might say or fear?"

Then, something dawned on me: I had just spent an entire graduate program with a focus on organizational development, cultural anthropology, and student development within the field of higher education. I was particularly reminded of Marcia Baxter Magolda's (2001) student development theory, which examines three domains of development (cognitive/epistemological, interpersonal, and intrapersonal) as they relate to an individual's ability to achieve self-authorship of their lives. I was specifically struck by the immature state from which I was enacting my intrapersonal understanding, or personal identity and beliefs, as it related to my decision-making process. I was internalizing external thoughts, meaning I was assuming the ideas and myths that others held, believing they were my own. I am confident my primary motivation for this was that I did not want to disappoint the people most important in my life. I had always been a people pleaser. However, if I let the career myths I internalized from others trap me into a decision that everyone else thought was a better choice instead of what I felt was a better choice, I would ultimately be disappointing myself.

Different, more authentic questions began to emerge. If I aspire to help students along their developmental journeys, why shouldn't I choose a job and an institution that enlivens me? Doesn't it make sense to select a place whose mission does not focus solely on cognitive and interpersonal development but requires students to focus on developing intrapersonal maturity through full and personal engagement with their course studies and use of contemplative practices to do so? After all, *Learning Reconsidered* states,

> transformative education instead places the student's reflective processes at the core of the learning experience and asks the student to evaluate both new information and the frames of reference through which the information acquires meaning. . . . In the transformative educational paradigm, the purpose of educational involvement is the evolution of multidimensional identity, including but not limited to cognitive, affective, behavioral and spiritual development. (Keeling, 2004, p. 9)

Upon this revelation, I realized that Naropa was getting it right! It was enacting the theories that had grounded my studies for the past two years. It was through my job one decision-making process that I began to listen to and gauge how my beliefs and values motivated and guided me, which is exactly what I wanted to inspire in the students and alumni/ae with whom I would be working. I trusted the transformational process that had taken place in my life over the past seven years since leaving for college.

If we actually dare to discover who we are in relation to those around us, we can then begin "to meet the world as it is and to change it for the better" just as Naropa University's mission statement claims. By standing in this space, my doubt began to diminish. I admit there is risk in every decision we make, but what I was unwilling to risk were my authenticity and integrity.

I knew then that I could admit that I truly wanted to work with the student artist and poet and peacemaker. I wanted to engage with people who approached our world's most pressing issues in innovative and creative ways. It was not that I wouldn't have received a similar kind of experience working with engineering students, some of our world's most creative individuals, it was that I was not excited by the opportunity. I was being called to a little, Buddhist-inspired institution that was doing great and wonderful things. I had discovered my mission fit. I could no longer deny that my professional and spiritual curiosity as well as my intuition and passions were the true compasses I must follow, so I stepped into the unknown, accepted my new role as the career services coordinator at Naropa University, and headed west.

OPENING OURSELVES TO NEW WAYS OF KNOWING AND BEING

After taking the time and space to make a career decision that allowed me to find an institution that was a mission fit, I was ready to begin job one. As I imagine most new professionals feel, I was initially overwhelmed with the responsibilities of the career services coordinator position. Also, my supervisor was someone who provided each of the student affairs professionals he supervised with much freedom and autonomy, primarily because at a small institution we all played highly specialized roles. So I had to quickly learn to navigate what my supervisor expected from me in the position and the opportunity that existed for me to create the position in the way that best fit my strengths. During my early days on the job, I relied heavily on the person who had formerly held the position and fellow career professionals at other institutions to help me understand how I might lay the foundation for my work as the career services coordinator.

Despite the tremendous and sincerely appreciated support I received, my colleagues did not fully prepare me for the type of student and alumni/ae with whom I would be working at Naropa. Although my Naropa colleagues described the student body in ways that were helpful, it was not until I sat across from the students and alumni/ae that I began to understand them. They were remarkable individuals who amazed me with the depth of reflection they presented about their career processes. I quickly realized I had much to learn from them.

The approaches I used with more traditional-aged college students at the mid-sized, public university from which I had just graduated were not going to cut it at Naropa. The students with whom I had previously worked would often sit across from me because faculty had required them to be there or one of the parents or siblings said they *should* talk with me. I found myself asking several open-ended yet direct questions to elicit any kind of meaningful reflection from them, because they lacked the personal motivation and inspiration to engage with me. As a result, I often assumed the role of service provider and fell into the habit of directing students to specific resources to help facilitate the exploration process.

At Naropa, on the other hand, rarely, if ever, did students or alumni/ae tell me they were required to meet with me. They were self-directed and personally chose to explore their career visioning and decision-making processes, and they expected me to engage with them on a much deeper level. As soon as I realized this, I knew as well as felt I needed to open myself to new ways of knowing and being. I needed to address old habits and embrace my vulnerability, because I could no longer rely on assuming the role of service provider. Otherwise, students and alumni/ae would see right through me, because they sought someone who could actively listen to and engage with them in their exploration processes.

Embracing my vulnerability to discover new ways of knowing and being has been the greatest lesson I have learned since arriving at Naropa. This lesson came in the form of assuming the role of learner first and foremost and then acknowledging the inherent wisdom of whomever I was engaging, whether it was the student during a one-on-one advising session, the group who decided to attend a workshop I facilitated or sponsored, or the colleague who had insight to share or a collaborative project on which to partner. Great learning can occur anytime, anywhere, with anyone. If we do not fear the vulnerability that arises when we do this and if we are willing to set aside our judgments and expectations, discoveries and learning abound. Believe me when I say this is not easy and is something I am only beginning to understand and practice.

I first began to practice this lesson in my individual sessions. For instance, when I was first sitting across from students who were looking for jobs, I was not fully focusing on what they were presenting to me, a result of bad habits I had developed. As they shared their goals for our time together and presented the questions or issues they were facing, I was in the habit of mentally creating a to-do list for this person or preparing my job search spiel. I was distracted by my expectation that this is what I should do. I was a career services professional after all. I was providing a service.

I had pondered and reflected on this tendency in graduate school but not to the depth I did at Naropa. After being exposed to some of the contemplative practices offered at the institution, I realized how chaotic my mind functioned and how distracted I was. During my individual sessions, I seldom honored the present moment or the person who was sitting across from me who had a unique and important story to share, so I began to monitor my thought patterns in these interactions. When I successfully suspended my ideas and my urge to give advice and instead truly listened to the person across from me, I discovered that the person often revealed two things: (a) other issues that were more pressing than what was first presented—the person only needed time to feel safe to share them with me—and (b) more often than not the person inherently held many solutions to the problems or questions being presented. I began to understand I was simply there to listen, to help tease out their ideas, and to help them discern the best next step for them.

This was a very similar process to my personal job one decision. Back in May 2008, I did not need advice or other peoples' ideas. I needed a sounding board. I needed someone to listen to me and to what I was thinking and to what I believed to be true for me. It has been a blessing to discover this in my work with others as I witness their career development processes; however, this would not have been possible if I was not willing to learn about myself and discover different ways to approach my interactions and work.

I have to admit that this lesson was likely easier to learn at an institution where faculty and staff expect students to critically and personally engage in their own discernment and developmental processes—that was a clear advantage to my decision to work at a contemplative university. I was engaging with students and alumni/ae who aspired to change the world in innovative ways. Most approached everyday problems and issues from such a unique perspective that listening was sometimes the most I could offer. And they were adept at sharing their stories and perspectives. This was unlike some of the career sessions I had at more traditional institutions where students might have been required to see me, or their parents insisted on scheduling the meeting. As I write this, I believe that it is in our best interest and in the best interest of those with whom we work to try to remain present and provide enough space and safety for the other person to enter into a place of deep and personally meaningful reflection, whoever that person may be. Otherwise, we are not engaging in transformative education and not fulfilling the aspirations of our profession.

The practice of letting go of our judgments and expectations can feel chaotic, overwhelming, and uncontrollable. I learned to trust the process and something—whatever it may be—will emerge. Some of you who are reading this essay may have training in counseling techniques and have practice doing exactly what I have described. I did not receive such training. My master's degree was an academically rigorous program that held the assumption that our work as higher education professionals should begin with the development of a strong theoretical foundation to then support practical application in the field. As a result, I never took a counseling course and only learned techniques during my internships and on-the-job training.

While I had been developing strategies for working with students and alumni/ae on various career issues, I also was fortunate to stumble upon a technique that allowed me to ground my ideas, name what I was doing, and build my capacities as a career counselor. It was called motivational interviewing. I took the training simply because my department offered to sponsor me, and I did not have any grand expectations it would change how I worked with others. In fact what I knew of motivational interviewing at the time was that it was a technique used primarily with people suffering from substance abuse issues; in light of this, it seemed like it may be a stretch to use in career counseling sessions.

I was pleasantly surprised to discover that motivational interviewing offered a wonderful framework from which to understand the way I wanted to work with students and alumni/ae at Naropa. According to the Mid-Atlantic Addiction Technology Transfer Center (n.d.),

> The [motivational interviewing or MI] method differs from more "coercive" or externally-driven methods for motivating change as it does not impose change . . . but rather supports change in a manner congruent with the person's own values and concerns. . . . MI is more than the use of a set of technical interventions. It is characterized by a particular "spirit" or clinical "way of being" which is the context or interpersonal relationship within which techniques are employed. The spirit of MI is based on three key elements: *collaboration* between the therapist and the client; *evoking or drawing out* the client's ideas about change; and emphasizing the *autonomy* of the client. (pp. 1-2)

This description has a clinical and therapeutic focus, but the key elements offered great insight into how I could motivate students and alumni/ae in their career development. Some motivational interviewing techniques include open-ended questions, affirmations, reflections, and summaries (Mid-Atlantic Addiction Technology Transfer Center, n.d.). Motivational interviewing begins with deep listening then continues with reflection and reframing. Rarely does the interviewer focus on asking questions. This process required me to trust that students and alumni/ae have the internal wisdom to discover for themselves their life paths/callings. It also required me to step away from the role of service provider and my urge to advise. By entering into this space, transformation becomes possible for the person with whom the counselor is working.

After discovering motivational interviewing and reflecting on the ways I wished to partner with the inspiring and unique students, alumni/ae, and colleagues of Naropa, I no longer view my work as a career services professional in the same way. I now understand that my role is not to match students with occupations and career fields. Instead, I must honor the dynamic, ever-changing world in which we live; the world needs people who are flexible, adaptable, open, and non-judgmental and people who can sit with chaos and emerge with a calm presence and ideas to make meaningful change. These are exactly the students and alumni/ae with whom I work. It simply does not make sense for me to use the same approach I once employed as a career services professional. I feel liberated by this discovery and transformation and hope those with whom I work feel the same.

CONCLUDING BOW

If you had asked me at the beginning of 2008 where I would be today, I never would have imagined I would be given the opportunity to work at Naropa University, a small yet uniquely important institution of higher education. I could have let the career myths I held around what my first job "should be" after graduation cloud my passion, excitement, and curiosity for, as well as my intuitive connection to, Naropa. However, I am drawn to be transformed in this lifetime and in turn to be a transformative educator and learner with others. By making what seemed to be a risky decision, I found a home. I discovered people in this world who are true change agents, and I am fortunate to continue to learn who I am along the way. It is an incredible honor.

I hope you have found my story meaningful and that the next time your heart tells you to go for it but your mind resists you make peace with the thoughts and myths you hold, suspend them for a moment, and listen to your true desire. I invite you to open up to the extraordinary opportunity that exists when you allow yourself to be professionally and personally transformed.

I bow to honor wherever you—the graduate student, the budding professional, the seasoned professional, the curious reader, my family and friends—may be in your lives. May you find the space to reflect on your deepest and truest beliefs and values and embrace the potential for transformation and growth along your journeys, acknowledging the here and now and all the gifts the present holds.

NOTE

1. Description of the bow adapted from personal interview experience as well as an explanation found in Simmer-Brown, J., & Grace, F. (Eds.). (2011). *Meditation and the classroom: Contemplative pedagogy for religious studies.* Albany, NY: State University of New York Press and on Naropa University's website at http://www.naropa.edu/the-naropa-experience/story-of-naropa/the-bow.php

REFERENCES

Baxter Magolda, M. B. (2001). *Making their own way: Narratives for transforming higher education to promote self-development.* Sterling, VA: Stylus.

Coburn, T. B. (2011). The convergence of liberal education and contemplative education—inevitable? In J. Simmer-Brown & F. Grace (Eds.), *Meditation and the classroom: Contemplative pedagogy for religious studies* (pp. 3-12). Albany, NY: State University of New York Press.

Keeling, R. P. (Ed.). (2004). *Learning reconsidered: A campus-wide focus on the student experience.* Washington, DC: NASPA and ACPA.

Mid-Atlantic Addiction Technology Transfer Center. (n.d.). *An overview of motivational interviewing.* Retrieved from http://www.motivationalinterview.org/quick_links/about_mi.html

CHAPTER 7 DISCUSSION QUESTIONS

New Professionals

- What myths do you have about working at faith-based institutions?
- What is occurring for you in this moment that calls for your attention?
- What career myths might you hold about working in student affairs?
- In what ways do you anticipate being transformed by job one?

Supporters of New Professionals

- What methods do you employ to help mentees share their stories, ideas, and lessons learned?
- To what extent do you truly listen to mentees?
- How can you apply the lessons learned in Sarah's story to your work with new professionals?
- What recommendations would you offer to new professionals who are missing out on their "present" moments?

— *QUESTIONS PREPARED BY KATIE SHOEMAKER*

CHAPTER 8

Risky Business: Securing and Surviving Job One

KIM RUTLEDGE

San Francisco, California is not a place I expected to call home. I had no ties to the west coast and had never once stepped foot in the great state of California, thousands of miles away from my Midwest home of Cincinnati, Ohio. Soon after I completed my master's degree in college student personnel, however, I knew that I had to widen my search to include universities across the entire United States to land a job in academic support services. During college and my graduate studies, I resided in two small college towns and spent a few months as a student in London, England. I was by no means an adventurer, yet I resisted the urge to return to Cincinnati. Would taking a risk to achieve my life goals bring me happiness?

Initially I aspired to work in a metropolitan area, close to Ohio and my family but not too close. As a single, African American woman from Cincinnati, I placed high importance on finding a community that was diverse, included a great nightlife, and possessed a decent mass transit system since I'm not much of a driver. I wanted to continue working in academic support due to my positive experience as a graduate assistant in a university learning center. Finally, I wanted to work with colleagues who were proud of their work, collaborative, constantly honing their craft, satisfied with their work–life balance, and professionally active. I sent resumes to numerous colleges along the east coast and in the Midwest and to the University of San Francisco (USF). The position at USF appealed to me because my values aligned with the university's mission and values, and the position would provide me the opportunity to work with multiple offices within academic support services. Intuitively, I felt San Francisco would be a city that also could satisfy my personal needs. Unfortunately, the vacancy was a ten-month temporary position. If hired, I would begin another job search soon after arriving in San Francisco.

After completing my undergraduate program in retail merchandising, I moved to Chicago and worked for several retail establishments in positions that were both overwhelming and unsatisfying. Like many of my peers, after graduating from college I was unsure about life in general and my career in particular. Eventually, I had enough confidence to stage a self-directed intervention. I carefully assessed my strengths and concluded that I might really find joy in higher education where I could work closely with students to assist them in attaining their goals. I wanted to help students understand that it was okay to leave college not knowing their final destinations in life and that it was equally important to keep learning and be willing to change course to find a career and life that was exciting and fulfilling. I began to practice what I aspired to teach and began to conduct research focused on academic advising and career counseling at the college level. I visited my local library to investigate the student affairs functional areas, the graduate school admission requirements, and the schools that provided the necessary education and experience to prepare me for this new career. I took a huge risk and quit my job.

I returned to Ohio and moved in with my sister and her family until I found work. My first position was again in retail, but I kept my eyes open for jobs in education to gain experience before applying to graduate schools. A former advisor connected me to a position with an organization whose programs I utilized in high school, a college access program working with middle school students. My work with the college access program provided me an opportunity to reflect on my own experiences and understanding of higher education before entering college. I helped underrepresented prospective college students understand that they could attend college, and I helped them develop the skills and knowledge that would best prepare them to achieve their life goals. We focused on their academics during the school year and visited nearby campuses to interact with college students, faculty, and staff during their breaks. Although this was an exciting and educational job, I knew that it did not exactly align with my career aspirations.

At the age of 28, I enrolled in a higher education graduate program in the Midwest. My graduate assistantship was in the learning center, supervising tutors and working one-on-one with students. I felt great pride in my work as a graduate assistant in the campus learning center. I forged bonds with students that centered on personal and academic development and satisfaction. Although I had an opportunity to work in other offices, I was most drawn to the type of work that I could do with students in learning centers and academic support. I had spent so many years professionally unfulfilled, and I was determined that once I graduated I would secure work that fulfilled me, no matter how difficult the task.

While attending graduate school I worked for six months as an academic advisor. I highly enjoyed the experience, interacting with students to discuss their academic progress and connecting them with campus resources, but the lack of sustained contact with individual students concerned me. This brought me back to my true passion: engaging with students through a role in a learning center community. As an academic support professional, I would have the opportunity to engage, support, and assist in the development of a variety of students on an ongoing basis. In my dream role as a learning center specialist, I could develop in-depth relationships with students as an academic coach, advisor, supervisor, instructor, and group facilitator. I was not ready to give up, but being unemployed was not easy.

Like most of my peers, I began my job search at the beginning of the 2008 spring semester. I allowed my need for community, diversity, and student contact to drive my search process. As the semester progressed, I noticed that many of my peers were applying to many more positions than I did and were securing on-campus interviews while I patiently waited for my search to "get into gear." Although I was not geographically bound, my career focus (i.e., student academic support) was limiting. My first phone interview invitation arrived the week following graduation. Several of my peers were either weighing job offers or en route to their new homes. This phone interview for a tutor coordinator position with a private east coast university excited me. I practiced responses to potential questions. I was extremely nervous but ready. The interview went exceptionally well, and the school invited me to campus for extensive interviews. While on campus I met with several stakeholders to discuss my qualifications and vision. I was so nervous I perspired the entire day. After returning home, I dropped my thank you cards in the mail and waited to learn about the outcome. Several weeks later I called my campus liaison for an update. I learned that another candidate accepted the university's offer, and I was the second choice. The news was heartbreaking, but my contact provided me with valuable feedback that I could use to improve my interview skills whenever the next opportunity arose. She discussed the need to demonstrate an understanding of the campus community and to provide concrete examples of what I may be able to contribute if selected.

Moments of doubt occurred more frequently. I followed the advice of several peers and mentors and widened my search to include positions within residence life and academic advising. I quickly realized that I was not qualified or suited for residence life, because I cherished the ability to walk away from work at the end of the day and separate my home and work worlds. Several advising roles interested me, especially the positions with large caseloads. However, I quickly concluded that these opportunities would limit my ability to establish in-depth relationships with each student the way that working in a learning center would.

Two months after my first interview, long after my peers had departed campus to begin their first jobs, I received a phone message from the University of San Francisco inviting me for a phone interview for the program coordinator assistant position. The university was unable to provide an on-campus interview because the position was temporary; therefore, everything I was to learn about the campus and the city would have to come from USF staff and my Internet research. The idea of accepting a position sight unseen was a little risky; had the position been a permanent one, I would have advocated for an in-person interview, even if it meant that I would have to pay. USF offered me the position, and I had to decide if I wanted to take the risk of accepting a temporary position in a state I had never entered or keep searching for something more permanent and a little closer to home.

Accepting the position at USF would be an adventure. I convinced myself that it would be like studying abroad for a year. I also felt that this position would provide me with more diverse experiences in academic support services, which would only strengthen my resume as I searched for a new position the next year. I was concerned that I was considering the job simply to have a job, but I knew that I wanted a job within a learning center. These positions were sparse, and many vacancies required more experience than I possessed. I was unwilling to take the risk that an entry-level position in a learning center might open, but I was willing to commit a year of my life to gain more experience to qualify for a greater number of positions. Accepting this full-time position also would help me understand the full scope of learning center duties and determine if this was indeed a path I wished to pursue. I accepted the job and prepared to face the perils connected with finding an appropriate home, developing a social network, and separating from family, friends and all that was familiar.

Risks were not confined to simply securing the job. Beginning a new job in an unfamiliar city is stressful enough, but setting up house and building a personal life without the support of friends and family was a temporary nightmare. After accepting the position of program coordinator assistant, I had two weeks to pack and move to San Francisco. Because the position was temporary, I bundled up some belongings and put everything else in storage. As I began to pack, I also began searching for apartments or rather rooms in my new city. I learned from my new coworkers that Craig's List was the way to go. I scoured the listings for affordable one-bedroom flats. I soon came to learn that one-bedroom apartments do not come cheap in San Francisco. My colleagues informed me that most people had roommates and that would be the best way to go given my entry-level salary. I had not had a roommate in years. The thought of waiting to take a shower or arguing over whose turn it was to take out the garbage made me terribly uneasy. I enjoyed the freedom of moving about without interrupting others, leaving messes everywhere, and knowing that only I was responsible. While I was striking out on my own at work, I felt that I was losing my independence at home, but I made the sacrifice. I convinced myself that roommates could mean connections in a city where I had none.

I sought out "Rooms for Rent" in neighborhoods that, according to local maps, were relatively close to campus and provided detail about the continuing occupants. Each post then asked for an email response with "a little about you." "Yikes," I thought, "are these people looking for a roommate or a date?" Fear aside, I played up my great roommate attributes—clean and quiet—and asked if I could Skype my interview as I was not yet in the city. Radio silence. I concluded that I might fare better once I was in the city.

With most of my belongings in storage, five bags of clothes accompanied me to the airport to begin my adventure. In San Francisco, my colleagues anticipated that I might have some difficulty locating permanent accommodations, and they arranged for me to stay one week in an empty residence hall on campus. The good news about San Francisco is that people are always moving out of apartments. The bad news about San Francisco is that people are always moving in and looking for apartments. On my second day in the city I attended an open house. Here people who have rooms to rent open their apartments for several hours to allow those interested in a room to view the apartment and meet the roommates. When I arrived the residents gave me a tour. The place was a dump, but I needed a home at least for a few months. After inspecting the apartment, I chatted with the occupants. Soon the buzzer rang, and a new person had arrived to view the room. In thirty minutes it was standing room only and people were bribing the couple with culinary skills and awesome furniture to secure their spot. I couldn't compete. I realized I was in "rental hell."

Opening up to others about my concerns has never been easy for me. I realized that I would only make things worse by not opening up and asking for help; the less time I spent in the apartment search, the more time I could spend focusing on my new job. The next day, I spoke with my new colleagues of my concerns. They assured me that finding an apartment in San Francisco was tough. They then dedicated their time to assisting me in my search. One coworker took me on drives at lunchtime to see the city and find vacancy signs in apartment windows. A few others bombarded my email inbox with apartment ads. I hitched rides to interviews during lunch, and colleagues provided necessary feedback on which neighborhoods were appropriate for a young, single woman. As my residence hall lease expired, I snagged a one-month sublease in an apartment within walking distance to campus. It wasn't ideal, but I was unwilling to risk the chance of being homeless and losing my savings on weekly hotel rates.

The weekend that I moved in to the sublet, I committed to a permanent room available the next month. By San Francisco standards, the room was reasonably priced; it was fully furnished, in a beautiful neighborhood, and came with a roommate who was very mature (twenty years my senior). There were of course some differences, and living with another person necessitated honing my negotiating and compromising skills. The support of my coworkers and my willingness to accept their support was key in making this transition. Not many are fortunate enough to have such caring colleagues on their side when starting a new life. After having experiences with both supportive and unsupportive coworkers and supervisory staff, I knew that care would be one of the most important attributes of any new team I would consider joining.

Settled comfortably in San Francisco, it was time to face the perils of developing a social network. Developing friendships outside of college is no easy task. Once I left college, the number of opportunities to interact with strangers who share my interests dwindled. Instead of making friends in the residence halls or in class, I had to create opportunities to meet like-minded people, especially when I moved to a place with no connection to my past. For me, the gamble was not making friends but opening myself to ridicule and rejection during the process.

I had started over several times before, but meeting new people was an activity that always made me anxious. Although I was brave enough to move across the country, I was less willing to step out of my comfort zone to meet new people. My coworkers were amazing and supportive at work, but I wanted to be less dependent on them outside of work. Many people in the city seemed closed off to the idea of making new acquaintances; my new roommates in the sublet seemed particularly opposed to the idea. Two of the roommates spent their time in the apartment going between each other's rooms, rarely stepping foot in the common areas. The third roommate stayed quietly in his own room. I managed to get a peek at his face only once while he scurried to and from the bathroom. A month later, when I moved in with my fifty-year-old roommate there was even less opportunity to mingle with people similar to me.

As I never got the hang of meeting people outside of school, I called on friends and peers from school to ask how they were going about the task in their new cities. It seemed that developing friendships was a slow and risky process for everyone, but they blazed forward making connections through work, religious affiliations, family friends, and organizations. I joined several groups through the website meetup.com. I felt that joining established groups and organizations was a great way to meet new people as they appeared more receptive to forming new bonds. I attended multiple socials and outdoor events; however, the connections I made were tenuous. Nothing crossed over to life outside of the organization as I had hoped. Although I did not find meaningful and long-lasting friendships, I participated in activities that I enjoyed or had never tried. I moved forward at a pace that was comfortable for me, but I still faced uncomfortable situations and rejection.

The process of developing friendships in my new community was slow. There were times that I felt alone and longed to return home to more familiar surroundings. Falling comfortably back into my old life would reduce the risk of ever getting hurt and ever having to put forth effort, but I had not come this far to stall once again out of fear. I was grateful to know that my friends and family in the Midwest were still there to support me, even though we were 2000 miles apart. This knowledge provided me the strength to go out and expose myself to the possibility of rejection and ridicule that came with meeting new people. Today I have built strong bonds within the USF community and throughout the Bay Area. The process of connecting with new people continues to be a difficult venture; however, the prospect of never moving forward and encountering new adventures forces me to take the risk and repeatedly put myself out there.

During my interviews for the USF program coordinator assistant position, I shared with my interviewers my need to observe and understand why rules, roles, processes, and traditions exist before initiating change. I share my perspective because I wanted interviewers to know that I valued the culture of the school and did not wish to trample well-established ideals that initially I did not fully understand. As I assumed this new role, I had no desire to make quick changes due to my ignorance of the culture. Based on past experiences, I knew that change is difficult for many to accept, especially change introduced by outsiders. And I was certain that my sudden presence at this university and in these offices would be change enough for those involved, at least for the time being.

Introducing change was made even more difficult by the precariousness of my temporary job. The university created my role to provide academic support while two of its key employees were on maternity leave during the academic year. During my first few weeks on the job, I simply wanted to learn from the students and professionals with whom I worked, to tend to the programs that had been placed in my care, and to meet the needs of the students. During my first few months of work, I studied the Learning Center's programs, became familiar with the campus, and interacted with my new colleagues and the few students who were present during the summer session. My job was to learn as much as I could from the available materials until my official job responsibilities began in a month's time, the start of the new academic year.

After several months, the Academic Support Services team learned that people were changing positions within the office. My current supervisor was going to become the Learning Center coordinator, and his supervisor, currently on maternity leave, was to assume the role of director of first-year student programs. These transitions left a vacant position—the Learning Center assistant coordinator. My supervisor, now coordinator of the Learning Center, suggested I apply. The decision was not as easy it should have been. Although this opportunity meant that I would have a secure position within the Learning Center and

Academic Support Services, I had to decide if I felt at home enough in San Francisco and at the university.

If I applied for the position, I also would have to relive the dreaded interview process. Was I willing to take the risk of being rejected? Did my colleagues think me capable and competent to assume these job responsibilities? Was I willing to put myself out there, yet again, to be scrutinized and evaluated? The doubts and fears that I faced during my most recent job search reemerged. I feared that I was not good enough and that I was underprepared for this new position. I was certain that there was a more qualified applicant in the pool, and one of them would most certainly get the job. This thought was bad enough, but knowing that I would still work alongside these individuals for another six to seven months as well as the person who accepted the position I desired was terrifying. Instead of letting this hypothetical scenario paralyze me, I pushed aside the fear of rejection and submitted an application. I decided I was ready to make a more permanent home at USF.

Multiple applicants interviewed for the position. As they visited the office during their interviews, I avoided sizing up the competition and instead focused on my work. In this round of interviews at USF, I had the opportunity not only to speak of my qualifications with my peers in Academic Support Services but also to interview with the student staff in our office. The rapport that I had already built with these individuals on campus lowered my stress, but I did not take anything for granted and answered their questions as thoroughly and respectfully as possible. A month later, my supervisor offered me the position; from there, we began planning for the future, starting with a discussion about our new roles.

We made the announcement to the student staff that I accepted the position of Learning Center assistant coordinator, a permanent position. We also shared with them who would assume specific programs and tasks in the Learning Center. The students were accepting of the news, but it seemed they were disappointed that the former director of the center would no longer work in the office. The students experienced a great deal of transition in that first year with me and my boss moving into our current positions and their former director and program assistant moving out. The students were unaccustomed to rapid change, and they felt somewhat betrayed because they had little input into these changes. This made my transition into the new position challenging, as I wanted to help them become more comfortable with all that was happening in their "work family."

I spent the remainder of my first year at USF working to introduce as little change as possible. I had the opportunity to identify key weaknesses based on my observations and those of the students with whom I worked, but my supervisor and I chose to implement changes at the start of the next academic year. Students, faculty, and staff had developed certain ways of doing things and were unwilling to take risks in exchange for potentially improved systems with so many unknowns. I wanted to respect established traditions and learn more of the politics before altering the environment.

As I contemplated future ideas and decisions, I solicited input from students and colleagues to avoid making huge blunders that could have negative consequences for all. However, at times I felt trapped in my inability to send a simple email without first getting input from my peers regarding its content and necessary addressees. I was sometimes uncomfortable with this process as communication was never one of my strong attributes, and communicating with so many people to complete a basic task was a nightmare. I did not want to endanger my tenuous position with the university by offending others. Over time, I realized that I was letting my fear and risk aversion hold me back from doing my best work. I was uncomfortable in my new role, so I began to confide in my supervisor about my concerns and the biases that were affecting my performance.

There was one interaction I had with a colleague during my first year at the university that is still with me to this day. She asked how I was getting involved on campus and what changes I had made. I confessed that I had done little of either but that I spent the year observing and getting to understand the culture. She seemed to disapprove of this strategy and told me it was important to jump right in. Again, I wondered if I was doing a good enough job.

Two years later, I still wonder if I am doing a good job. I constantly question when it is best to steam ahead or pull back. Every day I risk offending others or encountering disapproval based upon my personal approach. I have learned to appreciate the fact that we all take different roads to get to the same place, roads most appropriate for our own vehicles. The risks that I take have put me right where I am, and I am in a good place. Ahead I have nothing but choices; some days I may play it safe, but on those other days, I will take a chance on the unknown as it may result in something better.

My experiences thus far have shown me that taking risks to get what I want personally and professionally has paid off. Even if they had not, I have learned a great deal about myself. Everyone takes some risks when seeking their first jobs in higher education. We give up opportunities because they do not match our values. Some of us value closeness to family and friends, working in specific locations or institutions, or working with certain student populations. In my job search, I was unwilling to compromise and took some risks. I realized I was no longer content with standing still or playing it safe. I made the decision before arriving at graduate school that I would stop making choices based on my fear of failure.

In my first position, I gambled that accepting a temporary position would have a higher payoff than future offers. Working at the University of San Francisco, I have gained experience as a professional in a learning center. I have collaborated with individuals working in various roles throughout the university, including academic advising and residence life; through our interactions, I have gained a broader understanding of others' roles and how they assist students to develop as learners and individuals. I enjoy my work with USF students, and I no longer believe that I can only have such meaningful interactions through a role in a learning center. I am now open to greater possibilities within student affairs as compared to when I began my job search during graduate school.

When I moved to San Francisco, there was the very real possibility that I might go months without a permanent place to call home. This scenario was unacceptable to me as I needed home to be the one constant in my life. Unfortunately, I allowed my fear of rejection to slow down the process of finding a suitable home. To be sure, I was not pursuing as many leads during that first month as I could have. Soon I came to realize that it was my pride or my sanity, and sanity won. I would risk almost anything to ensure that I had a reliable sanctuary from the perils of everyday life; without that, facing my work life would be almost impossible. I knew that finding comfort at home was just as important as finding comfort at work.

Outside of work and home, my social interactions were very important in my new life. My family and friends in the Midwest always made me feel wanted and supported, but finding that in a new place was scary. At times, the risk of rejection held me back from interacting with new people. Knowing I had the support of family and friends in the Midwest, I was willing to make a go of it repeatedly until I gained the friendships I wanted and needed.

Taking a risk is always unpredictable; however, when the possibilities of that risk are more exciting than your current life, it is important to move forward. I did not know where I would end up a year after accepting my first position at the University of San Francisco, but I was certain that it would not be the same place as where I started. My experiences at USF have made me a different person than who I was; therefore, it is impossible to go back to where I started. Whether I received a permanent position or not, I achieved what I was after: both a satisfying work life as well as a satisfying personal life.

CHAPTER 8 DISCUSSION QUESTIONS

New Professionals

- How do you determine which risks you should push yourself to take?
- What are ideal characteristics in colleagues? How can you develop these characteristics in yourself and others?
- What important factors must you consider before implementing change in the workplace, particularly as a new professional?
- Kim wrote, "It is impossible to go back to where I started." In what ways have you outgrown your previous self? What aspects of your identity remain?

Supporters of New Professionals

- How do you orient new professionals to understand the complexities of new positions?
- In what ways can you help new professionals implement change in a positive and effective way?
- How can you provide insights about an institution's culture while balancing the need for new professionals to experience the culture for themselves?

— *QUESTIONS PREPARED BY KATIE SHOEMAKER*

CHAPTER 9

Common Ground, Classrooms, and Conversations: Finding Professional Development in Unexpected Places

CARRIE MILLER

As I write this essay, I am sitting in my office. Many of my books reside on the shelves that line its walls, and three semesters' worth of decorations cover my door. My office, drastically transformed from when I first moved in, has come to feel like home. I have held countless meetings and staff one-on-ones in this office, spent early mornings writing final exams, evenings reading, and hours on conference calls. Living only twenty feet down the hall, I spend more time in my office than most people probably do. It is a comfortable place to work, whether I am doing my "day job" or working on something else. Lately, I find my usual contentment when working in my office paired with a twinge of sadness. I am leaving the university at the end of this year to begin my doctoral studies. When I began to unpack my things in this office, I was unsure what this job would bring and if I would make a place for myself at Ohio Wesleyan University (OWU). As I prepare to leave, I know I had not considered the career path I am heading down when I started as a residential life coordinator. I have experienced many moments of uncertainty and revelations in my office that will make it sad to leave it.

NEW BEGINNINGS: HEADING THE RIGHT DIRECTION?

When I accepted a residential life coordinator position at OWU in 2010, I had only visited Ohio twice in my life. I could not fathom how I would create a life like the one I had in Boston—full of evenings on the patio, barbeques, coffee dates, and watching the world pass by on my daily commute. My partner, Chett, and I packed everything we owned, loaded our dog, Frank, in the car and headed west; neither of us sure what we were getting into. Chett made a career change and started graduate school at Ohio State University, and I could not help but feel that I was just along for the ride. Unsure about my choice to work in residential life, the consummate planner in me wrestled with the notion of where my career was going. Somewhere between finishing my undergraduate degree and completing my graduate studies, my career path had become less obvious. A graduate research assistantship and interest in qualitative inquiry and cultural studies had me trying to figure out how to integrate those interests and my work with students. I hoped this new start would allow me to explore ways to integrate what sometimes seemed to be divergent interests.

In part, my eclectic interests led me to accept the position at OWU. I began at OWU as the residential life coordinator (RLC) for Hayes Hall, an all women's hall, and nine small living units (SLUs). The SLUs, small family-style homes that house 10-17 students, each organized around a specific theme, played a major role in attracting me to OWU. Their themes spanned a broad range of topics from social justice to foreign languages. My excitement for working with this community stemmed from the unique perspective that each house offered. Many of the students in the SLU community do not identify as a part of the mainstream campus culture but rather have their own community, norms, and values. The SLU community appeared to provide opportunities to work with and informally observe students who participated in these campus subcultures. One of the cornerstones of qualitative inquiry is understanding the meaning of human action. Working directly with the SLU community provided opportunities not only to observe these students but also to develop meaningful relationships that could potentially enhance my understanding of the multiple perspectives and realities that comprised the students' experiences and interactions with the greater campus community. Accepting the position as the RLC for the SLUs felt like an extension of my academic life into my student affairs practice.

On my first day on the job, I opened my new file cabinet and retrieved the copious files within. I intended to peruse the files to discover the different policies and procedures that governed my buildings. Instead, I found flyers, completed work orders, old house rosters, and key receipts, none of which offered any insight into how to do my new job. On my second day, my supervisor and I toured all of the SLUs. The lack of cleanliness and amount of clutter surprised both of us. I knew that I needed to hold the residents accountable for the slovenly state of their houses. In additional meetings with both my supervisor and the staff in the student involvement office, it became evident that the programming model also needed some modification to adhere to new policies. My predecessor, who before joining the professional staff lived as a resident in a SLU, allowed the community to govern itself. I knew that I needed to impose some structure. Before student staff training began, I wanted to compile all of the policies and procedures in a single written document. As a result, I had to ask numerous questions to gather background information on how things had worked or not worked before my arrival.

During this investigation, I rarely felt like I said the "right" thing. At my core, I simply wanted to understand how things worked. Asking *why* questions allows me to understand not only the mechanics of a process but also how it influences those involved. I felt compelled to understand how and why OWU developed its policies, procedures, and traditions. I mostly posed my questions to my supervisor and the other RLCs; conversations with my supervisor never seemed to go well. My questions, and even more so my suggestions to change the SLU procedures, flustered her. After about a month, her discomfort came to a head during a staff meeting. Many of the returning RLCs had indicated that they wanted to change and improve student staff training. I suggested that we could put together an assessment plan in coordination with the Institutional Research Office to improve student staff training. My suggestion caused quite the fuss. My supervisor responded immediately with "You have never worked at a small college and should bother learning about that before suggesting what we should do." I felt humiliated and unsure why my suggestion had elicited such a strong reaction. This interaction set the tone for the next few months.

I had arrived and begun asking questions and making suggestions for how I might structure my own work with the SLUs. Eager to use the knowledge I had gained in graduate school, I took the information I received and created proposals that utilized the theories or research that supported goals. Now, with a better understanding of my supervisor, I know that she preferred questions in lists and time to ruminate on them. Often she interpreted my proposals as disregarding her insights, when in reality I wanted to integrate her insights about campus processes with, for example, student development theory. I did not know how to approach my supervisor to continue to develop as a professional and hone my skills. Reflecting on my interactions with my supervisor, I realized that I, too often, repeated the same experiment and hoped for different results. I would ask a series of questions, read about an idea, write and submit a proposal, each time being careful to include all of the components of program and proposal development I had learned in class. Rarely did this strategy yield a successful outcome. I had to rethink my approach. I needed to sit back and do more observing and less direct questioning. In doing so, I learned about the types of ideas that my supervisor received well and the appropriate forums in which to present them. It became clear that the way my department preferred to receive information differed from the formats I learned and fine-tuned in graduate school. I did not want to abandon opportunities to integrate theory and research with my everyday work responsibilities, but I knew had to change my approach.

How could I create space to discuss theory and its place in our department's work? I thought carefully about my own professional development experiences, particularly those that had been most meaningful to me. I realized that the professional development strategies and opportunities I employed always involved someone else. I worked with someone to share my learning, and the support of the other person or group was important to my learning. These relationships helped keep professional development near the top of my priority list. The kindness, patience, and generosity of educators who invested their time in me serve as the foundation of my career in student affairs. Numerous individuals, who gave generously of their time to teach me, shaped my experiences and beliefs about student affairs work. In graduate school, I developed a relationship with a faculty member that proved to be among my most influential and meaningful professional relationships. The faculty member challenged me to read material I would not have selected on my own and to think critically about its application to student affairs practice. Our scheduled discussions have remained a highlight of my professional development and have greatly influenced my career path. That relationship, as well as the relationships that I cultivated and maintained from my undergraduate years and professional organizations, allowed me to discuss and get advice on a variety of topics and ideas.

Before starting at OWU, I served on a variety of committees through ACPA-College Student Educators International, which allowed me to feel like I contributed in tangible ways. These experiences shared common elements such as support, challenge, accountability, and action and provided me the opportunity to work with colleagues to collectively solve problems and generate possibilities that were rooted in applying theories to our practice and vice-versa. I count being a member of ACPA's Next Generation Conference planning committee among my most valuable experiences. The sense of camaraderie, the shared work, and the discussions of our ideas (and joint effort to implement them), made the Next Generation planning committee experience so rewarding.

My supervisor seemed to see professional development as a solitary activity, centering around obtaining more information on a topic (e.g., addressing bed bugs in the residence halls, motivating student staff). I hoped to create a more collaborative environment in the OWU department by engaging my colleagues in what I believed were important discussions. I proposed the creation of an interdepartmental professional development committee. I thought that by creating a specific forum to discuss theory and reflect on our practice, my supervisor and colleagues would continue conversations in other meetings. I received permission and asked the staff to complete the Council for the Advancement of Standards in Higher Education (CAS) Characteristics of Individual Excellence for Professional Practice in Higher Education (Dean, 2009). The CAS Characteristics of Individual Excellence articulates skills that CAS considers essential for quality student affairs practice and services. I asked that the staff use the document to identify areas in which they would like to improve. I coordinated a book club to discuss the higher education-related readings over a potluck dinner. However, anytime I coordinated a professional development activity, a critical mass always backed out at the last minute, even if they initially championed the topics and activities. This experience helped me realize that although my colleagues were genuinely interested in pursuing professional development activities, the crisis du jour always seemed to trump professional development opportunities.

I felt frustrated that colleagues did not keep abreast of higher education issues and controversies. Participating in professional development opportunities seemed to be a burden for them, so I started exploring ways in which I could satisfy my own professional development needs. The gap between espousing the importance of professional development and enacting professional development opportunities remained wide.

Settling In: Looking for Alternative Routes

I had time to reflect about my first few months on the job over the Thanksgiving break. I felt frustrated and undervalued and never seemed to find a fit with my department. The things that I found exciting about student affairs work and that had been a central part of my experiences in graduate school, considering theory and ideas, were absent from my current experience. Navigating my relationship with my supervisor was also something I spent time contemplating, but ultimately I wanted to try to address the issues that I felt I had the most control over. I could not determine how to improve my relationship with my supervisor, and I missed engaging in discussion with others about ideas. So I thought about the types of professional development experiences I wanted. I missed participating in class and wanted to learn more about qualitative inquiry and cultural studies. I lived a reasonable distance from Ohio State University, so I started looking at the winter quarter class schedule to see if any course offering interested me. I discovered that the College of Education offered qualitative inquiry seminar on Thursday afternoons. I asked my supervisor if I could take the hour and a half a week off throughout the quarter. My supervisor approved my request, and I registered as a non-degree-seeking student for the class.

A stressful and nerve-wracking day awaited me on my first day of class. Ohio State University is a much larger university than any I had previously experienced as a student or employee. Simply finding my classroom challenged me. Reaching my destination, I waited in the hall with my classmates for our professor to arrive. When I registered, I knew that there would be students from multiple majors in education enrolled in the seminar. As the seminar began, I discovered I was the only student affairs educator in the class; for the first time in quite a while, I received quizzical looks when trying to explain my job as an RLC. Our professor brought coffee (an instant plus in my book) and started the lecture. The introduction to the class did little to settle my nerves. I had never heard of numerous terms she used: Comtean positivism, post-structuralism and post-colonialism. To make matters worse, my classmates wore knowing looks on their faces as if they had absolute understanding of the concepts. Thoughts of my inevitable failure created a feeling of foreboding and avoidance of my homework. I finally decided to tackle the reading a few days later and discovered that I did not find the concepts quite as obtuse as they originally seemed.

Over the course of the quarter, we delved into qualitative inquiry, and I began to see unexpected connections between the ideas we studied and my work as an RLC.

The spring semester also brought a series of what felt like successes with the SLU community. It took a while to find comfortable working relationships, but I had more positive experiences than negative ones. During the fall semester, I implemented health and safety inspections and added several steps to the students' program-planning process in coordination with the new student involvement policies. The community found these changes unnecessary and disconcerting. I proposed an all-community meeting to discuss the community's concerns. This meeting allowed students to air their concerns and gave me time to carefully explain the new procedures (and rationales) to the residents directly rather than through the student staff members. We continued to hold monthly meetings for the rest of the semester. These meetings gave me an opportunity to better understand the community and vice-versa. I found that many of the lessons that I was learning in my qualitative inquiry class about building rapport with study participants were applicable to building relationships with the students in the SLU community. When the students returned from spring break, I felt better equipped to consider their needs and concerns. I also felt respect from them and started to address what many of the community members perceived as an adversarial relationship with our department. Class discussions about representation in qualitative research made me consider not only how I represented students to my colleagues but also my limited ability to fully represent or understand their community. I found the most success in building relationships within the community when I spent more time listening and learning about their community than talking. The more I started to listen, the more I learned and found a rather unexpected source of both professional and personal development.

In working with students and staff members to sponsor house programming, I started asking students to tell me more about their programs than just the perfunctory planning details. I learned far more than I anticipated. I learned about urban gardening, interfaith initiatives on campus, linguistics, pottery, mountain top removal, and a myriad of other subjects. Occasionally, I even discussed what I studied in my classes with the students; we discussed feminism, social justice, and postmodernism. These conversations also challenged me to communicate the information I had learned or knew from my own graduate education to students in ways that were relatable. The time that I spent in class discussing power relationships between researchers and participants caused me to think about my power as a staff member and how that power dynamic affected my relationships with students but also the ways in which students possess and exercise power in their relationships with the residential life office. I found many examples, particularly in the ways in which colleagues described the SLU community and the assumptions made about the community based upon their outward appearances and actions, very informative in considering my class discussions.

The more opportunities I gave students to discuss their interests, the more meaningful and beneficial our relationships became. Not only was I learning from students but they were learning from me as well. A few staff members served as incredible teachers. Gabe always arrived early for our meetings and did not watch the clock like some of the other staff. He unabashedly asked me why I took a particular approach or how I had reached a certain conclusion. His upfront and sometimes challenging demeanor initially made me defensive; over time, I developed an appreciation for his curiosity and thoughtful questions. Another staff member, Glenn, also arrived early for our meetings and sat on my couch reading one of my many books. I valued these meetings and looked forward to them every week. We discussed the business on our agenda, and then Glenn offered a stream-of-consciousness review of the books she had read. Some books she enjoyed so much that she borrowed them over break periods to finish them. I found these conversations challenging and as informative as class discussions. I will always appreciate the moderators' (i.e., the student staff in the SLU community) penchant for debate and the lively discussions that we had about any number of topics. I had never thought of students as teachers in this way.

My semester-long conversations with students strengthened partnerships with other professionals on campus. I frequently worked with a variety of staffs across campus, but our interactions rarely extended beyond discussing program planning and details. The Chaplain's Office supported many of SLU students' house projects. After numerous email conversations about students' programs, I contacted the chaplain to see if we could meet and get to know each other better and discuss collaborative possibilities. Since our initial meeting, the chaplain and his staff have been invaluable resources for discussing ideas and developing programs. My supervisor fully supported my outreach efforts with other departments.

As I closed the buildings and completed my first academic year at OWU, I worked on my spring quarter mid-term exam for a cultural studies seminar in which I was enrolled. I initially viewed my coursework as something that would build skills, such as an understanding of qualitative research methods, that I could utilize in student affairs practice, but it offered so much more. My coursework made me think about my own perspective, about the way I view my work and higher education. I learned many things, but the more I learned, the more skeptical I became of grand theories. A given theory cannot explain every aspect of a situation. No one person's perspective is complete. I can have my own perspective, but I must acknowledge what my perspective allows me to see and, more importantly, what my perspective does not allow me to see. Acknowledging the limits of my perspective challenged me to consider what voices were absent from a story and to see stories as one interpretation of an issue rather than a definitive account. I started to wonder who determines what counts as knowledge and how we accept an idea as a truth. These concepts fundamentally changed my thinking about student affairs practice. I learned to appreciate the ways that work outside of higher education (e.g., scholarship about K-12 education, other countries, tribal villages, HIV education) often conveyed concepts applicable to my work in student affairs. Peter Magolda and Marcia Baxter

Magolda (2011) argued that engaging with multiple sources of knowledge is essential for student affairs educators; I concur. I find the student affairs literature extremely valuable, but stepping outside the traditional topics addressed in student affairs and thinking more broadly about education, society, culture, and the human condition challenges me to consider my work in a much broader context.

MOVING FORWARD: NO U-TURNS ALLOWED

During the summer, our department experienced a number of staffing changes, and I found myself the only remaining full-time RLC. My supervisor left the department, which caused me to reflect on our relationship. I acknowledge that I contributed to our frustrations; in hindsight, I could have avoided some of these tensions. I wish that I had listened more, explained my desire to help explicitly, and addressed situations as they arose, rather than leaving frustrating or hurtful situations unaddressed.

I wish that I invested more time and energy into understanding my supervisor's passions and beliefs about professional development. She regularly sent newsletters to all of the RLCs via email and circulated hard copies through our mailboxes, attaching to them a sheet with all of our names, so that we could check off when we had read it then pass it on to the next person, ensuring everyone had the chance to review. I looked through the newsletter once, found the articles of no particular interest, and after that never spent much time looking through it. In retrospect, I wish I invested some time to read a few of the articles. I had no idea how much my supervisor valued those publications and the diligence with which she read them. I learned just how much she valued these publications after Chett proctored the SATs with my supervisor. When Chett returned home, he told me that she had spent hours during the test reading and taking copious notes on this newsletter. I asked her about the newsletter in our next one-on-one meeting, and she excitedly told me about its contents for the better part of an hour. The newsletter, which seemed insignificant to me, held a great deal of value for her. Reading the newsletter and further immersing myself in the professional development activities she valued would have provided me with a better understanding of her ways of thinking about student affairs work.

I wish I had taken the time to find more common ground to discuss with her. Perhaps she would have found our exchanges about professional development to be more genuine and engaging if I had expressed a more sincere desire to understand her interests, rather than just sharing my own. Interestingly, many of the things that I found challenging about building a relationship with my supervisor were reflected in the challenges encountered by the researchers conducting the studies I was reading in my cultural studies course. Building a relationship, finding common ground, mutual understanding, and respect share many commonalities regardless of the setting in which they occur. The last few weeks we worked together were by far the most comfortable and enjoyable of the entire year, because we began to understand each other. I placed a premium on the types of professional development and ways of approaching a problem that I valued and did not perhaps consider the logic or value in my supervisor's approach.

During the summer, I added another family-style living unit, the honors house, and apartment style living to my area of responsibility as well as changed supervisors. I directly reported to the department's director rather than the assistant director. The addition of the honors house excited me. The honors house residents and their connection with the honors program allowed me to cultivate relationships with additional faculty and staff members as we assisted the students with their programming. As the only staff member other than the director remaining in their current positions, the department asked me to assume additional responsibilities. I immediately asked my supervisor if I could take responsibility for teaching Psychology 295, Counseling and Student Personnel Work in Higher Education, a half-semester course for residential life student staff. After speaking with my supervisor and the psychology department chair, I received approval to serve as the instructor for the course.

I spent the second half of the summer preparing for opening and welcoming new staff members as well as preparing to teach Psychology 295. As I fine-tuned the syllabus, I found myself incorporating student development theory, cultural studies, and a variety of topics I had discussed with other campus administrators. I wanted to provide the students with opportunities to explore different ideas and assigned a topic paper in which they would discuss a topic of their choice and how it related to their work in residential life. I had served as a teaching assistant and co-instructor, but I had never been solely responsible for a class and found that some classes were less successful than I hoped.

The students challenged me in ways I did not expect and sometimes I struggled with having members of my own staff in my class, particularly when they skipped class or failed to submit an assignment. Teaching allowed me to engage the students in the same types of conversations as I did with my individual staff members. I crashed and burned several times and was appreciative that I could talk to faculty mentors, particularly a professor from graduate school, about how I might approach things differently for the next class. I started my fall quarter class, Social Foundations of Education, with three doctoral students. None of us had taught at the college level previously and shared in the trials, tribulations, and triumphs of our first experiences teaching undergraduate students.

The fall semester provided other interesting opportunities to partner with students and colleagues across campus. Early in the semester, resident assistants in Hayes Hall and I began to notice an increased amount of profanity being written on the building white boards and what we perceived to be derogatory language being used by women to address other women on campus. I spoke to a colleague working in Greek Life about this apparent trend and she concurred with my assessment. We decided, in conjunction with a few students, that we would discuss the possibility of a program during women's month. We convened the student committee and their enthusiasm immediately impressed me. During our first committee meeting, I felt like the sum of my experiences of the past year was coming together. As I worked with the students, they taught me about trends in the media and online. They shared information with me about a campus climate survey they had access to through an internship, and I shared some of my own knowledge to structure the program. My colleague and I helped them organize logistics and discuss potential issues. When it came time to decide how to open the conversation, they talked about stories, a great personal interest of mine, and I described several digital storytelling methods they might be able to use. I had learned about digital storytelling in class, and the students decided to set up story telling booths in the campus center to allow students to share their own experiences with hurtful language. My colleague and I utilized our professional networks through ACPA and the Association of Fraternity/ Sorority Advisors to gather additional information on similar programs.

REFLECTIONS

The upcoming spring semester will be my last at OWU, as I am starting my doctoral studies in the fall. My experiences as an RLC challenged the way that I think about student affairs practice and the relationship between theory and practice. We cavalierly use terms like theory to practice and labels such as scholar and practitioner. However, I find the more I try to keep theory, practice, "academic work," and student affairs practice as discrete categories, the less I learn from the experience. The application of these clearly delineated categories to student affairs work only serves to create a false perception that ideas like scholarship and practice are separate, even in opposition to each other rather than interrelated and mutually beneficial ideas. Cultural studies scholars discuss these binaries as problematic, because they make it difficult for people to see shades of gray. Presented ideas as falling discretely into one of two categories obfuscates the connections between the ideas and their commonalities. When I began my coursework at OSU, I deemed that time as a separate part of my life. This was in part because I did not talk about what I was learning at work, and the end of the workday marked a shift to homework. That perception was ill conceived. The tangible tasks associated with work and classes were distinct and separate, but the experiences were inextricably linked. The more I learned in class, the more my thoughts about my work in student affairs changed. And in turn, my experiences as an RLC and in student affairs shaped the way that I interpreted and related to the information presented in class. Scholarship and practice exist in a mutually beneficial relationship: one informs the other. When we approach a problem, we bring the totality of our knowledge to bear; the amalgam of our experiences determines how we perceive and address the problem from the outset. My learning outside the "traditional" bounds of student affairs shapes my entire thinking about my work.

As an undergraduate, I wrote a final entry in the Student Government Association tome, a large leather book that contained the parting advice of several years' worth of graduating SGA members. In my entry I stated that our intent is often different from our impact. At the time I was referring to our words and actions, how the best of intentions can sometimes have a negative impact on others. When I reflect on this bit of advice now, I cannot help but think about my experiences at OWU and with professional development. What I planned to gain from an experience rarely corresponded with the result and far exceeded my expectations. Every experience has an impact on our trajectory; things that seem to take us off course simply redirect us to an unexpected, but often better, path.

REFERENCES

Baxter Magolda, M. B., & Magolda, P. (2011). Intellectual curiosity and lifelong learning. In P. Magolda & M. B. Baxter Magolda (Eds.), *Contested issues in student affairs: Diverse perspectives and respectful dialogue* (pp. 3-14). Sterling, VA: Stylus.

Dean, L. A. (Ed.). (2009). CAS characteristics of individual excellence for professional practice in higher education. In *CAS professional standards for higher education* (7th ed.; pp. 20-22). Washington, DC: Council for the Advancement of Standards in Higher Education.

Chapter 9 Discussion Questions

New Professionals

- With which student subcultures (e.g., Greeks, athletes, multicultural student organizations) do you prefer to work? How do you forge relationships with these students?
- How do these students perceive the office you work in and campus administration in general?
- How do campus administrators perceive that particular student subculture?
- How might you discover the expectations and preferences of those with whom you work (e.g., supervisors, colleagues) to avoid or directly address conflicts, such as those that Carrie experienced with her supervisor?
- What ideas do you have for developing professional resiliency?
- As a new professional, what constitutes meaningful professional development for you?
- How will you go about finding opportunities to engage in meaningful professional development?

Supporters of New Professionals

- How can you provide new professionals with opportunities to interact with a variety of constituencies across campus to allow them to observe the campus's multifaceted culture?
- How do you help new professionals integrate theory into their practice?
- As an experienced professional, what constitutes meaningful professional development, and how do you pursue meaningful development?
- What advice do you have for new professionals who are not connecting with their direct supervisors or who want to improve their relationships with their supervisors?
- How do you demonstrate that you are open to learning from new professionals and from direct reports?

— *Questions prepared by Katie Shoemaker*

CHAPTER 10

Go Ahead and Leap: The Rewards of Taking Risks

KATHLEEN GARDNER AND CRAIG WOODSMALL

Nine years have passed since we were new professionals and wrote our chapter for the *Job One* book. Since then we have changed jobs, transitioned institutions, altered career paths, bought our first home, and started a family. Reading the stories written by David Stanfield, Sarah Steward, Kim Rutledge, and Carrie Miller led us to reminisce about our own job one experiences. As we reread our chapter about being in a dual career relationship in student affairs, we marveled over where our journey has taken us. Our willingness to take calculated risks and to make ourselves vulnerable has been essential to our growth as individuals and as professionals, similar to the authors of the preceding four chapters. Reading and reflecting on these new professionals' narratives brought back memories of our early days in the field. Looking back with the benefit of hindsight, the risks we took are much clearer now. However, if asked about our choices, we would have said we were only doing what seemed necessary to move toward meeting our personal and professional goals.

We never considered ourselves risk takers. We would probably each describe ourselves as risk-averse. In hindsight—after reading the chapters penned by David, Sarah, Kim, and Carrie—it is obvious that risk taking has been central to our collective professional journey as well. I (Craig) turned down a first job offer after graduate school to follow Kathleen to Maryland. I (Kathleen) accepted a job in St. Louis without Craig having a job offer; I then accepted a second job at an institution unknown to me to further my career while allowing Craig to continue pursuing his dream of working as a psychologist in a college counseling center. I (Craig) chose to temporarily leave higher education to meet the needs of our growing family. All of these decisions demonstrated an element of risk taking. Growth and development occur when individuals venture outside of their comfort zones. In other words, risk taking is imperative for our professional development.

I (Kathleen) currently lead the residence life program at Southern Illinois University Edwardsville, and I have continued to take on leadership roles with ACPA-College Student Educators International. I (Craig) work full-time as a psychologist for a health insurance company and part-time as an adjunct faculty member at three different institutions of higher education. Our career paths have not been perfect or without fear or failure. We continue to challenge one another to be courageous, both personally and professionally. We also continue to embrace our vulnerability so that we can continue to grow as individuals, parents, partners, and professionals. Through our vulnerability we have learned to establish new ways of coping, which has strengthened our resiliency as a dual-career couple. Although the details of our story and the circumstances of each of these four new professionals differ greatly, one thread that connects us all is the element of risk and how new professionals face this challenge early in their careers.

FACING FEARS AND TAKING RISKS

Many individuals embarking on their first professional job search confront a variety of fears. The role of this basic human emotion in shaping our daily lives is difficult to underestimate. Evolutionary psychologists have written about how fear serves as a survival mechanism, an instinctual response to perceived danger. The dangers that confront potential job seekers, both seen and unseen, are too voluminous to list here but typically center on the following themes. What if I choose the wrong position or institution? What if my new community does not meet my needs? What if I do not connect with my new colleagues or supervisor? What if I am unable to fulfill my job duties and responsibilities? What if these experiences lead me to leave my job, or what if I am unsuccessful finding any employment? The nature of today's economy compounds these normal fears for new professionals. The average unemployment rate was 9.6% in 2010 and 8.9% in 2011 (Sicilia, n.d.). Although the rate fell below 8% at the end of 2012, it is still much higher than the rates at the start of the millennium. However, if we allow ourselves to ruminate on all the unknowns, we would be incapable of making decisions or taking action.

The authors of the preceding four chapters, although each unique, all describe strikingly similar fears as they progressed through their first search processes and the early days in their first jobs. David confronted fears about living and working far from his home, friends, and family while learning how to learn and understand a new culture. David noted that he is "adventurous at heart," but he recognized the need not to let his excitement for the position overshadow potential shortfalls: separation from friends and family, feeling safe in his new environment, and institutional fit. Sarah confronted her fears in relation to choosing to work at a nontraditional institution. She worried that this decision could limit future career growth and the loss of approval from people important to her for not seeking a position at a "reputable" institution. Kim faced a number of fears when considering the University of San Francisco position including accepting a temporary position in a new city without knowing anyone or having a place to live. She also experienced fear of rejection as she worked to forge new connections with others. Carrie faced her fear of criticism and potentially alienating herself from her supervisor and colleagues by asking questions and advocating for the adoption of new ideas.

Fear is both a biological event and a psychological experience. The physiological reactions that fear triggers include activation of the cardiovascular system, endocrine system, and neurological system. The emotion of fear is also a psychological event, producing a subjective feeling of terror. The role of our emotions, most theorists agree, is to motivate us to behave in certain ways (Lang, 1985, 1995; Lang, Bradley, & Cuthbert, 1998). For example, in a state of fear we may be motivated to flee or escape to decrease our terror or unpleasant state. Our thoughts and perceptions of the situation mediate our experience of fear. We appraise changes in our environment for their potential impact on us (Lazarus, 1991, 1995). How we perceive the situation could determine if we experience the emotion of fear or something else. In fact, fear and the emotion of excitement can be considered just different end points on a continuum of feelings associated with appraisal of a specific situation (Barlow, Rapee, & Reisner, 2001). In other words, our thoughts and perspectives, as much as the event itself, shape our emotional reactions. This is what enables some people to take risks more freely, but others may be paralyzed by a situation perceived as too risky.

The authors of the preceding four chapters faced their fears and took action, rather than fleeing. They took risks regarding their professional careers and personal lives. Their decisions were unconventional from the standpoint that they choose not to pursue the more "tried and true" traditional career options. David had to decide within days if he would fly to Qatar for an on-campus interview, traveling to an area of the world where most Americans would have serious fears about their safety. By taking decisive action, David demonstrated that he could manage such fears and re-focus his perspective on what could be gained from the experience of living and working in Qatar. Sarah's story illustrates many different types of risks and possible fears. She accepted a position without knowing the outcome of another search process. She risked loss of approval by selecting the non-traditional, Buddhist institution. Sarah recognized that "there is risk in every decision we make" (p. 74) and that "the practice of letting go of our judgments and expectations can feel chaotic, overwhelming, and uncontrollable" (p. 76).

Risk taking marked Kim's job search. She widened her job search beyond her geographical comfort zone. Kim accepted a temporary job with full knowledge that she would need to start her next job search soon after she settled in San Francisco. She also took a risk by taking the position sight unseen and without a place to call home. She questioned, "Would taking a risk to achieve my life goals bring me happiness?" (p. 80). Carrie's desire to understand her new institution's culture and her motivation to contribute immediately during her first months on the job guided her actions. Some professionals suggest that new professionals spend significant time learning a new environment and resist the urge to make changes too early in a new position. Although enthusiasm is admirable, sometimes supervisors view new professionals who challenge the status quo as professionally immature or as questioning authority. Carrie did both, which can be risky for a new professional.

In all four stories, each new professional identified what made the risk worth it for them. For David, it was the adventure of working overseas in student affairs. For Sarah, the opportunity to work at an institution that valued inner transformation of its students in ways that mirrored her personal values evoked "intrigue and enthusiasm" in her. Although Kim does not consider herself to be an adventurer, she perceived the position at USF as an adventure; one that was worth going after to have a chance at a satisfying work life.

Carrie took a risk by accepting a position at an institution that appeared to favor practice over theory, despite having a personal preference for the latter. Furthermore, she was uncomfortable working under an artificial theory–practice dichotomy and actively worked to integrate theory into her work. Carrie also took risks by challenging the supervisor–supervisee binary which tends to limit who can be the teacher versus learner—not by directly challenging her supervisor, but through a process of genuine questioning and offering of ideas. After Carrie encountered difficulties with her supervisor and resistance to her approach, she did not throw up her hands and give in to being stuck in a job that she needed to accept passively due to her circumstances. She took on additional risk when she sought an environment outside of her workplace that could stimulate her professional and personal growth. Her supervisor and colleagues could have perceived Carrie's decision to invest more of her time and energy outside of the department as a liability.

Each of the authors described the struggles they endured related to risk taking. Their decisions to take risks were at times uncomfortable. Kim noted her tendency toward risk aversion and at multiple points was keenly aware of the potential for receiving rejection or judgment from others as she attempted to forge new interpersonal connections with roommates and with the San Francisco community. The fear of not having a permanent home unsettled her. Sarah poignantly detailed the doubt and confusion created by the internalized career myths she absorbed from the external world. These myths work as guides for what is expected and what is desirable. The career myths Sarah encountered included the assumption that it is always best to seek the highest paying job at the most prestigious institution. In response to this myth, Sarah worried about limiting future career options by choosing to work at a lesser-known, non-traditional institution. In addition, it can be disorienting to open ourselves "to new ways of knowing and being" (p. 70)

Part of David's struggle was the uncertainty with just about everything in Qatar—a common cause of fear and risk-aversion. Not knowing how his family and friends would react to this decision or what would happen to his relationships with them being so far away could have been enough to deter him from getting on that plane. In addition, he took a risk by sharing his religious beliefs with students. David felt nervous about speaking with students about his faith because he identifies as a conservative Christian while a strong majority of the students identified as Muslim. David engaged students on a topic that many new professionals might see as risky, especially in a country where the law prohibits proselytizing by non-Muslims.

New professionals preparing to transition from graduate school programs into their first jobs are vulnerable to their fears, often overshadowing their ability to consider alternative paths. Many students have already moved away from familiar areas, family, and friends to attend graduate school and may be hesitant to move yet again. Student affairs work often requires individuals to tolerate multiple geographic moves, especially if they wish to further their careers or move up in the profession. The transient nature of student affairs work can add an additional layer of complexity. Preparation programs challenge students to question previously acquired knowledge and perspectives and to make room for new information and theories. This process often results in significant changes in the student's own beliefs and development, such that envisioning additional change and transformation may be overwhelming. The pull to "play it safe" and seek a traditional role at a reputable institution can be strong. The potentially exciting and inspiring outcomes that accompany risk taking may be easily missed or ignored. Taking risks may not be a choice we can manage to avoid completely; even playing it safe is a risk in itself. How could David avoid violating cultural norms while trying to empower students? Was there a better way for Kim to obtain experience in the area of student academic support without accepting a temporary position? Sarah wrote, "I admit there is risk in every decision we make" (p. 74), and she was unwilling to risk her own authenticity and integrity by not following her heart. Carrie came to a point where she felt compelled to rethink her approach and deliberated on whether she needed to observe more and question less.

Ultimately, David, Sarah, Kim, and Carrie saw the potential for new experiences, growth, and a chance to learn more about themselves by pursuing unconventional paths. Were they aware of the dangers? Yes, but that did not stop them from taking these risks, moving forward, and exploring the unknown. Because they took risks, they gained a great deal. David immersed himself in a new culture that provided "an intense opportunity to learn about oneself and other" (p. 68). Because he chose an institution that welcomed new ideas and encouraged innovative approaches to student learning, he thrived professionally. His supervisor rewarded David with additional job responsibilities, furthering his professional growth and development even more. Through Sarah's risk taking, she experienced an incredibly rich learning opportunity that sparked her intrapersonal growth. From this, she gained greater insight into new ways of learning and being. Working with Naropa students challenged her to engage with students on a much deeper level, and she gained greater insight into how learning occurs. "If we do not fear the vulnerability that arises when we do this and if we are willing to set aside our judgments and expectations, discoveries and learning abound" (p. 75). In turn, her work became more meaningful. Part of what Kim gained from her risk-taking was growth in her ability to tolerate the potential for rejection and not knowing what would happen. Kim noted, "Taking a risk is always unpredictable" (p. 89). Despite this unpredictability, she gained a full-time position in academic support services by taking a risk on a temporary position, sight unseen. She set aside her risk of rejection to find a more permanent home and to gain the friendships she wanted and needed. "I knew that finding comfort at home was just as important as finding comfort at work" (p. 89). All of these lessons will serve her well in her next job search. Carrie took a risk by seeking permission to enroll in a doctoral seminar. As a result, she learned a great deal about herself, her professional interests, students, and the culture at her institution. Carrie's risk taking culminated in the further development and clarification of her own career path. Finally, it is important to note that all four new professionals took one final risk: they each decided to participate in this publication and to document and share publicly their struggles, doubts, and fears as they embarked on their careers.

What enabled each of the authors to feel excitement more than fear, at least to the point they were not paralyzed by their fears? Each of the authors appears to share similar traits such as an openness to difference, willingness to engage in self-reflection, a desire for creativity or innovation, and the ability to appreciate where they are in the present rather than getting caught up in expectations and pursuit of the perfect job. Knowing that a person's choices could be wrong or result in negative outcomes requires a person to do what most people work hard to avoid, sometimes to disastrous results—be vulnerable.

VULNERABILITY AND COURAGE

Essential in all four stories is willingness to take some emotional risks, to be vulnerable: moving 7,000 miles away from friends and family, being open to new ways of knowing and being, moving to the West Coast without a place to call home, and sharing innovative ideas with new colleagues and supervisors are all vulnerable acts. Brown (2010) described vulnerability as the place where innovation, creativity and change come from. "Courage is about putting our vulnerability on the line" (Brown, 2010, p. 13).

One of the most common misconceptions in our society is that vulnerability equals weakness when in reality it is quite the opposite. Vulnerability is our most accurate measure of courage (Brown, 2010). Conducting a successful job search and thriving in a new environment, both personally and professionally, require both vulnerability and courage. To transition from graduate school into job one, individuals must identify their personal and professional values, needs, and aspirations then set about obtaining them. Courage is what propels us to enact our values, satisfy our needs, and reach for our aspirations. Courage assists us in creating connections, helps us make meaning out of our experiences, and helps us learn to work within the context of an imperfect work environment.

Sarah recognized the need to embrace her vulnerability during her time at Naropa University. Her courage to set aside her fear of being vulnerable allowed her to learn how to facilitate transformative learning. She learned to let go of her urge to advise students. Through her willingness to be vulnerable, Sarah learned how to "be the center of [her] own learning experience and be willing to undergo personal and professional transformation" (p. 70). Her vulnerability and courage changed her view of student affairs and brought greater meaning to her work as a career counselor.

David demonstrated professional vulnerability through the depth of his conversations with both his students and his supervisor. Through David's willingness to be vulnerable by discussing his faith with his students, he found common ground with them about a belief in a higher power and gained deeper insight into an often misunderstood religion. In addition, David engaged in regular reflective conversations with his supervisor about culture and its implications for his work. Reflection with someone in a position of power or authority requires a degree of vulnerability; reflection in supervision is about self-appraisal and not asserting a perfect self. Through his courage to be vulnerable with his supervisor, David gained deeper understanding and meaning from his experiences in Qatar.

Vulnerability requires us to let go of our desire for perfection. Each of the new professionals learned to become more comfortable with imperfection. When Kim applied for the permanent position, she had to reconcile her self-doubt with her desire to create a professional home at her institution. Her fear of not being the perfect candidate and her fear of rejection almost jeopardized her goals. No new professional is perfect or has all of the skills and experiences necessary for any one position; employers are looking for potential. Potential is very different from perfection. Recognizing one's own potential comes from knowing oneself: an awareness of needs, strengths, weaknesses, and values.

Carrie understood that she was not a perfect supervisee:

> I acknowledge that I contributed to our frustrations; in hindsight, I could have avoided some of these tensions. I wish that I had listened more, explained my desire to help explicitly, and addressed situations as they arose, rather than leaving frustrating or hurtful situations unaddressed. (p. 98)

This acknowledgement of imperfection helped Carrie make sense of her previous experiences and potentially bring deeper understanding and meaning to future supervisory relationships.

Brown (2010) reminded us that "perfectionism is self-destructive simply because there's no such thing as perfect. Perfection is an unattainable goal" (p. 57). In trying to avoid being vulnerable, new professionals often gravitate toward self-destructive behaviors such as perfection and become paralyzed. Embracing imperfection and vulnerability is necessary in the professional maturation process. We grow by identifying and addressing our weaknesses or imperfections. "Staying vulnerable is a risk we have to take if we want to experience connection" (Brown, 2010, p. 53). Brown defined connections as the "energy that exists between people when they feel seen, heard and valued; when they can give and receive without judgment; and when they derive sustenance and strength from the relationship" (p. 18). Each of the four authors articulated a need for connection. David wanted to connect with his new environment. Sarah wanted to connect with a deeper wisdom. Kim wanted to connect with peers who would offer social support. Carrie wanted to connect theory with practice in her new work setting and to be able to discuss with others. Each new professional experienced new connections by demonstrating vulnerability: moving abroad, letting go of previous forms of meaning, asking colleagues for help, and venturing out to find professional support beyond her department.

David, Sarah, Kim, and Carrie also demonstrated authenticity in their journeys. "Authenticity is a collection of choices that we have to make every day. It's about the choice to show up and be real. The choice to be honest. The choice to let our true selves be seen" (Brown, 2010, p. 49). It takes courage and vulnerability to be authentic. Student affairs educators require authenticity. New professionals often confuse transparency of thoughts and emotions with authenticity. How can graduate programs and practitioners weave concepts of authenticity into the classroom and supervisory relationship? Can conversations about authenticity encourage new professionals to forgo their quests for perfection? Through their ability to embrace vulnerability, each of the four authors created a sense of belonging for themselves. They sought something more than fitting in with their new environments. "Fitting in is about assessing the situation and becoming who you need to be accepted. Belonging, on the other hand, doesn't require us to change who we are; it requires us to be who we are" (Brown, 2010, p. 25).

RESILIENCY AND SELF-EFFICACY COPING SKILLS

All four case studies implicitly discuss sentiments associated with transition: transition to a new country, to a new job, to a new institutional culture, to a new supervisory relationship. To successfully navigate all of these transitions requires resiliency. Brown (2010) defined resiliency as "the ability to overcome adversity" (p. 63). It is not about avoiding feeling down or anxious but about how quickly one bounces back after encountering a setback. Brown listed five most common factors of resilient people:

1. They are resourceful and have good problem-solving skills.
2. They are more likely to seek help.
3. They hold the belief that they can do something that will help them manage their feelings and to cope.
4. They have social support available to them.

5. They are connected with others, such as family or friends. (p. 64)

Although adversity looked different to each of the new professionals, each experienced adversity and overcame it by employing some of the factors above.

Kim's story demonstrated both personal and professional resiliency. She quickly learned that she would need the help of others to successfully navigate the housing market in San Francisco. She accepted both advice and assistance from colleagues to find a permanent home. "The support of my coworkers and my willingness to accept their support was key in making this transition" (p. 85). Creating a support network also required resiliency. Roommates kept to themselves, and social groups she pursued did not yield the long-lasting friendships she craved. However, Kim continued to participate in new activities and tapped into the support of her friends and family in the Midwest. Once in the permanent position, Kim recognized that her fear of offending others and her self-doubt were holding her back. By confiding in her supervisor, she created support that strengthened her resiliency as she faced the challenges of her new, permanent position.

David moved overseas and faced his fears of safety and separation from friends and family. He tackled this adversity by treating his transition process "like a class research project aimed at discovering a new culture" (p. 61). David clearly believed that he could do something to manage the feelings associated with his transition. Through this experience, he learned how he would familiarize himself with future new environments. Once the initial excitement of being immersed in a new culture and environment wears off, people experience a state of disintegration. The familiar cues for behavior are gone and the person is bombarded by the requirements of the new culture (Pedersen, 1995). As the person slowly learns how to integrate new cues and regains the ability to function, the stress of culture shock starts to subside. As this process continues, people learn how to balance aspects of both cultures into their daily lives and reach a point where they can function autonomously in the new culture. For David to successfully navigate this process, he had to tolerate that state of disintegration and recover in time to start assimilating to aspects of his new cultural environment. He also obtained valuable insight from others who were further ahead in their cultural adjustments. Such a balanced outlook enables a person to appraise both the new and old cultural worldviews with greater insight. David wrote, "Once I returned to the United States, I promised myself that I would strive to make the familiar strange. I would assume less and question more" (p. 62).

Sarah demonstrated resilience through her ability to tolerate discomfort as she developed a new approach to her career services position. She quickly learned that she could not utilize the same advising strategies she used with the more traditional-aged students at her former institution. She had to discover new ways of knowing. "This lesson came in the form of assuming the role of learner first and foremost and then acknowledging the inherent wisdom of whomever I was engaging" (p. 75). Ceasing to constantly advise and beginning to listen to students disoriented her. Without judgment, she began to question her understanding of the situation at hand and examine her beliefs. Both Buddhism and modern psychological theories assert the human capacity to manage stress and alleviate suffering through a process of meditation or contemplation (Epstein, 1995). Through these processes, we can identify what we find disturbing; often it is some desire or craving we convince ourselves is critical to obtain. Once Sarah realized that she did not have the answers and embraced the unknown, she let go of simply advising students and began listening on a deeper level. Her understanding of how transformative learning occurs deepened as the obstacles that were preventing her from fully integrating into her new position faded. This illustrates resilience in the form of utilizing her inner resources and good problem-solving skills.

Carrie demonstrated her resilience through her belief that she could do something about some of the work issues that left her feeling frustrated and undervalued and let go of the rest. She recalled, "I could not determine how to improve my relationship with my supervisor, and I missed engaging in discussion with others about ideas" (p. 95). Carrie showed resilience by enrolling in coursework at a nearby institution. She also worked to strengthen her connections to others outside of the traditional supervisory and peer colleague spheres, such as the campus chaplain and a few of her staff members. Carrie stated that she "found these conversations challenging and as informative as class discussions" (p. 97). Such connections not only buffer stress but also can foster resilience. Because of these experiences, Carrie reconsidered her own perspective, not just about her work situation but how she viewed higher education, the limits of theory, and who determines truth. In a parallel fashion to her interpersonal resilience, Carrie began to investigate bodies of knowledge outside of student affairs and to think "more broadly about education, society, culture, and the human condition" (p. 98).

The situations the four authors faced required them to bring internal and external resources to bear when responding to their challenges. In doing so, the authors demonstrated the capacity to bounce back from the stressor(s) encountered—resilience. So where does this resilience come from? One significant factor that contributes to a person's resilience is self-efficacy.

According to psychologist Albert Bandura (1997), self-efficacy "refers to beliefs in one's capabilities to organize and execute the course of action required to produce given attainments" (p. 3). Bandura (1997) asserted self-efficacy determines

> the courses of action people choose to pursue, how much effort they put forth
> in given endeavors, how long they will persevere in the face of obstacles and
> failures, their resilience to adversity, whether their thought patterns are self-
> hindering or self-aiding, how much stress and depression they experience in
> coping with taxing environmental demands, and the level of accomplishments
> they realize. (p. 3)

In other words, self-efficacy is a person's belief in his or her ability to succeed in a particular situation. People with a strong sense of self-efficacy view challenging problems as tasks to be mastered, develop deeper interest in the activities in which they participate, form a stronger sense of commitment to their interests and activities, and recover more quickly from setbacks and disappointments.

Where does self-efficacy come from? Bandura (1995) asserted there are four major sources of self-efficacy: mastery experiences, social modeling, social persuasion, and psychological responses. Mastery experiences refer to strengthening self-efficacy as a result of task accomplishment. Performing a task successfully strengthens our sense of self-efficacy; however, failing to adequately deal with a task or challenge can undermine and weaken self-efficacy. Sarah strengthened her self-efficacy by doing her job using a new approach that required her to acquire new ways to connect with her students. Through her work with Naropa students and alumni/ae, Sarah became a better career counselor.

Social modeling, or watching peers successfully accomplish a similar task, is another source of self-efficacy. Seeing people similar to oneself succeed through consistent effort raises individuals' beliefs that they, too, possess the ability to accomplish a similar task or activity (Bandura, 1994). David engaged in conversation with other faculty and staff who had successfully transitioned into the new environment. They served as his sounding boards as he transitioned.

Social persuasion refers to the ability of individuals to persuade others to believe that they have the skills and abilities to succeed with a task (Bandura, 1994). Think about the impact supervisors, mentors, and peers can have by saying something positive and/or encouraging. Encouragement from others helps us overcome self-doubt. Kim received encouragement from her support network in the Midwest until she was able to develop a social network in San Francisco.

Finally, our own physical responses and emotional reactions to situations play an important role in self-efficacy. Moods, physical reactions, and stress levels can influence how a person feels about personal abilities in a particular situation (Bandura, 1994). By learning how to minimize stress when facing difficult or challenging tasks, people can improve their sense of self-efficacy. Carrie learned to minimize the stress of her new environment by working to create her own experience. She initiated staff development activities, enrolled in a course at another institution, and grew her circle of support through involvement with a professional association. New professionals must actively work to strengthen their self-efficacy because there is a positive, significant relationship between self-efficacy and performance.

CONCLUSION

Most people are afraid of change. Change increases the risk of being wrong and revealing imperfections. Taking risks means embracing discomfort and the unknown. Often, fear leads to a pattern of avoidance. By avoiding risk, individuals can reduce their vulnerabilities; however, this is an illusion. The effect is only temporary. And in the process, they miss out on what could be gained from risk taking. The new professionals in the preceding four chapters navigated their discomfort and reaped the benefits of risk taking. In doing so, these new professionals experienced new cultures and environments, applied theory to practice, and learned to work in imperfect situations. This kind of risk taking demands vulnerability and, to be sure, some mistakes are inevitable. However, the return is the opportunity to create individualized professional experiences, which enables new professionals to thrive. There is pride in knowing that they forged their own career path rather than following the dominant career myths or prescribed steps which sometimes requires one to compromise values or beliefs. leading to increased professional self-efficacy.

For students in graduate preparation programs who are nearing the start of job one, consider the lessons offered by Kim, David, Sarah, and Carrie's stories:

- Spend time investigating alternative paths, in addition to considering traditional career moves. The alternative paths look different for each individual, but could include working abroad, taking a temporary position, or working at a religiously affiliated institution. You never know which doors will open to alternative paths.
- Utilize support networks (peers, graduate program faculty, mentors, family, friends etc.) to develop a list of "non-negotiables" for job one. Non-negotiables could include geographic region, type of supervisory experience, access to professional development, or opportunity to use a particular skill set. Knowing one's non-negotiables increases comfort with taking calculated risks.
- Stop expecting perfection. Making mistakes is developmentally appropriate for new professionals. Supervisors are also human; they too will make mistakes. Accepting myths of perfection hurts others.
- Let go of perfection, the first step of learning to thrive within the context of an imperfect work environment. Enacting a support system helps individuals thrive. This could mean developing a social network outside of work, finding a mentor outside of the immediate work environment, or getting involved with a professional association, among other opportunities.
- Learn to ask for help from faculty, supervisors, colleagues and mentors. Seeking support, guidance, and professional kindness yields many rewards.

Each of the authors in the preceding four chapters took healthy risks, embraced their vulnerability, and demonstrated resiliency. Because of their choices, Kim, Carrie, Sarah and David will be better prepared for their next set of professional challenges, having further developed their professional self-efficacy. Taking risks spawns talents, interests, and dreams. Risk reveals new ideas and experiences and conquers fears. New professionals can safely leap, once they have a safety net in place. The rewards of risk taking are waiting for you!

REFERENCES

Bandura, A. (1994). Self-efficacy. In V. S. Ramachaudran (Ed.), *Encyclopedia of human behavior* (Vol. 4, pp. 71-81). New York, NY: Academic Press

Bandura, A. (1995). *Self efficacy in changing societies.* Cambridge, England: Cambridge University Press

Bandura, A. (1997). *Self-efficacy: The exercise of control.* New York, NY: W.H. Freeman.

Barlow, D. H., Rapee, R. M., & Reisner, I. C. (2001). *Mastering stress 2001: A lifestyle approach.* Dallas, TX: American Health.

Brown, B. (2010). The gifts of imperfection: Let go of who you think you're supposed to be and embrace who you are. Center City, MN: Hazelden.

Epstein, M. (1995). Psychotherapy from a Buddhist perspective: Thoughts without a thinker. New York, NY: Basic Books.

Lang, P. J. (1985). The cognitive psychophysiology of emotion: Fear and anxiety. In A. H. Tuma & J. D. Maser (Eds.), *Anxiety and the anxiety disorders* (pp. 131-170). Hillsdale, NJ: Erlbaum.

Lang, P. J. (1995). The emotion probe: Studies of motivation and attention. *American Psychologist, 50,* 372-385.

Lang, P. J., Bradley, M. M., & Cuthbert, B. N. (1998). Emotion, motivation, and anxiety: Brain mechanisms and psychophysiology. *Biological Psychiatry, 44,* 1248-1263.

Lazarus, R. S. (1991). Progress on a cognitive-motivational relational theory of emotion. *American Psychologist, 46,* 819-834.

Lazarus, R. S. (1995). Psychological stress in the workplace. In R. Crandall & P. L. Perrewe (Eds.), *Occupational stress: A handbook* (pp. 3-14). Philadelphia, PA: Taylor & Francis.

Pedersen, P. (1995). The five stages of culture shock: Critical incidents around the world. Westport, CT: Greenwood Press.

Sicilia, D. B. (n.d.), A brief history of U.S. unemployment. *The Washington Post.* Retrieved from http://www.washingtonpost.com/wp-srv/special/business/us-unemployment-rate-history/

UNIT II DISCUSSION QUESTIONS

- What do you know now that you did not know before reading David's, Sarah's, Kim's, and Carrie's stories?

New Professionals

- To what types of university cultures have you have grown accustomed throughout your undergraduate and graduate school experiences? And, how does this affect your work with students?
- How important is institutional culture for you when job searching?
- How can you learn more about, assess, and discuss the campus culture and climate during the job search and interview process?
- What professional development opportunities are important as you begin your first job? What can you gain from national conventions and conferences, regional conferences, or campus workshops?
- What role does theory play in your job search?

Supporters of New Professionals

- How do you communicate the culture and climate of your university to prospective candidates?
- How can a new professional act as an initial outsider and provide insight into your office's culture?
- What role does theory play in your everyday world? What role does theory play in the worlds of your colleagues and supervisors?

— *QUESTIONS PREPARED BY SARAH O'CONNELL*

UNIT III

CHAPTER 11

There's No Place Like Home?

SHAMIKA JOHNSON

TO STAY OR NOT TO STAY

Growing up, my relationship with family was close. I have vivid memories of family game nights, meetings, and meals. These daily activities socialized me to the importance of family in my life. Being an identical twin, I forged a strong and unique bond with Tosha—my "womb mate." We were inseparable growing up. We played the same sports, worked the same jobs, and spent most waking moments together. It was not until college that we parted ways to begin our individual lives. We attended different colleges and slowly established ourselves in two very distinct ways. Tosha's career path led her 500 miles away from our hometown of Cincinnati, Ohio, to pursue a career as a nuclear engineer. As a result of Tosha's new life on the east coast, I experienced an elevated sense of responsibility to my family. I wanted to stay geographically close to them, which definitely influenced my decision to accept the First Year Adviser position at Miami University in nearby Oxford, Ohio, after earning my master of science degree at the same institution.

The job search process was interesting, to say the least. I was a hyper-anxious graduate student hoping to secure a job that would allow me to showcase the knowledge and experiences I gained during my graduate studies. I was prepared to tackle any student affairs issue that could arise. I understood theory and its importance in everyday practice. I was excited, equipped, and expectant regarding my future. In April 2010, I knew I wanted to stay close to home because of my family responsibilities and the relationship with my partner, Emmanuel. Obviously, these parameters limited the institutions to which I applied. That said, I did not aspire to work full-time at my soon-to-be alma mater.

My Miami experience was not always the best. A defining moment for me was a beautiful sunny afternoon in April 2009. While strolling on the edge of campus and uptown Oxford with two of my friends, a truck with three White men appeared on the street. The occupants of the truck yelled racial slurs at me as it passed. My temporary shock and paralysis initially inhibited my reaction. My two White friends did not know how to respond either. How could the place I had called home for the past year now be an unwelcoming and unsafe place? How could this town, with close ties to a premier university, harbor racists? I had erroneously concluded that I had successfully assimilated into this predominantly White culture and that my identity as an African American would not be an issue. Clearly my assumption was incorrect. I felt naïve for believing that my skin color would not be a factor in how some individuals treated me in this college town. At that moment I decided I would complete my graduate studies, but I would not work in a small rural college town. I began to understand the importance of finding a school and town that accepted me. It was not enough to secure a desirable job, but I also had to be comfortable in my living environment. At that point, I did not believe Oxford could offer me the climate necessary to succeed. It wouldn't be until months later that I felt my heart soften to the idea of remaining at Miami.

Being geographically bound is both a blessing and a curse. The good news was that I aspired to work in residence life; historically, this functional area in student affairs has been highly receptive to hiring new student affairs professionals—even in a tough economy. I also wanted to focus on student academic success because of my rich graduate assistantship experience in Miami's Learning Center, where I supervised tutors and assisted students with academic concerns. I needed to find a progressive residence hall program that focused on residential and academic life. It was time to get my resume and cover letters in order. I crafted these masterpieces by describing my abilities, knowledge, and passion for working with students. I convinced myself that these documents would easily be the gateway for meaningful employment. *Rejection* soon became a word I added to my vocabulary. After several setbacks, I began to comprehend the stamina it would take to successfully navigate the job search process. I continued to submit applications at a pace equal to the rejections I received. I knew eventually that the right job would come my way. As I accepted interviews, my confidence grew and so did my receptiveness to working full-time at Miami University.

A job that combined my undergraduate love of residence life with my graduate assistantship experience in academic support existed at Miami University. I recognized "the obvious" after scrutinizing non-Miami job prospects. Looking at the First Year Adviser position at Miami, it looked increasingly appealing. It combined residence life responsibilities with academic advising and was close to home. It seemed too good to be true. I concluded that I should apply for this job as it closely aligned with my career aspirations. However, a question persisted: "How would I reconcile this decision with the negative experience I had last April?" I had to consider that I might not always get everything I wanted out of a job and might need to compromise to get a job.

I began to utilize the means I find most reliable during important decision-making times: my faith as a Christian. I began to pray and seek discernment on whether or not I should apply and seriously consider this position. I had to determine if the hate incident would disqualify Miami University. As I sought direction, I felt led that perhaps my work at Miami was not finished. I also realized that if every time something cruel or hurtful happened to me and I ran away, I would be running for the rest of my life. I concluded that was not the life I wanted to live or the example I wanted to set for others. Following these insights, I applied for the position, spoke candidly to staff in the department about the hate incident, and began to mentally envision what it would be like to work as a full-time staff member at Miami University. What would need to happen to ensure my success and growth? How would I get to a place of healing and restoration so I could fully embrace and engage as a new professional at Miami? I pondered these questions while radically altering my job search strategy.

Through all the questioning, there were never any solutions but instead more aspects to consider about the job search process. I found myself reminded of the discomfort I felt being in Oxford. I had to negotiate that with the comfort I felt of being in a familiar place with people I knew. Would I grow as a professional in an environment where I was already accustomed? I was not sure of the answer. I also could not ignore the discomfort I experienced at Miami. However, it was somewhat reassuring to be familiar with the racial environment in my current situation versus learning how to negotiate a new one. I had to determine how to balance the growth I wanted to receive with the comfort I needed to thrive.

YOU CAN'T ALWAYS GET WHAT YOU WANT

I applied and the Office of Residence Life granted me an interview for the First Year Adviser position. It's odd to interview on a campus where you have worked for almost two years. Do I pretend not to know the people who are interviewing me? Do I act friendly as usual or act "professional"? Will my knowledge of Miami be a benefit or liability? Will people expect more of me than other candidates? I struggled to devise satisfying answers to these questions as I prepared for my on-campus interview.

My on-campus interview began with dinner at a local restaurant, and my interview liaison asked if I wanted someone to escort me to dinner. Since I only lived two minutes from the restaurant, I respectfully declined and agreed to meet my host at the restaurant. Dinner was very casual and relaxing. I had never met my host, which made it feel more like a regular interview. I learned about Miami and Residence Life from a fresh perspective; however, all throughout dinner I was very critical of myself. I wondered if I was asking enough questions or if I was talking too much. I felt a lot of pressure to impress my host. I realized I needed to get over myself if I was ever going to be successful throughout the rest of the interview process. After a delicious meal and good conversation, I reviewed my schedule for the following day and we parted ways. I reflected on what the next day would be like for me; this time, I felt more confident about what I could contribute to the department.

As my alarm sounded the next morning, I was excited to begin my day. Adrenalin definitely carried me through the whirlwind interview experience. I went from breakfast to interviews with campus partners, interviews with professional staff, and then lunch with students. In the afternoon I continued to interview and meet prospective colleagues. Before I knew it, I was back in my apartment totally exhausted. Did I really just go through eight hours of "being on"? I had survived. Although I was physically exhausted, I felt professionally intrigued. I kept smiling as I thought back to the day's events and interactions. Was Miami really growing on me? Had I really been swayed? Even with my mind starting to shift, I also wondered if being an insider at Miami was a benefit or liability. Was more expected of me? Are they only interested in me because I am an African American? All things considered, I was on the verge of changing my views of my soon-to-be alma mater.

Three weeks later, I received a job offer. One week before it was time to make a final decision, I remained torn. I wanted to hold out a bit longer, because I was waiting to hear from another nearby institution where I had an on-campus interview that I *really* enjoyed. So, I waited and waited until the day before my decision deadline for Miami. It was then that I discovered that the other institution was no longer filling the position for which I had interviewed. Disappointment does not even begin to describe my feelings. I remember calling my twin sister as soon as I received the call to share with her what was happening with my job search. She reminded me how blessed I was to have Miami's job offer still on the table for a position that would be a great fit based upon my career aspirations. She gave me some tough love and told me to stop sulking and consider what could be gained by accepting Miami's job offer.

In that moment my sister reminded me that I don't always get what I want. I did some additional soul searching as I sorted out some lingering concerns about Miami University. One reservation was whether my colleagues would treat me as a professional when so many of these individuals knew me as a graduate student. I feared I would be asked questions such as, "How are classes going?" Would I have to continually remind colleagues that I earned my master's degree and was now a Miami full-time staff member? Would I be accepted as a professional?

As I contemplated my Miami offer, I realized I had a stake in crafting and communicating my new professional identity to colleagues. It was essential for me to understand how I wanted to be viewed by others. I could not allow others to define me. I knew this position could afford me the opportunity to make the climate at Miami more welcoming for all students. I could relate to students feeling unwelcomed in this environment, because I had experienced the same feelings. I recognized that I may not always get everything I want in a job. I had to accept the reality that no job is perfect. Most likely, there will be things I wish were better about my current situation; instead of dwelling on them, I could try to change them. These revelations affirmed that I had to be confident in my decision to accept the offer. I remember people in my cohort saying, "You're really going to stay here?" or "Good luck." Initially these statements shocked me, but I quickly realized that accepting this job was my decision and needed to own that it was mine to make.

THE GOOD AND THE BAD

Defining who I am and what is important to me were essential to my success in my first full-time position in student affairs. I could not allow others' doubts or criticisms about my decision to affect what I thought about myself. Tending to these issues is easier said than done. Some peers asserted that I was not a risk taker and only stayed at Miami because it was comfortable. Clearly, they did not know about my continual discomfort during my graduate studies and that starting anew elsewhere could be much more comfortable. I had to be confident that I was at Miami because I was qualified and had much to offer, not that I was trying "to play it safe." Knowing who I am and what I have to contribute were vital to my successful transition from graduate school to my first professional job. These realizations allowed me to continue pushing through when those around me questioned my decisions.

The courses I took allowed me the opportunity to reflect on who I was as an individual and how that translates to my work in student affairs. By writing papers about my identity, values, and skills, I formulated who I was, what was important to me, and how that contributed to my abilities and confidence. As well, class discussions allowed me to further explore my development alongside my classmates. These rich educational and developmental experiences were vital to my success and growing confidence. I am grateful that I learned this sooner rather than later as it helped me further formulate my professional identity.

Accepting the First Year Adviser position at Miami was a leap-of-faith decision. I had to trust that even with the reservations I had about staying that the benefits would far outweigh them. I had to let go of being in control of every aspect of my life and trust the process. Letting go was scary but necessary to fully embrace the next chapter in my life.

Questions about my identity, questions about institutional and departmental fit, and race and gender issues persisted long after I accepted the job offer in Residence Life. I fully acknowledge that I have the face and stature of an 18 year old; however, I am 25 years old! Not even my business attire or professional name badge seemed to mitigate my youthful appearance. During new student move-in day, I put on my Residence Life polo shirt, my name badge, and a smile that could light up a room. I was excited and ready to welcome our incoming class. As I walked around the building meeting parents and new students, a parent started talking to one of my undergraduate staff members about an issue, because the parent believed that the RA was in charge, not me. My RA explained to the parent that she was not in charge and pointed to me. The parent slowly walked over with a confused look on her face. I introduced myself to her and explained that I was the adviser of the hall. She said, "Oh . . . so you're the one I should speak to if I have any issues," to which I responded, "Yes, ma'am." She continued to look confused. I politely informed her that I was a full-time professional with a master's degree, and I was more than able to assist her with whatever she may need. At that moment, she understood.

The mixed feelings I had during the interview process persisted as I started work. All the things I feared about accepting this position were coming back to haunt me. As I reflect back on this specific instance with the mother, that resembles so many other incidents, I couldn't help but wonder, "What's going on?" Did the parent disregard me as a professional because I looked young? Or was it because of the color of my skin? Working at a historically and predominantly White institution always keeps the latter question in the back of my mind. I am constantly reminded of my skin color, so it was not anything new as a new professional, although the racial slurs incident definitely heightened my sense of being African American in Oxford, Ohio. It made me more aware of this particular aspect of my identity and its influence on all of my experiences.

Although I know I am valuable and have much to contribute, others may not afford me the opportunity to demonstrate that before dismissing me based solely on my appearance. It also reminded me that although society has "come a long way," we still have a way to go regarding social justice issues of race and inclusion.

Although I cannot control how others view me, I can control and influence my job satisfaction. During my two years of graduate study, I forged strong relationships with individuals who became mentors and colleagues. These existing relationships allowed me to get involved with professional development opportunities sooner rather than later. I am passionate about education. I taught a course during my first semester, which was a great professional development opportunity and one not readily afforded to a new staff member.

Because of connections I made during my graduate studies with faculty and staff around campus, I immediately got involved in the Association of Black Faculty and Staff and was elected to the executive board during my first semester as a full-time staff member. My already established network allowed me to get much needed support and encouragement from other African American colleagues across campus. These were people who could truly relate to my experience and some of the challenges I faced. I had the chance to learn and understand the campus climate and culture as a graduate student. While some of my colleagues struggled with understanding the "Miami student," I had a good grasp of who they were and that made the transition from student to staff that much easier for me. I also had an awareness of some of the campus politics. I knew who the "power players" were and how to "play the game." I learned when to speak up and share my opinion and when to keep my mouth shut. As a new professional, I learned to navigate this rather scary terrain; this process was easier for me than for some of my colleagues.

Reflecting on the liabilities and benefits of knowing an institution before starting full time assisted me in being able to manage the challenges that I encountered. Understanding the benefits afforded to insiders assisted me in my graduate student-to-new professional transition. I used the connections I already had established on campus to enhance my professional development and provide much needed support.

IF I KNEW THEN WHAT I KNOW NOW

After going through the entire process of researching jobs, applying for jobs, accepting a job offer, and then working a year and a half in my first position, I have gained invaluable insights and want to highlight them: risk taking, communication skills, personal and professional support systems, and staying true to myself.

I learned that it is essential to take risks when undertaking the first job search. I knew that if I wanted a great experience in my first job, I would have to be intentional about making that happen. It was a risk to seek veteran professionals for their wisdom and insights, but it was necessary for me to be successful. I also was nervous about asking to be more involved on campus as a new professional. I was afraid people would say "no" to me. I had to get to a point where I let go of the fear and just ask or I would never accomplish anything. To my surprise, colleagues were very willing to allow me to partner with them on various projects and get involved. I found that taking risks is a necessary and beneficial part of my professional life and developing this habit early has benefitted me.

I learned to listen more and speak less. I learned this lesson while observing some of my colleagues. I know that many new professionals, including myself, are anxious. I had learned theories and stood ready to save the world! I felt equipped, excited, and eager to begin this work called student affairs. I remember sitting in training and seeing my new professional colleagues always having their hands up to speak, always having to share their insights, and always believing that where they came from and their experiences were far superior to those around them. Now, perhaps these colleagues did not mean for it to come off this way, but it seemed to me that they knew it all and the rest of us were incompetent subordinates. I kept thinking to myself, I do not want to be *that* type of new professional. I learned that just because I have an idea or insight does not mean I always need to share it in a large group. I learned that I should only speak when I really have something important to say so people listen and do not think I am speaking only to hear myself talk. I learned the value of being tactful when sharing and respecting the experience and expertise that the more veteran colleagues have to offer. If someone has been at an institution for over 20 years, I am sure they have some keen insight on the student culture and can assist me in what things will work. Early on, I found it important to balance how much I speak and what I say. It is great to share my insights and new energy, but I have to be sure it is in a way that is respectful of those who have come before me.

Finding a support system is essential to my success as a professional. I need support professionally as well as personally. I was grateful to have both when I entered my first job. Working at my alma mater, I already had some established relationships. This made the transition much easier and was the foundation for gaining professional mentors who could assist me with my professional growth and development. I was able to teach with one of my mentors from graduate school. He is an alumnus of Miami's graduate program and was able to give me insights into the program and encourage me when it was difficult. Our mentoring relationship continued as I entered full-time work at Miami. I felt so grateful to have someone I trusted and who truly wanted me to succeed. He along with many others assisted me greatly as a professional transitioning into student affairs work.

Professional and personal support are equally important. Having a life outside of my job is what keeps me motivated to give my all while I am at work. I am blessed to have a fiancé who supports me—always pushing me to be better and strive for excellence. He challenges me to grow in my work and that has helped so much. It is nice to have someone to talk to after a long day and choose to talk about work or focus on other areas of my life. Having him in my life made the transition smoother. I also am grateful to family who support me in my professional endeavors. They instilled in me values and encourage me as they see those values play out in my life. It is encouraging to know I can call one of my siblings or my parents to vent or share successes. Ultimately, I learned that having professional and personal support is essential to my success in job one.

Lastly, I learned that it is important to stay true to myself. I must be able to go to bed every night knowing the decisions I made and interactions I had reflect my core values and embody who I truly am as a person. Being authentic is crucial for me to having a fulfilling and rich career. When I am genuine about who I am and what I believe, my values become evident. Sometimes it is hard to stay true to myself because I am pressured by those around me to change or fit in, but standing my ground in the midst of the pressure has benefitted me greatly. When I am free to truly be who I am in a work environment, I know I have found a fit.

CHAPTER 11 DISCUSSION QUESTIONS

New Professionals

- How important is your fit with an institution and region? How might these factors influence success in the workplace?
- What are the advantages and disadvantages of working at your alma mater?
- Shamika argues, "You can't always get what you want." What are your unyielding "wants" or "needs"?
- In what contexts is conformity an asset or a liability?

Supporters of New Professionals

- How can you encourage new professionals to define themselves, rather than succumbing to the pressures of conforming to others' perceptions of them? What is the importance of doing so?
- What are the advantages and disadvantages of hiring internal candidates for job openings?
- How might you assist new professionals as they negotiate the various challenges that their "new professional" identity creates for them?

— *QUESTIONS PREPARED BY KATIE SHOEMAKER*

CHAPTER 12

Breaking the Chains of my Segmented Life

MATT KWIATKOWSKI

It was spring 2010, and I was beginning my first professional job search. Like many of my graduate school colleagues, I could not believe our faculty expected us to focus not only on finding a job but also passing comprehensive exams on top of regular course work and assistantship responsibilities. Yes, I made it through that experience but only with the help of caffeine and "gripe sessions" in Harris Dining Hall.

Undoubtedly, the four months before earning my master's degree were the most stressful in my life. The stakes and my anxiety level were high. Amid roommate conflict mediations, late-night paper writing sessions, and Saturdays filled with reading books and journal articles, I needed to carve out time to plan for my future. There were many uncertainties related to my job search process, but one certainty held constant. I intended to work at a faith-based institution. I continually posed questions to myself. How is this job search going to be different? I really want to work at a faith-based institution, but what if I run out of time or options and have to work at a secular university? How long am I willing to wait for the perfect job one? Does an ideal job really exist?

My insistence on working at a faith-based institution resulted from recently living a dichotomous lifestyle. During college, I struggled to integrate my athlete and campus ministry identities. Are these identities incompatible? During graduate school, I struggled to blend my secular educator responsibilities with my sacred educator passions. Long ago, I created a sacred–secular binary that I struggled to reconcile as my days as a graduate student were ending. Is it possible to be a Christian and an effective student affairs professional at non-faith-based colleges? Ironically, I espoused the idea of tending to the needs of the whole student, yet I continued to treat aspects of my life as discrete and mutually exclusive entities. How do I de-compartmentalize my life? How can I understand students if I cannot understand myself?

Revisiting college student development theories as I studied for my comprehensive exams provided me opportunities to reflect and think critically about my life. While reading rich narratives in the crossroads phase of Marcia Baxter Magolda's (2001) self-authorship writings, I could not help but redefine my values, beliefs, relationships, and sense of self. I searched for the inner voice (that is God in my world) to help me discern my calling. Do I need to wrestle with the past to prepare for the future? How can my faith help me resolve these binary identity tensions at this important crossroads in my life?

DIGGING DEEP

I can best understand my current self by reflecting on the past. To borrow language from the StrengthsFinder assessment (Rath, 2007), the past is the "blueprint" that I must study to understand the present and make better decisions for the future. If I am unaware of this blueprint, developing a vision for my future is a formidable task. A significant portion of my blueprint has been my faith identity development, a passion I developed during high school.

I grew up in a Catholic household. My parents' beliefs informed the development of my values: honesty, integrity, working hard, love, following your heart, kindness, and generosity. I learned to accept responsibility for my actions. As a result, I was not a typical high school student living in western Pennsylvania. Although I had my fair share of fun, it was never solely defined by stereotypical coming-of-age activities such as partying and hooking up. Some of my peers argued that because these activities were not part of my high school experience, I missed out. I respectfully disagree. It was this sense of responsibility, coupled with the fear of disappointing my parents, that guided me inside and outside the classroom. These influences from my past still have an influence on my actions today.

I attended Sunday school classes and youth group activities; my values combined with the religious structure of the Catholic Church to help me to realize a stronger sense of God. I recognized God as a higher creator; however, this belief did not intersect with my day-to-day life as a high school student. Although I did not realize it at the time, I was leading a bifurcated life, where God conveniently garnered my attention only on Sundays for an hour and the busyness of the high school student lifestyle (e.g., studying, working, cross country, community service) consumed the rest of my week.

During my college years at Slippery Rock University, my faith developed. I recall thinking early in my college career that I should continue my relationship with God because it would be good for me to get involved in a campus fellowship. My motivations were less intrinsically motivated than wanting to gain approval from the authorities in my life, such as mentors, relatives, teachers, and youth group leaders. This motivation brought me to Fellowship of Christian Athletes, an organization I learned about in high school. Through involvement in this organization, I gained a full perspective of the Christian faith and what it meant for my life as someone who believed in God. Involvement in this organization as a peer leader led me to struggle to align my espoused values with my enacted values.

During my first two years of college, I lived a two-faced life. As an athlete, I was involved in the party scene. As my faith identity grew stronger, I realized that some of my behaviors did not align with Biblical behaviors—conduct unbecoming of a Christian leader. I existed between two worlds and two worldviews. Author Richard Rohr (2004) discussed this concept as an

> inner state and sometimes an outer situation where people can begin to think and act in genuinely new ways. It is when we are betwixt and between, have left one room but not yet entered the next room, any hiatus between stages of life, stages of faith, jobs, loves, or relationships. (p. 135)

What to choose? Who was I going to become? I enjoyed partying and being carefree, but I sure didn't feel better about it in the morning. I really did feel guilty. And the times I attended church hung over? Yeah, that wasn't good. Living for God seemed so restrictive. I really didn't understand this "freedom in Christ" concept. It just seemed like there were a lot more rules. I feared peers would view me as inauthentic: partying on the weekends then attending church during the week.

One particular evening I attended a party and consumed alcohol as a minor. A younger peer, whom I knew from my ministry involvement, approached me and confronted me about my inappropriate behavior. It was at this moment I fully realized the responsibility I had—to lead by my actions rather than by words.

I replayed a Biblical verse in my head: "Do not conform to the pattern of this world, but be transformed by the renewing of your mind. Then you will be able to test and approve what God's will is—his good, pleasing, and perfect will" (Romans 12:2, New International Version). Could I leave that "old" self behind and become renewed in my "new" self, renewed through my faith?

A NEW FRAMEWORK

Development of this faith offered me a new epistemological framework; more importantly, it allowed me to develop meaning and purpose for my life. My old self, the framework I grew up with, while value-laden, was unconcerned with living out faith on a daily basis. The new self was this new framework, a new way of knowing—a development of my inner voice, which started in college and became more refined during graduate school. This new framework gave me the tools, indeed the capacity I lacked before, to examine my newly espoused values and see how they compared to my enacted values. The old self versus new self was another binary with which I wrestled. It was helpful to change areas of my life in which I was not satisfied, but I later came to the realization that my past is always going to affect who I am in the present. Thus, this binary served me well for the time being. Working in my college residence hall was where I developed another framework for meaning: building relationships.

There was nothing quite like working the front desk of my college residence hall at 3:30 a.m. Buzzed from copious amounts of Mountain Dew just to get through the shift, I encountered many peers who allowed me to listen to their stories and understand their lives. Many of the interactions were superficial, but some allowed me to gaze into the souls of my peers and discern issues of meaning, faith, struggle, life, and love. It was then that I fell in love with learning about college students. As my college graduation approached, I began to look for ways to combine my passion for faith and passion for working with college students. I wanted to break down these binaries and pursue a more holistic career pathway where I could be true to myself.

My experiences as a front desk worker allowed me to speak with community assistants (i.e., RAs) and my hall director about the field of student affairs, which I never knew existed. Pursuing a career that centered on working with college students intrigued me. My senior year provided an up-close opportunity to explore the field of student affairs. My supervisor was a first-year graduate student in the student affairs program at Slippery Rock University. This afforded me the opportunity to talk with her about the field and about what she was learning in her graduate seminars. Over that year, our personal and professional relationship grew because of these conversations. She became my mentor through this exploratory process. The wisdom and friendship I gained through our interactions were invaluable in this discernment process and truly underscored the importance of having mentors in any experience, personal or professional.

Although my faith development and interest in student affairs were both very salient and focused, I struggled to find meaning in the classroom. I was a secondary education–social studies major, which meant after graduation I would be searching for teaching positions. It was probably a combination of discontent with the K-12 education system and a jaded teaching internship that prompted me to reexamine my career aspiration of becoming a history teacher. Once I made the decision to work with college students as a career, I next had to determine in what capacity. Two post-college options intrigued me: becoming a campus minister or a student affairs graduate student.

SACRED OR SECULAR?

These seemingly dichotomous options led me to the Coalition for Christian Outreach (CCO) organization. The CCO employs men and women as campus ministers on college campuses. In the most broad sense, these ministers bring their Christian faith to the students they serve. Their model is contextual, and placements are dependent upon the individual and the particular university or college he or she serves. Some ministers are residence hall educators at Christian schools; others work with on-campus religious organizations such as Fellowship of Christian Athletes. Some even work in coffee shops in the college town. In these relationships, the partner (e.g., a Christian college/university, church, coffee shop) pays half of the minister's salary, and the other half the minister must raise through monthly donations from family and friends.

In spring 2008, I saw my future career options as bifurcated. I could commit myself to working for the CCO and become a campus minister. Conversely, I could enroll in a graduate student affairs program. I did not possess the capacity to see how the merging of these two seemingly distinct pathways could help me achieve goals in my life: to dialogue directly about faith and to work with college students. Do I choose the sacred or the secular? Which option is best for me? These dichotomous categories caused me much stress and anxiety. At the time, it seemed like an either–or decision. Either I was going to be a campus minister or I would attend graduate school. I viewed campus ministry as aligning only with my faith passions and graduate school only with my college student interests. It was later that I was able to rupture these competing visions of the good life.

I decided to pursue both opportunities. As time progressed, negotiations with the CCO were not fruitful, and I questioned my capacity to work as a campus minister. Questions flooded my mind. Since I am so new in my faith, how can I inspire faith development in others? How can I encourage them to pursue God? Am I good enough, worthy enough, to do this? Oh, and not to mention, do I have the trust in God that he would help me to provide for myself financially?

I also attended a two-day interview program to gain admission to Miami University's College Student Personnel graduate program. I had no idea what to expect. Miami was one of two schools to which I applied, and I did not know if I was a viable candidate. Almost everyone I encountered welcomed me. En route back to Pennsylvania, I concluded that Miami would be a great fit. It would be the kind of place that I could expand my knowledge about student affairs and challenge myself intellectually. However, I did not know how this particular public university might influence my faith development.

As my college graduation neared, I became hyper-anxious. I got a letter from Miami informing me that I had been accepted to the program and that the Office of Residence Life had offered me an assistantship. The decision-making process quickly became simple, once I learned that neither of my options with the CCO had resulted in a job offer. Hence, I was going to Miami to attend graduate school.

At that time, I remember thinking that the decision was made for me. But having time to digest this experience, I recognize reasons why I did not ultimately work for the CCO. I sought out only two CCO positions, mainly because they were hall director positions. I was not receptive to working at a church, at a coffeehouse, or with any other agencies. I was not open to how God wanted to use me but how I viewed myself and what job I viewed myself having. Some may call this "just how the chips fall," but embracing a Christian worldview helped me to discern how God uses every situation. It is my choice how I view those decisions. Perhaps this logic can be best explained using the Biblical verse, "'For I know the plans I have for you,' declares the LORD, 'plans to prosper you and not to harm you, plans to give you hope and a future'" (Jeremiah 29:11). God is speaking to the prophet Jeremiah about his future and the promise of Israel, during a very difficult time in Jewish history, the Babylonian Captivity. The personal application for me is that the decisions God makes, although tough to swallow at times, are in my best interest.

I learned a critical lesson: I am not in control of my life. This may seem obvious and counter-intuitive. Since I am an adult, why aren't I in control of my life? However, this realization gave me great relief and solace. I do not have to predict the future! I do not have to worry and stress over the future, because whatever comes my way, God will help me to wrestle with it. Rohr (2004) stated, "Predictability might be good for science, but it is not helpful for the soul" (p. 71). This statement describes my gradual process of not worrying about every little detail about the future and focusing more on the bigger picture. God gave me the peace not to stress so much about the next step, because it would only be a small detail in the larger scheme of the events of my life.

I told myself after that experience that I would never again apply to work for CCO-like agencies unless I was totally committed to working for the organization, regardless of the opportunities afforded me. Working for an organization or in a particular job was less important than committing myself to God to do his work. Admittedly, my motivations for initially working for the CCO were more on my terms than on God's terms. In retrospect, if I had worked for the CCO my heart may not have been in it. This would have been a struggle as someone who strives to be open and authentic with my students.

LOVE AND HONOR

Before I knew it, I was packing my car and on my way across Ohio to begin graduate school at Miami University. I pondered many questions travelling the rural roads of Pennsylvania and Ohio. Is this going to be a good move? Will being six hours from my family result in homesickness? Will I get along with my cohort? I truthfully did not know what awaited me in Oxford, Ohio. Although the experience had its truly frustrating and exhausting moments, it ended up being a more rewarding experience than I could ever have imagined.

Miami was the first educational environment where I entered with a developed sense of my Christian faith. Sharing this important aspect of my identity with my peers, co-workers, and professors excited me. Surprisingly, what I discovered was an environment that was hostile to my faith. I cannot identify any single factor that provoked this hostility, but it existed and it confused me. Classroom discussions revealed that numerous colleagues had negative experiences with Christianity. Unfortunately, I found myself lumped into these gross Christian enclaves. I struggled to navigate this new environment. I felt, for the first time in my life, like a persecuted minority. I am sure my experience was mild compared to individuals (e.g., Latinos, homeless, African Americans, Asians) with more overt identity characteristics, but it was nonetheless a new-found experience for me—a White, middle-class, Christian, heterosexual man from Pennsylvania.

My first two months as a graduate student were difficult. I sought out relationships with others I surmised had some sort of faith background; to my surprise, I found many who shared my faith and were as exhilarated as I to find kindred spirits. I identified a local church that challenged me to think about my faith in new and different ways. During my two years as a graduate student, considerable personal faith development occurred; however, I had to actively seek out opportunities to challenge myself. My work and academic settings provided few avenues for faith development. As a result, I had to be intentional in seeking out faith-based venues.

As the end of my graduate studies approached, I wanted to work for a higher education institution that aligned with my faith values. I needed to find an institution that talked about faith and supported my faith. Although I talked about faith in my graduate program, the hidden curriculum (Snyder, 1973) made clear to me that this was taboo. The hidden curriculum consists of assumptions or expectations that every educational institution covertly and unintentionally teaches. At Miami, I perceived that a message in the hidden curriculum is that students tend to place heavy emphasis and value on high-risk alcohol consumption and lower value on their religious/faith development.

In searching for job one, it became increasingly important that this hidden curriculum message was flipped to where students valued their faith development more than partying. Applying to Christian institutions meant I would most likely be working at a place that valued my faith. I knew limiting my job search to faith-based institutions would make my job search more difficult, but I did not anticipate how much anxiety it would evoke in me. Four solid job prospects yielded no job and graduation was approaching. I panicked. Being an unemployed soon-to-be graduate was disconcerting. However, I knew that I needed to remain steadfast, patient, and willing to consider any professional opportunities.

In April 2010, I received an e-mail forwarded by one of my supervisors about a hall director position available at Baylor University. I immediately disregarded this e-mail as Baylor was located in Texas, and I had no desire to live in Texas. After spending some time researching the institution, I changed my mind and applied. I was just applying, right? Well to make a long story short, I moved to Texas. Having wrestled with the theme of dichotomies in my thinking before (i.e., secular graduate school program and campus ministry), I was able to look at Baylor through a different, a more holistic lens.

SIC 'EM BEARS

Getting to Baylor felt like divine influence, I genuinely felt called to work at Baylor. That, in and of itself, was a confirming feeling, yet fears and hesitations persisted. Arriving in Waco, Texas, was more than anxiety producing—complicated by a new state, a new school, and new colleagues. Keeping my faith during this uncertain time was no easy task.

Once I started working, calmness replaced my apprehension. I met colleagues who were supportive, welcoming, and willing to answer my seemingly endless questions. I encountered an authentic community of people who were willing to get to know me and welcome me into their everyday lives.

Our common faith as Christians at Baylor helped me during this transition. I remember attending a retreat with my new colleagues that involved pondering introspective questions and praying for one another, both very meaningful acts for me. Although it may not seem like much to those who work at Christian institutions, to me it was a completely different world. Being able to pray with my colleagues! After some years of feeling like my faith did not belong in the workplace, it was exciting and transforming to be openly praying at work. My colleagues and I were bound by this call to a larger purpose, which came down to supporting, encouraging, and acknowledging the Christian faith and helping students to come to a realization of their own personal faith. It was this sense of connectedness that defined my early experience at Baylor and gave me a new perspective on engaging students.

The faith-sharing environment that I first experienced during my retreat continued when I started working with student staff. Engaging with them on issues of their faith, both highs and lows, provided me with a meaningful way to forge relationships with them. During my graduate studies we often talked about educating the whole student. There were many moments at Miami, through in-depth student–staff relationships and mentoring relationships, that built the scaffolding for this holistic education. I recall working with one student in particular during my first year of graduate school. We had regular meetings to talk about troubles in his life: struggling with depression and anxiety and how these conditions affected his academic, work, and social identities. This was my first real experience tapping into many identities (familial, socio-economic, sexual, gender, and, yes, spiritual) to help a student make sense of the troubles he was experiencing. Through this specific interaction and others like it, there were many times when I wanted to insert ideals about Christianity but felt like it was not the place or the time. At Baylor, I was given the freedom to activate the spiritual dimension and truly educate holistically.

As the first several months of job one progressed, God confirmed his presence in getting me to Baylor. No longer did it feel like divine influence, I knew it was. Over the course of several conversations with friends and colleagues and several moments of prayer and meditation, God revealed himself and unveiled his master plan for the previous year of my life. It was so clear. Much like Baylor, the transition to Miami was also a risk, but once I got into the classroom, felt comfortable with my colleagues and student staff, and started to gain confidence in my own abilities, the risk was worth it. Another important lesson I learned through this process was those liminal spaces, not waiting for them to come to me. Whether it was the decision to move to Ohio or Texas, both of these life events transformed my personal and professional development. These transitional experiences have shown me that although taking risks can be a scary and unsettling process in the moment, they are absolutely necessary to personal and professional growth.

Through the job search journey, I learned there are people who are called to specific ministry opportunities; however, I learned that I did not need to have the title of campus minister to have my own ministry. My ministry is listening and providing feedback to student staff in one-on-ones, helping students resolve conflicts with each other, confronting students with policy violations in a loving way, supporting and challenging my colleagues in their work, and some days having those direct conversations about faith. The professional title on my door only offers glimpse of the work I do.

THE EVAPORATING BINARY

My experiences at Baylor proved the message wrong that I heard during my graduate studies: faith and student affairs are mutually exclusive. I have witnessed how acknowledging and supporting my faith and the faith of students can help me be a better student affairs educator. It was important not to buy into the binaries of sacred and secular and to be true to my identity, my faith, and myself.

In my time at Baylor, I am learning how to make the position my own—how to blend the requirements of my job description with my own passions, interests, and identity. I will not pretend that everything is perfect, but I have been able to be the most authentic self I have ever been. This experience, combined with my college and graduate school experiences, has made me a more holistic person, one who feels comfortable with the various dimensions of his identity, sharing those areas, and encouraging that development in others. I am confident that working at Miami prepared me well to work at Baylor and working at Baylor will prepare me well for job two. My experiences continue to build upon one another.

Before Baylor, I segmented my personal life, professional life, and faith life. Although I may still try to claim some parts of my life as solely professional or solely personal, I know that they cannot be separated from one another. The binaries are false. As a helping professional, I cannot just turn a switch off when a student comes to me in crisis or needs someone with whom to talk. For me, it was a process of first figuring out who I was, what I valued, and where I found meaning (i.e., college and graduate school), and then pursuing that purpose relentlessly. I need to pursue meaning and purpose in my personal and professional pathways. If I can do that, all the details will fall into place. The blueprint is evolving and flexible, but with a mind on the "things above" (Colossians 3:2). I do not need to stress over the blueprint.

REFERENCES

Baxter Magolda, M. B. (2001). *Making their own way: Narratives for transforming higher education to promote self-development.* Sterling, VA: Stylus.

Rath, T. (2007). *StrengthsFinder 2.0.* New York, NY: Gallup Press.

Rohr, R. (2004). *Adam's return: The five promises of male initiation.* New York, NY: Crossroads.

Snyder, B. (1973). *The hidden curriculum.* Cambridge, MA: MIT Press.

CHAPTER 12 DISCUSSION QUESTIONS

New Professionals

- Do your worldviews (in particular about faith) shape your professional life? If so, how?
- How do you find meaning and purpose in your work? How do you choose your path when there is a significant decision regarding career?
- In what ways do you hope to find community in your next position?
- What binaries do you create for yourself? How do these create and ease tension?

Supporters of New Professionals

- To what extent is it important or useful to share your worldview with new professionals?
- How can you help new professionals negotiate the need for community in a new place?
- Matt's story conveys the importance of faith in his life (and the lives of many new professionals). What are the advantages and disadvantages of engaging in dialogues about faith in the workplace?

— *QUESTIONS PREPARED BY KATIE SHOEMAKER*

CHAPTER 13

Risky Business: Why Playing It Safe Shouldn't Be the Only Option

SHILOH VENABLE

A year out of college I landed a job in the personnel department at an offshore oil drilling contractor in Houston, Texas. I am originally from Houston and had a bachelor's degree in human resources from Texas A&M, so in the opinion of nearly everyone, I had it made. My supervisor promoted me within a few months, and I was promoted again after the first year. I was on the fast track to management and was getting paid well in an economy that was spiraling downward. Knowing this context, it makes sense that the majority of my family and friends looked at me like I was crazy when I said I wanted to leave my stable and lucrative job in a booming industry to enroll in a graduate program in higher education administration to eventually work as a student group advisor and plan programs for college students. What is not apparent from this abbreviated story is what provoked this career switch and how incredibly unhappy I was at the time with nearly every aspect of my life.

When I reflect on my college years and the three years I worked full time (before enrolling in graduate school) and my life today, it is like looking at two totally different lives. These days, I am confident but not afraid to ask for help. I am self-assured but humble. And I love the experiences I am having at work. Back then, I was confused, lonely, and absolutely unsure of what I wanted to do with my life. I made choices based on what made sense or was convenient at the time; too often, those decisions led to boredom and career restlessness.

Until I decided to pursue a master's degree in student affairs administration, most of my decisions on what to study and where to work had been made in the moment. My bachelor's degree is in educational human resources. When the business school at Texas A&M did not accept me, I picked a major that interested me but, more importantly, required less than a 3.0 GPA for admittance. I applied to and enrolled in law school after graduating from college because I had no idea what else to do and many of my friends had pursued legal careers. I blindly followed their lead. Subsequently, I dropped out of law school before the end of my first semester. I learned very quickly, albeit a few months late, that I absolutely did not want to be a lawyer. It took another year of waiting tables and working as a receptionist at a car dealership to get a job where I could apply my HR background. Only six months into that I realized I needed to spend more time thinking about what I actually wanted to get out of my professional life, because I definitely had not found it. Despite the success at the oil company, I was finally ready to really commit to a career that ignited my passions.

I remember vividly the feeling of finally having clarity when it came to my future. I was sitting at my desk at the oil company, fingers on my keyboard in the middle of a daily task, and I was suddenly distracted by an answer to a question I had been asking myself for weeks. After being prompted by the morning news that consisted of reports on the dwindling economy and the impending presidential election, the idea of being able to create some kind of change kept rattling around in my head. I did not know where to start, but in that moment I was almost assaulted by the realization that if I could do anything I wanted for the rest of my life, it would be to work for positive change in the world. I had the same reaction you probably are having right now: "That's great, but how?" I concluded that if I could prepare other people for great careers that would lead to positive change, then I was changing the world. I figured out quickly that, in my opinion, the greatest place to have that influence was on a college campus and student affairs was the career I should pursue.

Everything happens for a reason, and my career path is something that illustrates this point perfectly. Thinking back, the decision to pursue a career in student affairs could have been made much earlier. All the signs were there; I was obsessed with my membership in Alpha Phi Omega, a national co-ed service fraternity, and wanted to figure out a way to inform others about this wonderful and one-of-a-kind opportunity. I had several conversations with advisors before leaving college about their careers, and leadership development interested me. I even crafted the internship required by my major to happen at a summer camp, where I developed and implemented a leadership-training program for the burgeoning counselors. All signs pointed to student affairs but I did not go that route immediately; for that, I am grateful.

The time away from a college campus allowed me to gain invaluable insight into the "real world." I had no idea what it was like to move back to your hometown after being away for three years and have virtually no local friends left, because they had all moved away. Although I had worked nearly full-time hours during my senior year of high school and the first few semesters of college, I had no idea what it was like to work a "real" full-time job. Having an 8:00 a.m. to 5:00 p.m., Monday through Friday work schedule and having nights and weekends free all the time, with no commitments, was definitely a novel experience. I had no idea what it was like to be the youngest staff member in an office and the only one who was not married with children. I also had no idea how difficult it would be to explore my own identity outside of the safety of a college campus. These were all lessons that I learned in what I sometimes call the "in between years," when I was figuring out that student affairs was where I belonged. Although these work experiences are not directly related to my student affairs education or skills, I draw on them every day in my work with college students. I have true real-world experiences to pull from and the hindsight necessary to offer sound advice as students plan service projects and work in groups to bring about change in their communities.

Those in-between years provided a strong foundation for my student affairs career. First, they framed my approach to graduate school in a much different way than that of my classmates who enrolled immediately following their undergraduate program. I approached my graduate studies as a job. I had the privilege of being there and had so much to gain from the professors and my peers, so I devoted as much energy and time as possible to my academics. I treated my assistantships and practica as if they were full-time positions, because I wanted to be treated like a full-time professional and knew that I would be one in no time. I also knew I needed to learn the craft, and I took every opportunity I could to be exposed to various aspects of student affairs. Because I had already dabbled in other careers, I had generated many important questions I needed to ask professors, supervisors, and myself. I also knew that just being present every day was physically and emotionally taxing, so I needed to give myself a break occasionally. Most importantly, I knew what it was like not to be passionate about the work I was doing, and I was not willing to let that happen again. I am so thankful for giving myself permission to truly dig into what it was I wanted out of my life. The ability to reflect on my past experiences was the key to determining a course that has led to more happiness than I could have expected.

When I applied to the Student Affairs Administration in Higher Education (SAAHE) graduate program at Texas A&M, I knew it would be perfect for me. Personal experience as an undergraduate and conversations with advisors and faculty in the SAAHE program and current and former students all told me it was a phenomenal program. It was exactly what I wanted in a graduate educational experience: a focus on practical application of the theory and honing skills inside and outside the classroom. The faculty was world class, and the assistantship opportunities seemed limitless. I was driving when the SAAHE program director called me about the faculty's admission decisions. I had to pull over before she shared the results with me, because I knew whatever she was about to say would evoke an emotional reaction. My life changed in the parking lot of a gas station when I learned I had been accepted into the program. I immediately felt a shift in the direction of my life. Finally, I knew I was on track for the ultimate career.

I did quite a bit of preparatory work before starting graduate school. I researched my course schedule, professors, places to live around the university, and what types of jobs might be available when I graduated. I thought I was set when I arrived on campus in August, but I actually had no idea what I was getting into—in a wonderful sort of way. The first week at my assistantship before classes began was routine; I did paperwork, met many coworkers, read manuals, and met with my supervisor Becca to discuss our goals for the year. I was taken aback the first time Becca asked, "What do you want to get out of this experience?" I had no idea how to answer this question. No one had ever asked me what I wanted out of an employment experience, because it had never been about anything other than the employer's expectations. What I learned in that moment was that I was not just expected to complete tasks or go to meetings. I learned that jobs in student affairs can be just as much about the education and development of a professional as they are about fulfilling job responsibilities. I was elated.

During all of my preparations for graduate school, I had not considered that it would be okay for me to talk about my own personal goals on a regular basis. My community-service-oriented family taught me to do the work because it needed to be done and to keep my personal goals to myself. The expectation to know and regularly discuss my goals seemed a bit contrary to my upbringing. As I became more comfortable asking myself the questions about what I wanted to learn and achieve, I became increasingly excited about beginning a career in the field. The realization that I could define my own journey and that I had a tremendous support network for doing so was both liberating and empowering. During those first few months of graduate school, I resolved to do things in ways that made sense to me. I was not going to settle again. I was going to pour myself into the experiences I was having, and I was going to achieve those goals I was being asked to set for myself.

There were several moments in graduate school that stand out as "game changers" for my career path. During my first assistantship, I served on the Risk Management and Organizational Development team within the Department of Student Activities at Texas A&M. The team focused on helping student organizations plan major events and ensuring the safety of on- and off-campus activities. Although the work was rewarding and I loved being a part of the team, I learned quickly that I did not enjoy the administrative portions of my work as much as I had anticipated. I was attracted to the position because of my previous work experience in interpreting policy and the opportunity to help students get the most out of their experiences; as it turned out, I found myself wanting to apply those skills in much different ways. I did not enjoy completing paper work and the tedious risk assessments as much as I loved working face-to-face with the student group that I directly advised. This realization was a clear indication that I needed to reassess my goals. I enjoyed the programming and advising much more than the administrative work. This was an odd realization to have because it also meant that if I were to pursue work more concentrated on these things, I would have to venture into uncomfortable terrain and build a different set of skills. It was a bit daunting at first, but taking the chance has paid off remarkably.

One experience that greatly influenced my career path was my summer internship and the events that occurred in my life as a result. During the phone interview, I had an instant connection with the supervisor for the position of Summer Training and Development Coordinator for Residence Life. I knew when I hung up that if she called to offer me the internship, I would depart for the east coast without a second thought. A couple of weeks later, I got that call and would be heading across the country for the summer to design a new training program for professional and graduate residence hall directors. I knew getting experience in a residence life department could be crucial to the impending job search, and I could apply my human resources background to the work I would be doing. I was going to the east coast, so I knew I would travel to places I had never been before. Overall, the internship was going to be one of those once-in-a-lifetime experiences. Not only was it once-in-a-lifetime but also wholly life changing.

I experienced some of the best and worst moments in my life that summer, moments that shaped my career and my personal life in ways that I could never have anticipated. When my supervisor was given an additional assignment about two weeks after I arrived on campus, she trusted a co-intern and me to build the training program. Knowing how much she trusted me was empowering and truly helped build my confidence as a professional. At the same time that I had been entrusted with an entire staff-training program, I also was learning the way an overly political work environment can be painful and toxic to the productivity of an entire department.

My supervisor had been hired the year before as an assistant director in residence life to create change within the staff development program. When she started implementing those changes, it quickly became a struggle with several members of the staff. Instead of talking to her about those changes, they approached the other assistant directors who chose to placate them instead of challenging them to approach the changes with an open mind. My supervisor did not get support from the department director, and it created a fragmented and distrusting atmosphere. The tension from day to day was palpable and made me thankful that my position was temporary. Although some of the internship experience was negative, I learned firsthand the importance of trusting and supporting the people who work for and with you. I made a commitment that summer that I would do everything I could to create an empowering environment for people I advised and supervised in the future, and I would always go directly to the source of any issue I was having, provided that was an option. Despite a workplace environment that left something to be desired, the personal connections and experiences I encountered that summer taught me so much about myself and led me to determine my ultimate goals for my job search and life after graduate school.

The day I sat at my desk at the oil company and decided to return to school, I also realized that after I graduated I wanted to leave Texas. I had lived there my entire life and was increasingly distressed by the extreme conservatism of the state. My summer away from Texas was just what I needed to confirm that plan, as I experienced what it was like to live somewhere that I felt I could be myself and where I felt a part of a community like I never had before. I ended up spending a great deal of time with my supervisor and her family and friends when we were not at work. They welcomed me into their lives as if I had been there for years, and those are some of my strongest friendships today.

Through the friendships I developed with my supervisor and her partner and several of their coupled friends, I was exposed to healthy and functioning lesbian relationships, and this was a critical moment in my own identity development as a queer woman. I was not quite ready to come out publicly; that would come a bit later, but I did finally have examples of how two women could live together happily, raise children, and thrive without being surrounded by constant stigma. During the final days of my internship, I had another distracted moment of clarity. I resolved to frame my job search in such a way that I would end up in a place where I felt equally as comfortable. My summer on the east coast turned out to be the foundation for serious self-reflection and laid the groundwork for one of the most personally rewarding years of my life.

When I returned to Texas A&M the following fall semester, I was inspired and determined to make the final year of graduate school count. I had had so many conversations over the summer about how to approach my job search and career, and I was committed to using my time and resources effectively. I began the second year of my assistantship in the Department of Student Activities working in the Leadership and Service Center, and I primarily focused on the community service initiatives. I also advised a new student group and was thrilled with the opportunity for new professional challenges. In addition to my assistantship and nine hours of coursework, I also had an internship with the Department of Disability Services and was serving as the secondary advisor to the service organization in which I was a member as an undergraduate. One goal for the year was to gain a wide range of experience through multiple areas of student affairs and broaden the way I thought about my work, so I would be as prepared as possible for entering the field as a full-time professional.

An additional responsibility I had as a graduate student was as a facilitator for the Aggie Allies program, the LGBT safe-zones training at Texas A&M. This was something that was extremely important to me, because I knew the conservative nature of Texas A&M and the importance of the Allies program in this repressive context. I also wanted to do whatever I could to foster a caring community at the university. At the time I became a facilitator, I had a boyfriend and identified as straight, although I had had a relationship with a woman a few years earlier. Shortly after returning to Texas, my boyfriend and I broke up. I was happily single with a bit more free time to devote to other things, like my steadily increasing involvement with activism related to LGBT civil rights. As I became more vocal about my beliefs, I also began to question my motivation for speaking out. Subsequently, I developed a slight crush on one of my women friends and was rocked by the sudden awareness that my feelings for women were not confined to my ex-girlfriend.

I was 26 years old and coming out to myself. I knew my attraction to men was real and apparently so was my attraction to women, but for some reason, I was not comfortable with the conclusion that I was bisexual. I have never been one for labels, but I felt a compulsion to define myself at the time. When I spoke with my friends about my quandary, they repeatedly said that I should focus on being comfortable with myself, not the labels. Strangely, the coming-out process was not all consuming as I had feared it might be. I thought about it often, but it was actually more liberating than it was overwhelming. I was finding an inner peace that I had not known before, and it gave me a renewed sense of self as I headed into a major decision-making time in my life.

As I began my last semester of graduate school and was really focusing on the job search, I felt myself come alive. For the first time in my life, I felt almost completely in control of where I was headed and knew that I was solely responsible for defining my journey. I made the decision early on that I was going to be open minded and let the search take me where it would. Yet, I also was going to heed the advice I received from advisors, faculty, and colleagues about finding that "perfect" job. There were two pieces of advice that stuck with me throughout the entire process:

- Be authentically you. Know that if the institution you are interviewing with does not like what they see, you would not have found a good fit there anyway.
- Know your "must haves" and "must not haves" and do not compromise those—the size/type of institution, the location, or the job responsibilities.

When I combined the goals I had set for myself over the last two and a half years with the process of coming out and my newfound personal liberation, I knew I was going to follow this advice to the letter. I had an open mind going into the search process and knew that the parameters I set were about more than just a job. They were about starting my life over in the way I wanted to define it. The goals I set were not overly complicated. I wanted to live in a city in a state outside of Texas that was less oppressive and homophobic. I wanted to work at an institution that shared my values for social justice and would allow me to be open about my sexual orientation (whenever I decided how I wanted to identify myself). I also wanted a position that would allow me to work with student organizations and had some element of social justice-related programming. There were other things I knew I would like to have or avoid, but I did not count them among the essentials as I was serious about not restricting myself. I did want to actually end up with a job after all.

After I registered for the Placement Exchange, I received a few offers for interviews from schools where I had not applied. I know the requests were most likely sent to a filtered list of conference registrants, but that did not make it any less real or flattering. Some of the positions were attractive, but I had a real gut-check moment regarding my "deal-breakers" when I got my first offer for an interview. I was so excited about the fact that a school wanted to talk to me! My peers were all talking about the interviews they had gotten, and I wanted to have that first one on the books. If I took the interview, it would mean that I had a chance and that was all I needed to get hired and begin to achieve my goals. If I declined, it would mean that I was ruling out what could end up being my only shot. The problem was that the interview was for a school in Alabama, and I had said I would not move to the South. It was a risk, but I ended up turning down that opportunity and holding out hope that other opportunities would present themselves. Looking back, it was such a small thing, but it seemed huge at the time. It was good practice and a relatively low-risk way to feel what being authentic in the job search process would be like.

I wanted my odds for getting a job to be in my favor, so I applied to several positions. By the time the placement process at the conference had begun, I had submitted somewhere between 35 and 40 resumes, cover letters, and applications for positions and institutions that aligned with my goals and values. I kept a detailed spreadsheet of the schools and positions where I had applied, color coded to denote where I was in the process, dates for interviews, and notes on the conversations I had with staff members. I also ended up buying a very large United States map and hanging it on my bedroom wall to help me keep track of the locations where I could end up after graduation. When I submitted an application, I attached a pin with a tiny paper tag that noted the institution and the position. I was looking for more liberal places to live, so the most concentrated areas were on the east and west coasts. I was more interested in going east because it would mean I was closer to the friends I had made the previous summer, but I was still keeping my options open. And suddenly I found the perfect job description that led to one pin in the middle of it all.

I was doing my daily scouring of one of the student affairs job posting websites, and I came across a position description that caused me to think twice about moving to either coast and instead had me seriously considering a move to the Midwest. It was like the job should have had my name on it from the beginning. Working in the Community Service Office at Washington University in St. Louis would combine my background of service work, interest in social justice, and passion for student group advising and would get me to a large city. I knew this was THE job for me, because I felt immediately invested in the position. I cared about whether I got it. I wanted to be the Coordinator for Community Service at Washington University in St. Louis, and I was going to do everything in my power to make that happen. I worked on my application materials for days and finally placed that one single pin in the middle of my United States map that ended up being the only one left when all was said and done.

The Placement Exchange is like a blur of suits, resumes, and countless interviews. It was so fast and so intense that it is difficult for me to recount details, but there are a few things that stand out years later. First, I left the conference having narrowed down my search immensely after participating in countless first- and second-round interviews. Some interviews had excited me and others bored me, so it was easy to make some very important decisions. I also had confirmed Washington University (WashU) as my first choice. I soared through the first interview; the search committee invited me for a second and during that time something powerful clicked inside me. Without even thinking about it, I came out during the interview. All it took was being asked about the social justice issue that I was most passionate about, and it ended with my answer of "standing up for the LGBT community and figuring out where I belong in it myself." I was floored. I was still in the stage of being very careful with whom I told about my new personal revelation, but I felt completely comfortable with the people from WashU sitting across the table from me. I had not shared that information in any of the other interviews and knew that meant something as well. After a few more incredible conversations, all I could do was go back to school and wait.

As I pulled pins out of the east and west sides of my map, the one positioned on St. Louis, where WashU is located, remained. I got the invitation for an on-campus interview and could barely contain my excitement as I traveled to campus and tried to let those who could be my colleagues and students get to know the real me. I answered questions and offered honest accounts of my philosophies and experiences. I asked questions about the work environment, the expectations of advisors, and what it was that got people to stay at WashU. I tried everything to ensure it was as perfect a fit as it had seemed so far. I went home with the same feeling I had had about attending Texas A&M and about my summer internship; if I got the call offering me the position, I would take it. When my eventual supervisor called to offer me the position, doubt had begun to creep in and I was sure she was going to tell me that they had selected someone else. It had been a few days longer than she indicated it would take to call, and I even heard the first few words she said as, "Thanks for applying, but we picked someone else." But in a stroke of incredibly humbling luck, what she actually said was I was the one that they wanted on campus! I was overwhelmed when I got off the phone. I had done it. I had been selected for a position that would allow me to help people change the world, and I had done it all while being completely and totally myself.

Moving to St. Louis is one of the best things that has ever happened to me. The questions I asked and the information I gathered through the interview process helped me gain a clear idea of what to expect when I got to campus; because of that, I did not face many surprises after joining the staff at Washington University. Moving to a new place where no one really knows you is also extremely beneficial when you have had a major change in your life, like coming out as queer. To the people at WashU and in St. Louis, I had always dated women. I still have not come up with that perfect label to describe my sexuality, but I am more comfortable now with using queer than anything else and that is all I have to say if it comes up. Because people in St. Louis did not know me "when I was straight," I never got inquisitive looks that I know come with questions like "But what about all those guys you dated?"

With all the wonderful things that came out of my move to St. Louis, I also faced some significant challenges. I was so enamored by the perfect job description, the exciting possibilities for working with incredibly intelligent and engaged students, and the chance to get out of Texas, that I did not realize how difficult it actually would be to be so far from my entire family. I learned the very hard way that although your family says they understand that you are a thousand miles from home and busier than you have ever been, sometimes they do not really understand, and although it may be unconscious, they will be mad at you. I had to remind myself and my family that this move was something I wanted for a long time, and that just because I was physically removed from the family, I was not any less a part of it. The rising cost of air travel also affected my ability to see friends and family, and that is something that sneaked up on me emotionally.

All of this is not to say that I would have done anything differently. Today, I am happier than I have ever been. My work fulfills my professional and personal goals. I was promoted to Assistant Director of the Community Service Office, I have a partner (a woman) with whom I plan to spend my life, we have relocated back to Texas, and I have some of the best friends I could ever imagine. I am so thankful I had the courage and strength it took to find what I really wanted. My goals are evolving each day. I know that someday what I am doing now will not be enough, but the difference between current me and past me is that now I know what it feels like to have the risk of figuring it all out pay off.

As I reflect on the years since I graduated from college, my three years in St. Louis and at WashU, and my recent move, I can point to several critical lessons learned. The first is the importance of giving myself permission to recognize unhappiness. When I finally admitted that I needed to dig deeper into what I wanted out of my career, I was able to do the work necessary to get to the point where I am now: happy in my life and fulfilled in my work.

Another lesson, a humbling one, was the realization that no matter how well-crafted my life plan is, things will change. My trip to law school and short career in human resources showed me that decisions made because they are the most convenient options hardly ever work out to be the best option. Along with the realization that decisions made in the moment may not be the best approach to major life choices, I must keep in mind that agility and fluidity are also essential. Although moving to the Midwest was unexpected, it is a choice I am so glad I made. I am thankful every day for the growth I have experienced in the last decade of my life. This growth has allowed me to take risks while maintaining confidence in my choices, and this is something I know will lead to many great opportunities in my career.

CHAPTER 13 DISCUSSION QUESTIONS

New Professionals

- Shiloh shared that previous decisions regarding the direction of her life had been "made in the moment." What choices in your professional life have you made in a similar fashion, and are there any you might want or need to rethink?
- In what ways does your individual path to student affairs shape your professional viewpoint?
- To what extent is personal disclosure comfortable, prudent, or liberating for you in various professional contexts?

Supporters of New Professionals

- How do you encourage new professionals to refine, monitor, and attain their professional goals?
- How can you help new professionals learn from both positive and negative experiences?
- How important is reflection for new professionals?

— *QUESTIONS PREPARED BY KATIE SHOEMAKER*

CHAPTER 14

Demanding Identities: Multiple Identities, Self-Authorship, and Career Development

WILL SIMPKINS

Eight years after the first publication of *Job One* (Magolda & Carnaghi, 2004), I am pleased to return as a seasoned, rather than new, professional contributor. As a respondent to the essays written by Shamika Johnson, Matt Kwiatkowski, and Shiloh Venable, I recognize similarities between their stories and my job one story. My original *Job One* chapter, entitled "Part of a Crowd: One Man's Journey through Identity," discussed an issue that dominated my early years in student affairs: managing competing demands during the job search, on the job, and in my life beyond work—demands that were informed and complicated by my own personal identity development as a gay man. Shamika, Matt, and Shiloh, too, implicitly and explicitly discuss identity issues.

Each of these three narratives illuminates experiences that many new professionals might share: an African-American woman seeking a meaningful career in a safe place, a Christian man seeking a position where his faith explicitly informs his day-to-day practice, and a woman exploring her sexuality and seeking the right balance of place, personality, and purpose. Their words triggered many memories, including an overwhelming anxiety about a future that seemed just beyond my grasp. In the job search, there are often more questions than there are answers. Sometimes making a decision feels like a game of Pin the

Tail—blindly searching for the prize you know is right in front of you. As I read the narratives written by Shamika, Matt, and Shiloh, I remembered when the questions were overpowering and the answers too abundant and overwhelming. At the root of the anxiety produced by searching for and doing well in the first job are hosts of competing demands, each weighing differently upon the new professional. These demands emanate from internal stimuli like personal values such as Matt's faith or professional interests, like Shamika's clear desire to work in residential life, as well as from external pressures like colleagues and families when Shiloh was questioned by her family about her choice to go back to graduate school.

Understanding these competing demands and the diverse ways these three new professionals navigated them benefits the four primary audiences of this book: graduate students seeking employment, new professionals, supervisors and mentors of new professionals, and faculty who teach in graduate preparation programs. In this chapter, I will discuss how Shamika, Matt, and Shiloh identified and managed their multiple identities throughout the job search process, making connections between their experiences as well as with my own experiences. I then will identify several competing demands in common among these three authors and reveal how successfully navigating competing demands can lead to career satisfaction.

A WILL UPDATE

A goal of this chapter is to illuminate issues that transcend the narratives written by Shamika, Matt, and Shiloh. I will use my career story to illuminate how early job decisions influenced my career over the long term and how my personal and professional identities intersect with that process. By juxtaposing new professionals' stories with my own, I am able to illustrate how we as professionals face similar choices throughout our careers.

My career path has been unexpected. In *Job One*, I wrote about building a professional identity as an undergraduate student who took on a great deal of responsibility for shaping the experiences of other lesbian, gay, bisexual, or transgender (LGBT) students at my alma mater. I also described my experiences dealing with the clash of identities within a graduate program focused on cultivating multicultural competence. I wrote about my first job experiences as a gay man working at a women's college located in a progressive city. During my first job search, I had a clear preference for working in student activities designing student leadership programs. I accomplished these aims at Barnard College in New York City where I enjoyed interactions with students, faculty, and administrators. In 2004, after working for three years with student clubs and orientation and creating the college's first leadership program, I began to administer the college's new civic engagement program in partnership with an energetic faculty member. The program was housed in Career Development and was the idea of the provost, dean of the college (who was also the chief student affairs officer), and the director of career development. As the program director, I built new partnerships and learned how to be a career counselor—a role for which I had neither previous experience nor interest.

Six years later and nine years after starting my professional career at Barnard College, I knew that the time was right to move into a mid-manager's role, and I applied for career development vacancies in New York City. I accepted the position of Director of the Center for Career and Professional Development at John Jay College of Criminal Justice. This position combines several important aspects that align with my values: a mission focused on public service, the opportunity to restructure a department that needed to transform itself to match the college's recent move toward the liberal arts, and the opportunities to be a student counselor, department manager, part-time fundraiser, and spokesperson for students' career interests. During the interview process I quickly concluded that this position was the "perfect" job for me—a feeling that became even stronger after several visits to the campus in midtown Manhattan and was reminiscent of the emotions I felt after first interviewing at Barnard College nine years earlier. Shamika, Matt, and Shiloh also echoed this quest for the perfect job.

My efforts on college campuses are not the only forces shaping my career. Membership in professional associations has shaped my experience, particularly my engagement with NASPA–Student Affairs Administrators in Higher Education. Throughout my career, I have been involved in NASPA as a graduate student intern, an enthusiastic member, regional knowledge community representative, a national co-chair for the GLBT Issues Knowledge Community, and currently a NASPA Region 2 co-coordinator of Knowledge Communities. Involvement in leadership teams, advisory boards, and conference committees has introduced me to a broad spectrum of colleagues from near and far, similar and dissimilar institutions, shared and divergent identities. These individuals have kept me grounded in times of stress, challenged me to look beyond common assumptions, and affirmed my contributions to the profession. Each of the current authors, too, has collegial networks. My experience with professional associations has affirmed for me that having a network from which to solicit feedback has enhanced my professional confidence and competence. Encouraging graduate students and new professionals to become actively engaged in professional networks is one way that faculty and supervisors are able to provide additional support mechanisms during the job search, a period of high stress and anxiety.

PERSONAL IDENTITIES, PROFESSIONAL ROLES

Race, faith, and gender and sexuality are among the most obvious personal identities showcased in the preceding three chapters, but each author also was pondering life questions ranging from vocation to voice to geography and to age, a process which also lends to better understanding personal identities. These multiple identities, continually shifting and competing, are also sources of many of the stressors facing these three new professionals. Each author spoke to feelings of living two lives or of fearing inauthenticity because of the difficult work of attempting to untangle issues of personal as well as professional identities. Why, in a profession so in tune with the concepts of change, are we so unwilling to allow ourselves the same space for growth over time that we demand for our students?

For Shamika, there exists a strong connection between her personal identity and her job search as well as her success in her first job. She said, "Defining who I am and what is important to me were essential to my success in my first full-time position in student affairs" (p. 123). She continued, "Questions about my identity, questions about institutional and departmental fit, and race and gender issues persisted long after I accepted the job offer" (p. 123). She clearly cited several identities that played a significant role in her experience: race ("Are they only interested in me because I am an African American?" p. 122), spirituality ("the means I find most reliable during important decision-making times: my faith as a Christian" p. 121), and age ("Did the parent disregard me as a professional because I looked young?" p. 124). It was her racial identity that she revisited throughout the chapter. She first exposed the role her race played in her job search through the revelation that she may not have "assimilated into this predominantly White culture" (p. 120) as successfully as she had thought and that her identity as an African American could be a factor in the types of jobs to which she aspires. No doubt, a racially motivated incident influenced these aspirations. For many people with marginalized identities, including myself, Shamika's negative racial incident is sadly too common.

In *Job One,* I discussed an incident that took place during a class discussion when several colleagues used threatening language toward me, because they perceived that I only raised gay issues during class discussions. This incident played a large role in determining the types of departments where and colleagues with whom I would consider working, although I do not believe that I could have verbalized these feelings at that time. What I now know is that these incidents regularly take place throughout our lives and have less connection to geography or institutional culture; instead, they are the result of an American society continuing to evolve into a more global society. A recent supervisor asserted that the students with whom I worked in a civic engagement program were only interested in issues of HIV and public health because of who I am. I interpreted her meaning to be that as an out, queer-identified administrator, students wanted to please me by getting involved with an issue personally related to me. Given that I do not identify as HIV-positive and had never discussed the topic with this supervisor, I harbored guilt ("What if she was right and I am abusing my power?"), shame ("Does she really think that all gay men are HIV-positive?"), and rage ("What gives her the right to say something like that and get away with it?"). Because she threatened my queer identity and held a position of power and because I respected her abilities, it took me several years to sort out my feelings and publicly share my thoughts with her. Had this occurred during a job search, I would have most likely declined any invitation to work at this institution and missed out on nine wonderful years of work for an institution I greatly admire—not to mention the opportunity to build relationships with hundreds of bright, motivated students. Shamika's experience in Oxford and my own in New York show that negative events can shape our careers in powerful ways. Safe campuses are not defined solely by individual bias incidents but by how the college community and individuals respond and make meaning of them. This understanding of a campus culture takes time to develop and is difficult to do during a job search.

Unlike Shamika, Matt did not identify any single factor that he deemed overtly hostile to his faith, but resistance existed and it confused him. From Matt's chapter, his spirituality appears to be the most salient aspect of his identity. He identified himself as a "White, middle-class, Christian, heterosexual man from Pennsylvania" (p. 134), and his strong sense of faith in an environment he perceived to be unwelcoming to Christians made him feel for the first time in his life like a persecuted minority. Throughout his essay, Matt returned to the theme of "living a dichotomous lifestyle" (p. 128) throughout his graduate studies and job search. During his undergraduate years, this bifurcation existed as he reconciled the organizational cultures of athletics and campus ministries. During his graduate studies, he struggled to blend his secular educator responsibilities with his sacred educator passions. He doubted whether he could merge his faith identity with his student affairs identity. His solution was to limit his job search to faith-based institutions. Ultimately accepting a position at Baylor University, a Christian university in Texas, Matt found a place that allowed him to "be the most authentic self" (p. 136) he had ever been.

Fowler (1981), in *Stages of Faith*, identified a state of spiritual development typically occurring in one's late 20s and early 30s. Struggle and angst mark the individuative–reflective stage, when an individual builds accountability for faith-based beliefs. During this stage, Fowler posited that there is a heightened awareness of the conflicts regarding one's beliefs. Other identity development theories include a phase marked by the surrounding of oneself with other like-identified individuals; Cass (1979) called this stage identity pride and Cross, Parham, and Helms (1991) called it immersion/emersion. Given that Matt's identity as a Christian was still somewhat evolving, it is understandable that he wanted to surround himself with like-minded individuals to nurture this critical aspect of his worldview and self, just as I did when applying for jobs in major urban areas with vibrant queer communities. By immersing himself in Christian culture, and because his residential life position includes both personal and professional spaces, Matt continues to build his sense of self and better understand how to marry his faith with his student affairs position. Matt seeks to live in the universalizing faith stage of Fowler's theory, when all persons are treated with compassion and the universal principles of love and justice—ideas that resonate with the basic tenets and values of the student affairs profession.

The most profound question of Matt's chapter centers on *fit*: "Is it possible to be a Christian and an effective student affairs professional at non-faith-based colleges?" (p. 129). I, too, remember grappling with a similar question concerning what type of institution would be the best fit for me—the "me" being the fullest combination of my various identities. In 2001, when I left behind rural

Virginia and suburban Maryland to move to New York City, I expected that the community at Barnard College would welcome me. Of course, I was primarily concerned with my queer identity. I found this to be true; Barnard was very open to me as a gay man and self-identified feminist. Yet there were times when the college's culture and my own values collided. Over nine years, I never overcame "feeling like a fraud" (McIntosh, 1985) or feeling like I had "pulled the wool over others' eyes" (McIntosh, 1985, p. 1) and being full of self-doubt when it came to my intelligence and socioeconomic class background. Nor did I ever feel that I fit in with this bastion of New York City intelligentsia. It was, however, when I began working with the college community to address the needs of our transgender students that I felt the full force of a schism between my personal values and my role as a campus administrator.

Toward the end of my tenure at Barnard I became involved in a campus conflict about the college's policy toward transgender students. Although Barnard (a women's college) allowed upperclass students who came out in their later years to use masculine pronouns and even to graduate after legally changing their genders and names, how the philosophy of women's education would be carried out was challenged when a first-year student came forward as transgender, preferring to use male pronouns, only two days after the start of orientation. So much was at stake—the student's well-being, the needs of the student's roommates, parents on both sides of the equation, and on a greater level an unease about how public inclusion of students from throughout the gender spectrum would jeopardize the legal status of women's colleges and create negative publicity and alumnae backlash. Was I disappointed in the reactions of some of my peers and proud of the support from others? Yes. Did this situation, where my own values ran counter to the enacted values of the institution, eventually lead to my decision to move to a new institution? Not at all. Although I lost the battle, I felt secure knowing that I left Barnard having contributed to building a much stronger LGBTQ community and putting into place policies and cultivating trainings for faculty and staff that might eventually lead the college to a different perspective on transgender students.

Matt, in concluding his essay, said, "I am learning how to make the position my own—how to blend the requirements of my job description with my own passions, interests, and identity. I will not pretend that everything is perfect, but I have been able to be the most authentic self I have ever been" (p. 136). The lesson from these two very different stories is that through reconciling personal identities and needs with professional roles and responsibilities, student affairs practitioners can move closer to a more authentic mode of practice and career success.

"I was 26 years old and coming out to myself" (p. 144). These words from Shiloh who, having worked for several years before returning to graduate school, had a more developed sense of self and found herself facing unanticipated questions about her identity during her job search. During her time as a graduate student at Texas A&M, Shiloh recounted an attraction to one of her female friends. She was "rocked by the sudden awareness that [her] feelings for women were not confined" to a previous singular relationship with a woman (p. 144). That word *rocked* carries tremendous power and signifies how meaningful the self-discovery process inherent in a student development-based graduate program can be. Shiloh attributed much of this self-discovery to a significant mentoring relationship with her summer internship supervisor who modeled a successful lesbian relationship. She used potent language to describe how natural the product of self-discovery can be: "Something powerful clicked inside me. Without even thinking about it, I came out during the interview" (p. 146). The power of many student affairs graduate programs is a curriculum centered on self-discovery, cultivating empathic advocates for our students and acting as caretakers of their learning. Participating in guided self-discovery reveals the importance of being open to identity development as a process. Shiloh summed up this idea when she said, "I still have not come up with that perfect label to describe my sexuality, but I am more comfortable now with using queer than anything else and that is all I have to say if it comes up" (p. 146).

Matt, Shamika, and Shiloh each presented a compelling story of how personal identity affected the job search process. Whether race, faith, or gender and sexuality, these identities were at the center of their thinking about what sorts of positions, institutions, and places could provide the best fit. The next section of this chapter extends this assertion to reveal how managing multiple identities is but one of the demands placed upon student affairs professionals during the job search.

MULTIPLE IDENTITIES, COMPETING DEMANDS, AND SELF-AUTHORSHIP

All three essays focus on the imperative to land a job in a tough economy while finding a place that will affirm one's core values. These authors were not simply looking for a job; they were looking for jobs that aligned with their values. The competing demands—managing multiple identities, developing self-authorship, and balancing life roles—placed on new student affairs job-seekers, especially those who have undergone a rigorous graduate program that encourage self-discovery, are many.

Jones and McEwen (2000) reminded us that the weight of any one of an individual's multiple identities depends greatly on the context. At any given time, the identity that is the most useful, the most marginalized, or even the most understood will be what we "work with" while our other identities take a backseat. For Shamika, her identity as an African-American carried special weight in her career decision-making process, especially after being the victim of a racially motivated hate incident off-campus. For Matt, the importance of his Christian identity in job decision-making rested on a long-term revelation that he was living "a two-faced life" (p. 130) and "really did feel guilty" (p. 130) after participating in activities that did not align with his Christian faith. Shiloh revealed how the power of relationships altered her worldview, simply by exposing possibilities for happiness that she had not considered. Observing a "healthy and functioning lesbian relationship . . . was a critical moment" (p. 143) in her identity development.

Graduate faculty and the supervisors of new professionals often make the mistake of expecting their students or new hires to be further along in the development of a personal identity than they may be. We must challenge ourselves to remember that self-authorship—a "capacity to define one's beliefs, identity, and social relations" (Baxter Magolda, 2008, p. 269)—develops over time. Our new professionals are busy answering life questions: "How do I know, who am I, and how do I want to construct relationships with others?" (Baxter Magolda, 2001, p. 15). Too often, we expect them to arrive on our campuses having already answered these questions, when in fact we are attempting to answer the same questions ourselves! Self-authorship advocates the moving away from external influences and moving toward developing an inner voice that assists us in making meaning of our world.

The three authors identify several external influences regarding their job decision-making. Shamika revealed, "Sometimes it is hard to stay true to myself because I am pressured by those around me to change or fit in" (p. 126). The racial hate incident was one of the greatest influences on Shamika's job search. However, she also identified other external influences, such as wondering whether her colleagues would treat her as a professional when so many of these individuals knew her as a graduate student. She also recounted the peer influence of members of her cohort asking, "You're really going to stay here?" (p. 123) and asserting that she "was not a risk taker and only stayed at Miami because it was comfortable" (p. 123). Then, once she was on the job, Shamika encountered a parent who did not believe she was old enough to be in charge. Shamika challenged herself to move past these peripheral voices; through introspection, she made a job decision based on an honest evaluation of all available data.

When Matt spoke about the role of religion and faith in his decision-making process, he often used the language of Christianity. "God revealed himself and unveiled his master plan for the previous year of my life. It was so clear" (p. 135). Matt gave his inner voice external properties: "I could not help but redefine my values, beliefs, relationships, and sense of self. I searched for the inner voice (that is God in my world) to help me discern my calling" (p. 129). Given his statements about his inner voice, the authority Matt gave to an external voice (i.e., God) could be seen as running contrary to Baxter Magolda's (2008) concept of self-authorship where one moves away from following external formulas and toward the development of an inner voice and making meaning of the world based on internal foundations. On my first read of Matt's chapter, I initially was challenged by Matt's use of language to describe his inner foundations because it seemed, to me, to expose an over-reliance on external motivators to make life decisions. My own reaction to Matt's narrative might lend credence to his desire to work at a Christian college—a place where this aspect of his identity is understood, shared, encouraged, and cultivated. After a deeper read of his story, I realized that through spiritual growth, Matt developed an inner voice that models his faith beliefs and thus his actions became congruent with his values. My initial reaction to Matt's story suggests that our profession needs to better understand how personal faith intersects and influences professional identity. So that other graduate students, like Matt, do not have to feel like outliers among their peers, student affairs professionals must do more to understand how spirituality complements, rather than hinders, authentic identity development.

Shiloh's story includes guidance about how seasoned professionals can best assist in guiding new professionals toward self-authorship. She also recounted how her family and friends looked at her strangely when she said she "wanted to leave my stable and lucrative job in a booming industry to enroll in a graduate program in higher education administration" (p. 138). Through her first assistantship she discovered a way forward. She recounted that her supervisor asked her, "What do you want to get out of this experience?" Her reaction is revealing. "No one had ever asked me what I wanted out of an employment experience, because it had never been about anything other than the employer's expectations" (p. 142). It took her supervisor to assist Shiloh in trusting her internal voice. For many young adults, "their personal reflection skills and the extent to which they had good support systems mediated the intensity and duration of excursions into [times of confusion, ambiguity, fear, and despair]" (Baxter Magolda, 2008, p. 280). Student affairs supervisors are uniquely positioned to incorporate our understanding of college student development into our understanding of new professional development. Asking thoughtful, open-ended questions, such as "What do you want to get out of this experience?" is one way supportive supervisors can assist supervisees in building confidence in themselves and with their responsibilities.

If supervisors approached new professionals with strategies to promote self-authorship, a result could be more confident, empowered team members who can carry out the mission of their departments. Baxter Magolda (2008) challenged us to move toward self-authorship by (a) respecting the thoughts and feelings of others, (b) helping them view experiences as opportunities for growth, (c) collaborating with them to analyze their own problems, and (d) viewing the learning as mutual. These four tenets, and the questions that emanate from them, have the power to allow new professionals to build meaning from satisfaction of all of their experiences and not to search for the perfect job as something that is "out there" if they could just find it. Shamika, Matt, and Shiloh each illuminated the challenges to developing self-authorship while searching for the first job, either from becoming overwhelmed by the volume of external influences (Shamika), or from developing congruence between an institution's values and one's own (Matt), or from establishing a trusting supervisory relationship (Shiloh).

Whereas self-authorship denotes a broader perspective of the self in the world, how new professionals develop a professional identity is also a critical aspect of the transition to job one. Super, Savickas, and Super (1996), in the life span, life space theory of career development, suggested that career decisions represent the application of our self-concept. Vocational self-concept develops through observation and identification with various professionals and is ultimately about self-expression. Professionals are diverse beings with skills, personalities, and values. So, too, are organizations. Super et al. argued there is no such thing as the perfect job—that elusive entity that Shamika, Matt, and Shiloh and hundreds of other new professionals seek. Our satisfaction with our work lives increases proportionately with our ability to apply our self-concept to any given life role. Super et al. identified six roles: child, student, leisurite, citizen, worker, and homemaker or parent. Rather than viewing time as corresponding to age, Super argued the developmental timeline as having more to do with vocational development in five stages—growth, exploration, establishment, maintenance, and decline—that recycle anytime we make a career transition. This multi-dimensional model, where we are simultaneously balancing the development of a professional identity with the multiple roles we play in life, shows how complex job satisfaction and success can be (Super et al., 1996).

Student affairs professionals and graduate faculty have learned how to support graduate students' and new professionals' growth and development through person-centered graduate programs, orientations and training programs, and valuing life-long professional development and involvement. What many student affairs professionals do poorly is acknowledge our life roles and balance. Shamika, Matt, and Shiloh clearly identified multiple roles that they struggle to balance. For Shamika, they are sister/twin, child, friend, and partner. Matt identified some of his roles as secular educator, sacred educator, and athlete. Shiloh identified strongly with Super et al.'s (1996) citizen role (e.g., her affinity for community service programming) as well as child, partner, administrator, and Texan. As a career counselor at Barnard College, I primarily worked with traditional, socially savvy young women. At John Jay College, I mostly interact with nontraditional, first generation students, struggling to develop the social capital to be successful in their selected careers. I talk with students about how to manage multiple roles and make the best decisions at each point in their lives. In some cases, they will take jobs because their status as family members requires them to make sacrifices. In others, they may make career transitions that recognize their desire to focus on the citizen role and shape our society by working at a nonprofit or governmental agency.

Similarly, Shiloh, Shamika, and Matt have each made life decisions based in part on their roles: Shamika to remain close to her family, Matt to further develop his spiritual identity, and Shiloh to move to a new location where no one knew her, seeking new experiences in work and life outside of Texas. However, their transitions to jobs two, three, or four might be based on the influence of any of the other roles. Mentors and supervisors should focus on two tasks. First, be transparent about one's own career decision-making so that new professionals can at least understand our processes and identify with them (or not). Second, engage with new professionals and learn about the other roles in their lives beyond worker, assisting them with various roles in ways to allow for career satisfaction and improved performance.

CONCLUSION

The experiences of new professionals in student affairs should be a priority for graduate students, new professionals, supervisors/mentors, and graduate preparation faculty. A better understanding of the experiences of graduate students transitioning to new professionals is essential. Graduate program faculty must use this understanding to construct meaningful graduate programs that incorporate guided self-discovery along with the theory and history of the profession. The supervisors of graduate students and new professionals should use their knowledge of competing demands of their employees, including identity, the development of self-authorship, and grappling with various life roles, and provide the best possible mentorship and feedback to guide these individuals forward in their own growth and development. Graduate students and new professionals can gain awareness that their experiences resonate with many, regardless of shared identities.

Graduate students and new professionals can begin this process by asking themselves Baxter Magolda's (2001) three questions: (a) "How do I know?" (b) "Who am I?" and (c) "How do I want to construct relationships with others?" (p. 4). They also could ask additional questions.

1. What identities matter to me right now? How do these identities influence career decisions and job satisfaction?
2. How can I challenge myself to move toward self-authorship and away from following external formulas? How can I use this self-awareness to do well on the job?
3. What value do I place on my life roles in this moment? How might my life roles change in the coming years, affecting my job satisfaction?

Shamika Johnson, Matt Kwiatkowski, and Shiloh Venable discuss how personal identities influence career decision-making and job satisfaction. For me, these three stories reveal how Super et al.'s (1996) belief that we recycle through various career stages with each career transition still holds true. Two months after starting my current position, I went for a jog and was consumed by self-doubt and the sense that I had gotten in over my head. How could I possibly be ready to lead a department? Did I have enough experience as a career services professional to manage everyone's expectations? Would I be able to effectively work with various deans and vice presidents? Cresting a hill, I had an "aha!" moment and remembered that I had similar feelings before—when I took my first position at Barnard in 2001. I recalled that the second year was better than the first and the third better than the second. I recalled mistakes, tough conversations, and celebrated accomplishments and successes. This is development. Perhaps Shiloh Venable said it best: "This growth has allowed me to take risks while maintaining confidence in my choices, and this is something I know will lead to many great opportunities in my career" (p. 147).

REFERENCES

Baxter Magolda, M. B. (2001). *Making their own way: Narratives for transforming higher education to promote self-development.* Sterling, VA: Stylus.

Baxter Magolda, M. B. (2008). Three elements of self-authorship. *Journal of College Student Development, 49,* 269-284.

Cass, V. C. (1979). Homosexual identity formation: A theoretical model. *Journal of Homosexuality, 4,* 219-235.

Cross, W. E., Jr., Parham, T. A., & Helms, J. E. (1991). The stages of Black identity development: Nigrescence models. In R. L. Jones (Ed.), *Black psychology* (3rd ed., pp. 319-338). Los Angeles, CA: Cobb & Henry.

Fowler, J. W. (1981). *Stages of faith.* New York, NY: Harper & Row.

Jones, S. R., & McEwen, M. K. (2000). A conceptual model of multiple dimensions of identity. *Journal of College Student Development, 41,* 405-414.

McIntosh, P. (1985). *Feeling like a fraud.* Wellesley, MA: Stone Center for Developmental Services and Studies at Wellesley College.

Super, D. E., Savickas, M. L., & Super, C. M. (1996). The life-span, life-space approach to careers. In D. Brown, L. Brooks, & Associates (Eds.), *Career choice and development* (pp. 121-178). San Francisco, CA: Jossey-Bass.

Unit III Discussion Questions

- What do you know now that you did not know before reading Shamika, Matt, and Shiloh's stories?

New Professionals

- How would you determine if a university is ambivalent toward marginalized groups, especially those you support or are a part of?
- How do you support marginalized groups in your work setting?
- How has your identity changed since enrolling in college? How has this change influenced your work and views about student affairs and higher education?
- What institutional values are necessary for you to consider before accepting a job offer?

Supporters of New Professionals

- Are there any aspects of identity a candidate should reveal or avoid revealing during the search process?
- What identity-related topics make you uncomfortable, and how do you address this discomfort?
- What forms of support do you provide mentees?

— *Questions Prepared by Sarah O'Connell*

CHAPTER 15

Job One: Continuing the Journey toward Self-Authorship

ROZANA CARDUCCI AND DIANA JARAMILLO

Diana: Hey Rozana! I'm so glad to be reconnecting with you. It's been far too long.

Rozana: I know. Can you believe it has been fourteen years since we earned master's degrees and embarked upon our own job one journeys? I still recall the excitement of signing my solo apartment lease. Finally, no roommate! I couldn't wait to start my dream job as the Coordinator of Leadership Development. Armed with my knowledge of student affairs theory, I was going to make a difference. Looking back, I chuckle at my idealism, or what some might call naiveté. I had so much to learn. Refresh my memory, where did you head after grad school?

Diana: I accepted a job in Texas, where I spent two years. That "perfect job" did not turn out as I had expected. Looking back at my younger and more idealistic self, I had so much more to learn than I realized. One of my biggest after-the-fact realizations was the importance of cultivating and maintaining a support network. That's what led me back to Los Angeles. I felt like I needed to get back to a familiar, comfortable place after having had such a difficult time in job one. When I left Texas, I interviewed in a variety of student affairs functional areas. I admit, accepting a job at University of Southern California (USC)—

my alma mater—as a career counselor surprised me. I had never considered working in career services, but I was open-minded because I needed a job. That move did not feel like a big risk because I worked on a familiar campus, lived with my best friend, and had my parents and friends nearby.

I stayed in career services for four years, but I itched to try academic advising. I liked the idea of having more sustained relationships with students. In 2004, I accepted an academic advising position at USC. It was a good fit, and my role expanded to include leadership functions. I stayed in that job for eight years.

Rozana: What are you up to now? I know you moved to Portland earlier in the year without a job. Any developments on that front?

Diana: My job search continues. I maintained my job at USC by telecommuting for several months. After I trained my successor, it was time to close that chapter of my life. I'm so glad to be living here in Portland, but "funemployment" is not as fun as I expected. It is very typical for me to be uncomfortable without a clear next step. I am having a hard time relaxing while out of work. I don't know how long it will last. The last couple of times I actively searched for a job, the economy was stronger. These days I am more vulnerable. As I explore opportunities, I frequently feel over- or under-qualified. Finding the right match is a challenge. So, co-authoring this *Job One 2.0* chapter is great for me. Having something to do besides job searching makes me feel like less of a layabout. I admit to being intimidated, though, because it has been quite some time since I have done this kind of thinking or writing.

Rozana: I completely understand. Although writing for publication is a high priority in my job as an assistant professor, I too am a little intimidated by our charge. I thoroughly enjoyed reading the personal narratives included in *Job One 2.0*. The diversity of voices, experiences, and insights captured in the new professional and analysis chapters was incredibly engaging. However, given the large number of complex issues and themes addressed by the contributing authors, our task to "tie it all together" is formidable. Perhaps we should just dive right in.

I found reading the new professional narratives in *Job One 2.0* to be a stroll down memory lane. It brought back vivid images of sitting at my computer in 2001, struggling to write my own job one narrative as I searched for a way to respectfully, yet truthfully, describe my disappointment with my supervisor and my frustrations with a department culture that did not value my commitment to linking theory and practice. Carrie Miller's story (Chapter 9) about her supervisor's resistance to theory resonated with me.

Collectively, I was struck by the timelessness of issues discussed in the *Job One 2.0* essays. The new professionals featured in this volume are dealing with many of the same struggles and tensions I confronted in my first student affairs professional position fourteen years ago. Familiar struggles and tensions included the risks and challenges associated with starting a new life in an unfamiliar environment, establishing personal and professional boundaries, building support networks, (re)negotiating multiple identities in the construction of a new professional identity (e.g., race, gender, nationality, sexual orientation, religion, family), and initiating change. Although the student affairs profession and colleges and universities have undergone significant change since we first embarked upon our job one journeys—changes related to funding, learning technology, globalization, student demographics—some dimensions of the new professional experience appear eternal.

Diana: There were familiar stories for me as well, but my experience reading the narratives and analysis chapters was not as much about comparing them with my *Job One* story as it was connecting the stories to my contemporary quest to find a job. Granted, I do not have the same idealistic view of what a job can be for me as I did when I first entered the field, but I do harbor some of the questions and doubts that the new professionals expressed in their stories, particularly Craig Berger (Chapter 3).

The intersection of my job search with these new stories reminded me of the power of reflection, especially for individuals who are coping with the stressors of the job search and a quest for fit. My own job four search still involves vulnerability, courage, and fear. Perhaps I will soon be on the other side of my most recent risk, reaping the rewards of that leap toward an unknown future.

Rozana: I am so glad you mentioned that many of the job one themes still resonate with you today in your search for job four. I was also struck by the continued salience of several new professional struggles to my own career development. I, too, struggle to cultivate a productive relationship with my immediate supervisor, the department chair. And although I may not be the same inexperienced twenty-something I was when we left graduate school in 1998, reading and reflecting on these *Job One 2.0* narratives helped me recognize that my current professional discontent is likely a function of holding on to unrealistic expectations for the work of a student affairs faculty member. Here I am thinking specifically about Sarah Steward's description in Chapter 7 of career myths that construct images of the perfect student affairs job, images that foster feelings of disappointment when professional reality does not match idealized expectations.

Diana: Just as you and I made connections between the new professionals' narratives and our current work experiences, the authors of the analysis chapters (who wrote new professional chapters in the first edition of *Job One*) appear to have had similar insights. Craig Woodsmall and Kathleen Gardner (Chapter 10) shared that they never stopped encountering fear or vulnerability. Kevin Piskadlo (Chapter 5) and Will Simpkins (Chapter 14) separately acknowledged that their most recent career transitions were tinged with familiar uncertainties. Christana Johnson (Chapter 5) reflected on the continued importance of fit and support networks in her professional life.

Another common theme I noted in several of the analysis chapters was the importance of self-authorship in job one. Molly Reas Hall (Chapter 1), Kathleen and Craig, and Will all touched on Baxter Magolda's work in their analyses. In the interest of tying the narrative and analysis chapters together, I suggest we use self-authorship as the theoretical centerpiece for our chapter.

Rozana: Yes, self-authorship makes complete sense as an organizing framework for our chapter, because the common transition issues associated with searching for and starting the first full-time student affairs position are not merely a function of embarking upon a new career, they are issues of adult development that are not easily resolved. Productively navigating this important professional milestone—one's first full-time student affairs job—is an important step in a much longer developmental journey (Baxter Magolda, 2009).

Diana: In addition to analyzing the job one experience though the lens of self-authorship, I would like to build in some recommendations for the readers to make this analysis chapter a useful tool.

Rozana: Agreed. One of the aims of our chapter is to situate the *Job One 2.0* personal narratives within contemporary scholarship on new student affairs professionals and employment transitions. Several student affairs scholar-practitioners—Cilente, Henning, Skinner, Kennedy, and Sloane, 2007; Renn and Hodges, 2007; Renn and Jessup-Anger, 2008; Tull, Hirt, and Saunders, 2009—have explored the needs and experiences of new student affairs professionals since the publication of *Job One* in 2004. Although each of these studies adopts slightly different approaches to researching new student affairs professionals, collectively this scholarship affirms several common themes (e.g., the importance of mentorship, the need to reconcile expectations and reality, and the challenges of adjusting to a new environment) noted by the new professionals in this book.

Diana: Molly Reas Hall (Chapter 1) provided a valuable summary of this scholarship, and the authors of the three analysis chapters (Chapters 5, 10, and 14) also described multiple theoretical lenses through which to understand these stories (e.g., generational theories, career development theories, identity development theories, psychological theories, and human development theories).

Rozana: Let's begin with a discussion of the contemporary challenges that characterize young adulthood. We'll provide a formal introduction to the theory of self-authorship and draw upon excerpts from the new professional narratives to illustrate the developmental dimensions of job one. I like your idea of concluding the chapter with recommendations. We can connect lessons learned from our review of the new professionals' stories with the conditions for self-authorship articulated by Baxter Magolda (2002, 2009). Given the broad audience for this book—graduate students, new professionals and their supervisors, as well as graduate preparation faculty—we will need to develop recommendations that speak to all four groups.

JOB ONE AND SELF-AUTHORSHIP

This chapter situates the *Job One 2.0* narratives within contemporary scholarship on new student affairs professionals and employment transitions. Because of the congruence between the transition issues we experienced fourteen years ago and the challenges confronting the new professionals featured in this book, the ease with which we connected *Job One 2.0* insights to the findings and implications for practice highlighted in recent studies of new professionals did not surprise us. Renn and Jessup-Anger (2008) underscored the timelessness of new professional transition issues, noting that many of the themes highlighted in studies of new student affairs professionals conducted during the 1980s remain relevant today.

The cross-case analyses presented by Molly Reas Hall (Chapter 1), Kevin Piskadlo and Christana Johnson (Chapter 5), Kathleen Gardner and Craig Woodsmall (Chapter 10) and Will Simpkins (Chapter 14) offer in-depth explorations of a number of these timeless transition themes, including building relationships; exploring professional and organizational fit; establishing competence and confidence; managing differences between expectations and lived realities; the value of taking risks, exhibiting courage, and cultivating resiliency in job one; and integrating personal and professional identities. We will not rehash these topics in this chapter. Instead, we will examine the important role job one plays in facilitating the development of self-authorship, highlighting both individual and collective efforts that may help new student affairs professionals productively navigate the complexities of adulthood.

The developmental journey of self-authorship was referenced repeatedly in both the new professional narratives and cross-case analyses that precede our chapter, underscoring the importance of this framework for making meaning of the student affairs job one experience. Contributing authors mentioned the concepts of self-authorship—developing one's internal voice, the power of reflection and the need for support— but we want to provide a more coherent and in-depth exploration of this framework. We will begin this discussion by examining the challenges of young adulthood that call upon new student affairs professionals to develop and exercise their internal voices.

The Complexity of Young Adulthood

Marcia Baxter Magolda (2002, 2007) asserted that complexity is the mainstay of adulthood, noting "the early years of the journey into adult life are particularly difficult because they are marked by profound transformations—transformation from reliance on external authority to taking ownership and responsibility for one's life" (Baxter Magolda, 2002, p. 2). The personal narratives featured in *Job One 2.0* vividly illustrate the diverse array of challenges and transformational opportunities encountered by new student affairs professionals as they transition from graduate school to full-time positions. For example, in Chapter 2, DuJuan Smith recounted his decision to take responsibility for his professional development, opting to pursue a master's degree in clinical mental health counseling rather than follow the counsel of mentors (i.e., an important source of external authority) who urged DuJuan to pursue the more traditional path of a master's in higher education/student affairs. Similarly, in Chapter 7, Sarah Steward called attention to the powerful influence exhibited by external authorities. Rather than allowing externally defined career myths to artificially constrain her postgraduate school options, she, too, acted upon her internal values and beliefs, accepting a professional position at the Buddhist-inspired Naropa University.

In addition to acknowledging and disrupting career myths about ideal educational pathways and first professional positions, the new professionals' narratives highlight the transitions and transformations embedded within the developmental task of (re)negotiating relationships with family members, significant others, and co-workers. Molly Pierson (Chapter 4) struggled to balance the constraints of a dual career search with her career ambitions. Carrie Miller (Chapter 9) grappled with cultivating a mutually respectful relationship with her new supervisor.

The complexities of adulthood also are evident in the common task of moving to a new city (or in the case of David Stanfield [Chapter 6]—a new country) and engaging in the time-consuming and exhausting processes of setting up a household and cultivating new personal and professional networks. Kim Rutledge's story (Chapter 8) of searching for an apartment and friends in San Francisco powerfully illustrates this point.

Forging new personal and professional identities that integrate multiple identity dimensions (e.g., age, physical ability, sexual orientation, gender identity and expression, religion, race, ethnicity, nationality) is also an important, yet incredibly complex, developmental task encountered by new student affairs professionals seeking to identify a job one position that will allow them to live congruent and authentic lives at work, at home, and in the community. Here we are reminded of Matt Kwiatkowski's (Chapter 12) moving journey to find an organization that honored his religious values, Shiloh Venable's (Chapter 13) enactment of authenticity when she decided to come out as queer during a job interview, and Shamika Johnson's (Chapter 11) efforts to integrate her age, family, racial, and new professional identities at Miami University, the institution where just months earlier she was a graduate student.

In addition, the transition into young adulthood and job one is frequently a time of tremendous anxiety, pressure (both internally and externally imposed), and self-doubt. Craig Berger (Chapter 3) eloquently described the angst he experienced while searching for job one:

> Although I recognized that the circumstances of each job search do not make for easy or fair comparisons to peers' searches, I felt increasing pressure to get a job. . . . Telling classmates, former colleagues, and mentors that I was living with my parents, who continued to support me into my mid-20s and while my bachelor's and master's degrees collected dust, was difficult and embarrassing. With each passing day, my self-imposed pressure intensified. . . . With no opportunities on the proverbial horizon, I questioned the clarity of my career plans. Did I need to revise my plans in the face of this seemingly brutal job market? (pp. 22-23)

Craig's was certainly not the only narrative to prominently feature the emotional and physical toll associated with transitioning from graduate school to full-time employment. Matt Kwiatkowski described the last four months of graduate school as "the most stressful in my life" (p. 128) as he struggled to simultaneously balance coursework, comprehensive exam preparations, assistantship responsibilities, and job search tasks.

The anxiety did not dissipate, however, when these new professionals accepted job offers. For many the focus of self-doubt transitioned from whether or not they would find a job to questioning whether or not they possessed the knowledge and skills necessary to successfully fulfill their new professional responsibilities. Sarah Steward questioned whether or not she possessed "enough" experience to be Naropa University's sole career counselor. Shamika Johnson was uncertain if her new colleagues would recognize her professional identity and authority given her recent transition from student to full-time employee. Kim Rutledge confronted a second wave of anxiety when she applied for a permanent position at the University of San Francisco.

> Did my colleagues think me capable and competent to assume these job responsibilities? Was I willing to put myself out there, yet again, to be scrutinized and evaluated? The doubts and fears that I faced during my most recent job search reemerged. I feared that I was not good enough and that I was underprepared for this new position. I was certain that there was a more qualified applicant in the pool, and one of them would most certainly get the job. (p. 87)

Kim's story and the stories of the other nine new professionals reveal the complexities of young adulthood embedded within the search for and transition into an entry-level student affairs professional position. Congruent with the findings of Marcia Baxter Magolda's (2001) longitudinal study of adult development, the new professionals featured in *Job One 2.0* were wrestling with the "driving questions of the twenties" (Baxter Magolda, 2001, p. 4): How do I know? Who am I? and What relationships do I want with others? Accordingly, the challenges facing new student affairs professionals are similar to the challenges facing young adults pursuing other professional paths—to cultivate and enact responses to these driving questions that reflect a coherent, internally derived sense of knowledge, self, and others. Thus, to make meaning of job one and facilitate the concomitant transitions, it is essential that we delve deeper into the journey of self-authorship.

Job One and the Developmental Journey Toward Self-Authorship

Self-authorship is "the internal capacity to define one's belief system, identity, and social relationships" (Baxter Magolda, 2007, p. 69). It is an integrated view of development (Jones, 2009) that acknowledges the inextricable connection between cognitive (How do I know?), intrapersonal (Who am I?), and interpersonal (How do I construct relationships with others?) dimensions of adult development (Baxter Magolda, 2001). Baxter Magolda's (1992, 2001, 2009) longitudinal study of adult development revealed three phases in the journey toward self-authorship: following external formulas, navigating the crossroads, and self-authorship.

Heavy reliance on external authorities (e.g., parents, professors, supervisors) for guidance in formulating beliefs, constructing a self-identity, building relationships, and defining success characterizes the following external formulas developmental phase that students navigate during the college years. The decisions of young adults guided by external formulas are driven by the expectations of authority figures rather than internal interests and needs (Baxter Magolda, 2001, 2009).

During the mid-twenties, dissatisfaction with outcomes arising from following externally imposed expectations leads young adults to enter the crossroads, "the place where participants recognized that they needed to shift from external to internal authority or were unsure how to do so and afraid of the costs involved" (Baxter Magolda, 2002, p. 4). During the crossroads, individuals begin to listen to and cultivate their internal voices, actively engaging in reflective activities and experiences (e.g., journaling, meditation, new professional responsibilities) that facilitate the identification and exploration of internally formulated beliefs, needs, interests and hopes.

For some new student affairs professionals, the highly reflective nature of student affairs graduate programs facilitates movement through the developmental crossroads; course assignments and experiential learning opportunities challenge students, perhaps for the first time, to articulate, reflect on, and enact personal values and professional interests. Shiloh Venable eloquently described how graduate school helped cultivate her internal voice.

> During all of my preparations for graduate school, I had not considered that it would be okay for me to talk about my own personal goals on a regular basis. My community-service-oriented family taught me to do the work because it needed to be done and to keep my personal goals to myself. The expectation to know and regularly discuss my goals seemed a bit contrary to my upbringing. As I became more comfortable asking myself the questions about what I wanted to learn and achieve, I became increasingly excited about beginning a career in the field. The realization that I could define my own journey and that I had a tremendous support network for doing so was both liberating and empowering. During those first few months of graduate school, I resolved to do things in ways that made sense to me. (p. 141)

Beyond the general challenge and support for self-directed learning that characterizes many student affairs graduate programs, student development courses can be particularly powerful vehicles for helping student affairs graduate students listen to and cultivate their internal voices. These courses foster deep engagement with diverse theories of development and frequently require students to demonstrate their knowledge by analyzing their own cognitive, intrapersonal, and interpersonal development.

The experiential learning opportunities embedded in most student affairs graduate preparation programs (e.g., assistantships, internships, study abroad) also provide students with opportunities to listen to and cultivate their internal voices, allowing them to explore and focus their professional interests (e.g., functional area, institutional type, professional role) prior to searching for a full-time position. Kim Rutledge described tuning into her internal voice and the fulfillment she experienced as a graduate assistant.

> I felt great pride in my work as a graduate assistant in the campus learning center. I forged bonds with students that centered on personal and academic development and satisfaction. Although I had an opportunity to work in other offices, I was most drawn to the type of work that I could do with students in learning centers and academic support. I had spent so many years professionally unfulfilled, and I was determined that once I graduated I would secure work that fulfilled me, no matter how difficult the task. (p. 82)

As a result of a positive graduate assistantship, Kim formulated an internally driven vision for the future. Enacting this vision was the next developmental challenge Kim faced. During the transition from the crossroads to the self-authorship phase of development, a journey often undertaken in the mid to late twenties, individuals become increasingly less reliant on external formulas, adopting instead expectations and visions for the future shaped by their internal voices.

Baxter Magolda's (1992, 2001, 2009) longitudinal research identified three essential elements of the self-authorship phase of adult development: trusting one's internal voice, building an internal foundation, and securing internal commitments. Often navigating this developmental phase in their late twenties and early thirties, individuals face the "overarching challenge . . . to integrate their beliefs, values, identities, and relationships into a core sense of self or psychological home" (Baxter Magolda, 2009, pp. 10-11). The *Job One 2.0* new professional authors described both the excitement and trepidation characteristic of this developmental phase, suggesting that this segment of the journey to self-authorship is of particular relevance to new student affairs professionals and, therefore, merits substantive consideration by those seeking to facilitate the transition from graduate school to full-time employment.

Trusting one's internal voice necessitates that individuals develop the capacity to distinguish between reality (e.g., events in the local context or broader society over which they have little control) and reactions to reality (i.e., behavioral and emotional responses to events of the day over which individuals do have control; Baxter Magolda, 2008). For the young adults in Baxter Magolda's study,

> trusting their internal voices heightened their ability to take ownership of how they made meaning of external events. They recognized that they could create their own emotions and happiness by choosing how to react to reality. This led to a better sense of when to make something happen versus when to let something happen. (Baxter Magolda, 2008, p. 279)

Several new professionals discussed the process of learning to trust their internal voices, intentionally focusing on what they could control when dealing with the disappointing realities of their job searches and new professional positions. Craig struggled with self-doubt as he faced slow progress in his job search. Rather than continue to lose self-confidence, Craig engaged in meaningful activities (e.g., blogging, organizing his academic papers) and created structures that facilitated his journey through self-authorship. Similarly, as Shamika reflected on her doubts concerning the wisdom of accepting a position at the same institution where she completed her master's degree, she realized that she could not control every aspect of her life, opting instead to "trust the process" (p. 123).

Carrie dealt with her disappointment in her new environment by identifying elements that were within her control. The interpersonal difficulty she had with her supervisor presented a complex challenge; in her uncertainty about how to proceed there, she chose to focus on the unsatisfactory condition that she felt confident about controlling, namely professional development.

> The things that I found exciting about student affairs work and that had been a central part of my experiences in graduate school, considering theory and ideas, were absent from my current experience. Navigating my relationship with my supervisor was also something I spent time contemplating, but ultimately I wanted to try to address the issues that I felt I had the most control over. I could not determine how to improve my relationship with my supervisor, and I missed engaging in discussion with others about ideas. So I thought about the types of professional development experiences I wanted. (p. 95)

Baxter Magolda (2009) explained that individuals who have trusted their internal voices to guide their actions progress toward self-authorship by building an internal foundation. Adults in this phase of self-authorship construct internal commitments or a framework for living life that is anchored by their internally defined values and beliefs about themselves and their relationships to knowledge and others. Internal foundations guide self-authoring people as they respond to reality.

Molly Pierson's description of her efforts to address the mismatch between her professional interests in residential life and the duties of her first full-time student affairs position as an honors program coordinator illustrates the challenge and process of building an internal foundation. Dissatisfied with the nature of her job one professional roles and responsibilities, Molly looked for a new position and took steps to make the best of her situation by shifting more of her energy to those tasks that most connected with her interests and goals. Molly took control of what she could as well as honored and enacted her internal voice.

DuJuan Smith learned to trust his internal voice early in life. His reflection on his job one experience offers numerous examples of the overt and subtle ways he articulated and enacted a personal philosophy of life informed by his internal voice. In describing his work as a judicial affairs officer, DuJuan recounted his commitment to enacting a humanistic perspective in the adjudication process, a paradigm congruent with his personal values but one at odds with traditional judicial affairs perspectives that all too often treat students who violate the conduct code as "bad people." In addition to adopting a philosophy of practice that reflected internally-derived principles of humanism and respect, DuJuan intentionally cultivated the value of self-care, engaging in numerous behaviors designed to help him separate his work and personal life.

> For me, the drive home was my relaxation time. I listened to music that calmed me or made phone calls to people I had been meaning to contact. When I ar-

rived at home, the first thing I did was change my clothes. It helped me to make the transition from one part of the day to the next. I rarely discussed work outside of the job. . . . Although I had my work email linked to my phone and occasionally checked for messages, I never addressed nonemergency emails when I was not at work. Most of this sounds simple, yet I was surprised how these small acts preserved my sanity. (p. 19)

Although student affairs faculty, supervisors, and new professionals often speak about the importance of establishing boundaries and practicing self-care, we have encountered few individuals who are as intentional as DuJuan with respect to living this principle. DuJuan trusts his internal voice to provide sound guidance and consistently engages in behaviors that reflect a coherent set of internal commitments—both hallmarks of self-authorship.

The third phase of the self-authorship journey, securing internal commitments, is characterized by a movement from understanding to enacting internal commitments in all dimensions of life (Baxter Magolda, 2008). As Baxter Magolda (2009) noted,

the commitments and foundations shifted from something being constructed to a solid home in which to live. . . . Being secure in these internal commitments left participants feeling less afraid of change, more open to deep relationships with others, and more open to continued personal growth. (p. 9)

Baxter Magolda suggested that adults traverse this segment of self-authorship during their thirties. We struggled to identify new professional narrative excerpts that might illustrate this phase of development. We did, however, recognize the hallmarks of securing internal commitments in Kathleen Gardner and Craig Woodsmall's reflections on the developmental journeys they traversed since contributing to the first edition of *Job One*. Continued personal and professional development beyond their first student affairs positions required risk, courage, and a willingness to embrace vulnerability. Fortunately, Kathleen and Craig provided good company for each other as they learned to trust their internal voices and make decisions that reflected their deep commitment to their relationship and to their continued personal growth.

Given the abbreviated nature of the personal stories shared in this book, it is impossible (and ill-advised) to assess and assign self-authorship developmental levels to each author. It is possible, however, to look across the chapters and identify a shared movement toward identifying and enacting an internal voice. At their core, the stories shared by the featured new professionals are stories of complexity, adult development, and journeys of self-authorship that are inevitably traversed as individuals confront the challenges of transitioning from full-time student to full-time professional.

The journey toward self-authorship is not a direct path. Baxter Magolda (2009) framed it as a cyclical and complex process, suggesting that individuals will likely circle back and renavigate segments of the journey as they find themselves exploring new contexts (e.g., professional, geographic), forging new relationships, and assuming new roles. The cyclical nature of self-authorship underscores the theme of timelessness we noted in our opening dialogue. Although we are fourteen years removed from our job ones, we continue to confront and navigate challenges similar to the ones described by the new professionals of *Job One 2.0* (e.g., relocating, new family and professional roles, building relationships, making tough decisions in the face of competing interests). We continue to find ourselves cycling through the elements of trusting our internal voices, building internal foundations, and securing internal commitments. Fortunately, Baxter Magolda and other self-authorship scholars have identified specific experiences and conditions that facilitate adult development.

Experiences that Promote Self-Authorship

In *Authoring Your Life*, Baxter Magolda (2009) identified three experiences that facilitate the development of self-authorship: pain, perspective, and support. Although individuals often seek to avoid pain in the interest of self-preservation, the cognitive dissonance associated with painful experiences provides a powerful impetus for questioning externally derived assumptions and formulating internally defined beliefs, identities, and relationships (Baxter Magolda, 2009). Engagement in reflective activities (e.g., talking with friends, journaling) and new experiences (e.g., professional responsibilities, traveling) allow individuals to gain a new perspective on their lives, one that recognizes the internal authority they possess for navigating painful experiences and taking actions congruent with their internal commitments. Although self-reflection is a key component of gaining perspective, Baxter Magolda (2001, 2002, 2009) did not describe the journey to self-authorship as a solo endeavor, but rather one that requires good company in the form of support from family members, significant others, friends, educators, supervisors, mentors, clergy, and/or therapists. Members of a support network promote self-authorship through the facilitation of conversations and experiences that help individuals listen to and enact their internal voices.

The self-authorship themes of pain, perspective, and support are prominent throughout the new professional narratives, underscoring the relevance of this framework for making meaning of the transition from graduate school to full-time student affairs employee. As mentioned in our preceding discussion of the complexities of adulthood, new student affairs professionals searching for and starting a full-time job encountered numerous painful experiences that prompt a reexamination of their beliefs, identities, and relationships.

To productively resolve the cognitive dissonance they experienced as a result of challenging externally imposed career expectations (DuJuan and Sarah), navigating a stressful job search (Craig), balancing personal and professional interests (Molly Pierson), building community in a new place (Kim and David), cultivating productive relationships with colleagues and supervisors (Carrie), and integrating and (re)negotiating multiple identities (Matt, Shamika, and Shiloh), the new professionals engaged in reflective activities (e.g., Craig's job search blog) and pursued new experiences (e.g., Carrie's qualitative graduate research seminar) that allowed them to develop a new, internally authored per-spective on their personal and professional lives. Although the scope of this chapter precludes us from providing an in-depth analysis of the diverse array of activities and experiences pursued by the new professionals in the interest of gaining new perspective on their pain, we call your attention to two intercon-nected approaches highlighted in several of the new professional narratives—adopting a learning orientation and actively engaging with identity.

Adopting a Learning Orientation in Job One

Contemporary dialogues on the mission of student affairs in higher educa-tion place student affairs professionals at the center of the student learning movement and identify the facilitation of transformational learning opportuni-ties, those that help individuals learn to "negotiate and act on [their] own pur-poses, values, feelings, and meanings rather than those [they] have uncritically assimilated" (Mezirow as quoted in Baxter Magolda, 2008, p. 270) to be an es-sential student affairs competency (ACPA & NASPA, 2010; Baxter Magolda, 2003; Benjamin & Hamrick, 2011; Keeling, 2004, 2006; Reason & Broido, 2011). Although a great deal of attention centers on helping student affairs pro-fessionals learn how to facilitate and assess meaningful, learning-centered pro-grams and services for participating students, comparatively little consideration has been given to strategies for facilitating the transformational learning of stu-dent affairs professionals, a problematic observation given Kolb and Yaganeh's (2012) assertion that "expertise at learning has become the key capability for survival, success, and fulfillment" (p. 2).

We concur with Kolb and Yaganeh's (2012) finding that the adoption of a learning orientation is an important means for new professionals to gain per-spective on their job transitions and the pain of adult development. As Renn and Jessup-Anger's (2008) study of new student affairs professionals revealed,

> whether it was dependent upon professional acculturation ("being a student af-fairs professional means never stop learning about the world of higher ed or the most recent group of incoming students") or a personal commitment to growth ("I fully wish to use my first year as a learning experience and to grow in my knowledge of the job") respondents who placed a high priority on learning from their experiences were likely to frame challenging experiences as oppor-tunities instead of setbacks. (p. 327)

Learning is an important storyline in the *Job One 2.0* narratives. Specifical-ly, tasked with making sense of new environments and (re)negotiating identities in unfamiliar contexts, several of the new professionals engaged in what Kolb and Yaganeh (2012) described as the learning way:

> The learning way is about approaching life experiences with a learning attitude. It involves a deep trust in one's own experience and a healthy skepticism about received knowledge. It requires the perspective of quiet reflection and a pas-sionate commitment to action in the face of uncertainty. (p. 2)

The preceding quote illuminates the inextricable connection between the adoption of a learning orientation and the development of self-authorship. Engagement in the learning way calls upon individuals to challenge received knowledge (i.e., external formulas) and value personal experience (i.e., internal voice) as a source of guidance in times of doubt and pain. David Stanfield's journey from the United States to Qatar is a particularly powerful example of the role learning plays in productively navigating the job one transition and cultivating self-authorship.

Having realized his dream of securing a student affairs position abroad, David confronted the challenge of living and working in a new cultural context, and he intentionally adopted a learning orientation as he attempted to settle into his new home.

> I approached my assimilation process like a class research project aimed at discovering a new culture. First, I spent time exploring my surroundings by identifying various artifacts and customs and attempting to interpret their meaning. I also sought to apply advice I heard repeatedly throughout graduate school: "Make the strange familiar and the familiar strange." (p. 61)

David juxtaposed his observations of familiar American restaurant chains and grocery items with unfamiliar cultural norms (e.g., Muslim prayer practices, strict guidelines regarding interactions between members of the opposite sex, and the significance of national identity). Active reflection on these cultural observations and lessons encouraged David to challenge implicit, externally imposed assumptions and listen instead to his emerging internal beliefs and knowledge regarding student identity development, the role of faith and religion in higher education, and the importance of context in professional practice.

David's commitment to the learning way also was evident in his approach to making sense of the high number of academic integrity cases he adjudicated. Questioning the assumption that the prevalence of plagiarism in Qatar was a function of a culture of academic dishonesty, David relied on insight gained from personal experience (i.e., student interactions) to reframe the problem and develop a research study that revealed significant cultural differences in academic integrity norms and practices.

David's story offers wise advice for all new student affairs professionals navigating the journey to self-authorship—assuming less and questioning more is a key step in taking responsibility and ownership for one's life (Baxter Magolda, 2009). The adoption of a learning way is not a solo venture. David described the excellent company he encountered along his journey, including students, colleagues, and a supervisor that encouraged David to trust his internal voice when confronted with new professional challenges. Although David's narrative is not the only story to exhibit the adoption of a learning orientation (Sarah Steward's and Carrie Miller's stories are equally compelling), we opted to provide an extended analysis of David's journey because it illustrates the three experiences that support self-authorship in job one: pain (disorientation in a new professional environment), perspective (reflection on experiences and professional practices), and support (good company).

Beyond the general observation that self-authoring individuals exhibit a learning orientation, Baxter Magolda (2003, 2008) and Jones (2009) shed specific insight on the importance role identity plays in shaping learning and the journey toward self-authorship. As Baxter Magolda (2003) asserted, recognizing the capacity of one's internal voice to construct knowledge and beliefs "requires acknowledging that one's identity is part of knowing" (p. 232). Accordingly, we now turn to the second strategy new professionals called upon to gain perspective on their job one transitions: engaging with their multiple identities.

Engaging With Identity on the Pathway Through Development.

While each new professional encountered learning tasks as they navigated new experiences and environments, they also further explored and defined their identities. Fried (2006) extended an elegant definition of identity, calling it "a process of individual consciousness in context, with an inner, relatively consistent set of core perspectives and beliefs and numerous external interactions with the social and physical environment that influence or shape identity in particular settings" (p. 5). Sometimes the interplay between the evolving sense of self and the encountered environmental demands and expectations challenged the new professionals. DuJuan described the low-income, urban environment where he grew up and how it shaped his life choices and professional practice. Craig connected with his identities as an introvert, an empathetic listener, and a writer to more capably navigate through his job search. Molly Pierson wrote about her identities as a partner, a colleague, and a friend and how they contributed to her personal and professional development. David reflected on being a global citizen, a Christian, an American, and an innovator. Sarah's journey was shaped by being a partner and a spiritual being. Kim considered how being a single, African American woman from the Midwest influenced her experience in San Francisco. Carrie conveyed the challenge of identifying as a scholar–practitioner in an environment where those identities were understood as discrete.

Will Simpkins discussed identity development issues raised by Shamika, Matt, and Shiloh. These Unit III stories presented complex individuals who define themselves as a family-oriented twin with a partner (Shamika), an athlete from Pennsylvania (Matt), and a servant-leader who is a champion for social justice (Shiloh). However, the primary social identities that anchor the narratives of Unit III's new professionals most clearly illustrate how actively engaging with identity can be productive in the process of developing self-authored lives.

Connections between identity development and development of self-authorship have been drawn by Baxter Magolda (2003), Pizzolato (2003, 2004, 2005), and Torres and Hernandez (2007). Pizzolato (2003) reimagined Piaget's concept of disequilibrium when she described the experience her high-risk student research subjects had when their conceptions of self were called into question by important others. Disequilibrium provides an opportunity for development when the individual reflects on the dissonance (or pain as it is understood in Baxter Magolda's work) and makes a choice to embrace the self-authored perspective. Pizzolato observed that disequilibrium is an opportunity for an individual to make a commitment to a new way of being, ultimately taking a further step in the journey toward self-authorship. Shamika, Matt, and Shiloh described feelings of discomfort and self-doubt related to significant social identities that could be characterized as disequilibrium.

Shamika reflected on an awkward conversation with a mother on student housing move-in day and on being the target of hateful speech on an earlier occasion.

> Did the parent disregard me as a professional because I looked young? Or was it because of the color of my skin? Working at a historically and predominantly White institution always keeps the latter question in the back of my mind. I am constantly reminded of my skin color, so it was not anything new as a new professional, although the racial slurs incident definitely heightened my sense of being African American in Oxford, Ohio. It made me more aware of this particular aspect of my identity and its influence on all of my experiences. (p. 124)

Although being conscious of her skin color was a familiar experience, the incident required Shamika to consider it in a new context as it intersected with her formation of identity as a student affairs professional. In fact, Shamika's initial conclusion drawn from her experience as a target of hate speech in Oxford, Ohio, was that she would not choose to stay in that environment. Shamika's peers also questioned the challenges associated with her transitioning to a professional role at Miami University. As she struggled with the decision, Shamika turned to reflection that led to a different conclusion altogether, determining that remaining at Miami provided her an opportunity to set an example for others by refusing to "run away" from hurtful speech and actions.

With new perspective on the Miami option, Shamika accepted a position there and worked to build on existing support systems to optimize her transition. As she reflected on her job one experience, Shamika observed,

> I must be able to go to bed every night knowing the decisions I made and interactions I had reflect my core values and embody who I truly am as a person. Being authentic is crucial for me to having a fulfilling and rich career. When I am genuine about who I am and what I believe, my values become evident. Sometimes it is hard to stay true to myself because I am pressured by those around me to change or fit in, but standing my ground in the midst of the pressure has benefitted me greatly. (p. 126).

Shamika articulated the cyclical process of reconciling her internal foundation with the reality of the challenges she encountered in her lived experience.

Jones (2009) observed that reflection on multiple social identities engages individuals in a constant negotiation with the environment that results in a more fluid experience of identity than might be experienced by individuals who do not identify with a marginalized population. Because this process of negotiating identity is regularly occurring for persons in marginalized groups, these individuals have an obvious hallmark they can use to process and engage their development. The unavoidable engagement with Shamika's identity as an African American and the intentional engagement with her identity as a new student affairs professional provided her with multiple reflection points in her ongoing developmental journey.

Christians are seldom considered a marginalized population in the United States, so Matt described his surprise at the reaction from some of his new graduate school colleagues as he proudly revealed his Christian identity. "I cannot identify any single factor that provoked this hostility, but it existed and it confused me." (p. 133). Rather than retreat from the challenge he experienced, Matt remained committed to embracing this element of his identity, seeking out support among his peers and others in the community, and ultimately finding an institution for job one that would align with his faith.

> In my time at Baylor, I am learning how to make the position my own—how to blend the requirements of my job description with my own passions, interests, and identity. I will not pretend that everything is perfect, but I have been able to be the most authentic self I have ever been. This experience, combined with my college and graduate school experiences, has made me a more holistic person, one who feels comfortable with the various dimensions of his identity, sharing those areas, and encouraging that development in others. (p. 136)

Matt's active reflection on his Christian identity as one of many integrated layers of identity provided him with a natural framework to address one of Baxter Magolda's (2001) driving questions in self-authorship development: Who am I? The process Matt underwent to answer that question led him to a more solid foundation from which he will perform his work with college students.

The social identities highlighted in Unit III offer explicit examples of new professionals engaging with their identities as they reflected on their experiences; however, each narrative referenced various identities, marginalized or otherwise, that were useful reflection points in the search for establishing oneself in job one. The extent to which new professionals access support while they actively engage with their various identities significantly influences their ability to successfully navigate new environments and gain confidence in their self-authored perspectives. We now consider what forms of support best serve the newest members of our profession as they face numerous professional and developmental challenges.

Being Good Company

A thoughtful construction of job one serves our collective interests as educators. Whenever we facilitate human development, we are infusing our organizations with professionals who have agency "to work in a proactive and collaborative manner with institutional partners to create . . . powerful learning environments" (Keeling, 2004, pp. 29-30). Individuals experience self-authorship development in ways that are as unique as they are, yet every individual will benefit from reflection, appropriate support, and intentionality during the sometimes difficult journey.

Baxter Magolda (2001, 2002, 2009) has written extensively on the conditions that promote self-authorship within others. Specifically, findings from her longitudinal study suggest three assumptions and three corresponding principles shared by the environments that provide the balance of challenge and support necessary for individuals to listen to, trust, and live out their internal voices. Each assumption and principle links to a dimension of holistic development (i.e., epistemological, intrapersonal, and interpersonal), building a foundation upon which a self-authoring individual may develop. Collectively, the six assumptions and principles contribute to the establishment of learning partnerships.

Within the dimension of epistemological development, Baxter Magolda (2002) encouraged learning partners to acknowledge that *knowledge is complex and socially constructed*, necessitating that individuals work through ambiguity and the lack of a single right answer or perspective. Closely associated with this assumption is the principle of valuing the knowledge and feelings of others, or what Baxter Magolda described as *validating the learners' capacity to know*. Within learning partnerships, supervisors, instructors, and others share their expertise while inviting employees, students, etc., to contribute their own insights and solutions, thereby supporting the capacity to wisely choose among multiple alternatives. This complex cognitive task is necessary for effectively authoring one's perspective and was evident in several of the new professional narratives. DuJuan reflected fondly on the learning partnership he forged with a supervisor who explicitly valued DuJuan's contribution to the organization despite his status as an entry-level professional. DuJuan benefitted tremendously from the company of supportive mentors, supervisors, and coworkers who trusted his professional judgment, providing DuJuan with meaningful opportunities to cultivate, listen to, and enact his internal voice.

The intrapersonal assumption that *self is central to knowledge construction* honors burgeoning internal voices. By explicitly encouraging people to place their values and identities in the context of their learning, work, and relationships (i.e., *situating learning in the learners' experience*), environments "modeled the intrapersonal growth, the internal sense of self, needed for self-authorship" (Baxter Magolda, 2002, p. 6). When enacting this dimension within learning partnerships, supervisors, instructors, and important others intentionally discuss how their identities and internal voices intersect with and shape the experience of transitioning into job one. In doing so, they support the developmental process that underlies the success of new professionals. Shamika described the insight and confidence she gained as a result of her engagement in learning activities that placed the self at the center of professional inquiry.

> The courses I took allowed me the opportunity to reflect on who I was as an individual and how that translates to my work in student affairs. By writing papers about my identity, values, and skills, I formulated who I was, what was important to me, and how that contributed to my abilities and confidence. As well, class discussions allowed me to further explore my development along-

side my classmates. These rich educational and developmental experiences were vital to my success and growing confidence. I am grateful that I learned this sooner rather than later as it helped me further formulate my professional identity. (p. 123)

Echoing the significance Shamika ascribed to the facilitation of learning activities that emphasize the exploration of self, Baxter Magolda (2002) contended, "The crucial role of the intrapersonal dimension for self-authorship requires that educators take up this dimension as a primary focus" (p. 8).

The interpersonal dimension of development is bolstered by the assumption that *authority and expertise are shared in the mutual construction of knowledge among peers.* When translated into an action-oriented principle, learning partners seek to *mutually construct meaning with others,* modeling the process of integrating multiple perspectives in the interest of developing "more complex understandings and decisions" (Baxter Magolda, 2002, p. 7). When supervisors, instructors, and others with more formal status in an organization frame relationships with junior colleagues as partnerships in which both parties are equally vital to developing solutions and making meaning in the environment, new professionals may access a greater confidence, allowing for more dynamic collaborations. Carrie called attention to the disappointment and tension that can arise when supervisory relationships do not meet expectations for a shared commitment to the mutual construction of knowledge. Socialized to value collaborative approaches to learning and professional development in graduate school, Carrie struggled to forge a productive relationship with a supervisor who did not seem to value Carrie's organizational contributions and her suggestions for improvement.

Although it might have been easy to blame her supervisor for their unproductive relationship, Carrie realized that she also played a role in their protracted struggle to find common ground. Enacting the commitment to mutually constructing meaning with others necessitates that all parties work to value the diverse perspectives and work styles of others. Although the supervisor's response to Carrie's suggestions for improvement certainly could have been offered in a more constructive manner, Carrie admitted that she too could have adopted a more respectful attitude toward her supervisor.

Enacting the assumptions and principles associated with Baxter Magolda's (2009) learning partnerships framework is a collaborative endeavor that requires the commitment and energy of those pursuing self-authorship (i.e., graduate students, new professionals) as well as their partners who seek to be good company along the journey (e.g., faculty, supervisors, mentors). Accordingly, we close this chapter with specific suggestions for cultivating self-authorship in entry-level student affairs professional positions.

CULTIVATING SELF-AUTHORSHIP IN JOB ONE

Informed by a heightened awareness of the developmental challenges confronting new student affairs professionals and a deeper understanding of the assumptions and principles that promote self-authorship, we offer specific suggestions and strategies for facilitating the student affairs job one transition—recommendations that target the four distinct audiences of *Job One 2.0*: professional preparation faculty, graduate students, new professionals, and their supervisors and mentors. Whatever your role in supporting the self-authorship development of new professionals (including yourself), you wield significant influence on that process and by extension on the growth and success of the student affairs profession.

Graduate Program Faculty

As a professional preparation faculty member, you share responsibility for ensuring that the next generation of student affairs professionals possesses the knowledge, competencies, and dispositions essential for promoting the holistic development and learning of college students. You also are called upon to provide new student affairs professionals with good company on their journey toward self-authorship. Several new professionals featured in this book acknowledged the significant cognitive, intrapersonal, and interpersonal development they experienced as graduate students, reflecting fondly on the powerful learning partnerships they forged with their program faculty, peers, and supervisors.

Cultivating self-authorship among graduate students necessitates the validation of students' capacities to know. One strategy for operationalizing this principle is to design experiential learning opportunities (e.g., internships, assistantships) and course assignments that emphasize the application of acquired knowledge and competencies in the resolution of complex professional problems. Case studies, problem-based learning assignments, and simulations provide students with meaningful vehicles to integrate multiple knowledge bases (e.g., student development, campus environments, professional ethics) and articulate relevant action plans, emulating the independent professional judgment expected of entry-level student affairs professionals. The thoughtful integration of active learning assignments throughout the curriculum fosters student self-confidence and increases trust in their internal voices to make sound professional decisions.

The inclusion of self-assessment exercises, reflective essays, and required professional engagement (e.g., webinars, professional association membership) while in graduate school facilitates the development of what Kolb and Yaganeh (2012) described as the learning way, an approach to professional practice that recognizes personal experience (and thus one's internal voice) as a legitimate source of knowledge. Stories penned by Sarah, Carrie, David, and Shamika illustrate the important role graduate studies play in fostering a learning orientation toward student affairs work. All four individuals thoughtfully described their efforts to draw upon the principles and practices of self-directed learning acquired in graduate school to make meaning of their new professional roles and environments.

Additionally, Sarah, Shamika, and Shiloh's narratives explicitly described the powerful insights derived from graduate coursework to situate learning in their personal experiences. Faculty encouraged these emerging new professionals to articulate their professional goals; explore the influence of multiple identities, values, and beliefs on their evolving professional practice; make meaning of their own developmental journeys; and challenge externally imposed formulas for career success. Of particular relevance to the job one transition process are faculty efforts to facilitate learning activities that assist students in the identification of their preferred work environments (e.g., institutional type, geographic location, organizational culture). Equipped with insight into their unique professional preferences, emerging student affairs professionals will be better able to assess their potential fit with particular higher education institutions. Fit plays an essential role in the transition experiences of new professionals (Magolda & Baxter Magolda, 2011; Renn & Hodges, 2007).

Student affairs graduate students will be well served by the intentional development of learning activities that help them recognize the importance of self in knowledge construction. Specific recommendations for assignments that emphasize self-reflection include journaling, blogging, self-assessment exercises, analyzing student affairs job descriptions, and cultural audits of experiential learning sites.

To help students recognize that authority and expertise are shared in the mutual construction of knowledge among peers, we invite you, graduate faculty members, to provide students with opportunities to engage in mutual construction of meaning with others. The *Job One 2.0* narratives coupled with findings from recent studies of new professional transition experiences (Cilente et al., 2007; Renn & Hodges, 2007; Renn & Jessup-Anger, 2008) highlight a specific dimension of mutual meaning making that has historically been problematic for graduate students transitioning into full-time employment: developing productive relationships with supervisors.

Team projects undoubtedly help emerging professionals recognize the presence and value of multiple perspectives; however, given peers (with equal positional power) typically comprise teams, group assignments rarely offer guidance on how to navigate the tensions that inevitably arise when supervisors and new professionals disagree or expectations are not met—two challenges confronted frequently in job one (Cilente et al., 2007; Magolda & Baxter Magolda, 2011; Renn & Hodges, 2007; Renn & Jessup-Anger, 2008). The goal is to help students develop realistic expectations for supervision and acquire the knowledge, competencies, and attitudes essential for mutually constructing meaning with those in formal positions of authority (e.g., active listening, respect for differences, capacity to read and navigate organizational politics, clear communication; Carducci, 2011; Meyerson, 2008). Specific strategies for addressing this topic include analysis of supervision case studies (Hamrick & Benjamin, 2009), engagement in supervision simulations and role play activities, and incorporation of experiential learning reflective exercises (e.g., internship blogs, journals, essays, peer debrief) challenging students to identify and articulate action plans for resolving supervision concerns encountered in their assistantships and practica.

Many of the challenges and tensions described by the new professionals featured in this book and recent scholarship on entry-level student affairs professionals (Cilente et al., 2007; Collins, 2009; Renn & Hodges, 2007; Renn & Jessup-Anger, 2008) center on the mismatch between professional expectations formed in graduate school and the lived reality of the job one search process and full-time employment. Indeed, frustration with unmet expectation emerged as a central theme in ACPA's 2007 study of new professional needs. Cilente and her colleagues (2007) observed, "In transitioning from graduate school to their new positions, new professionals indicated that they entered into their positions with unrealistic expectations that they would 'change the world and create wonderful theory-based programs that change the face of the college'" (p. 13).

Similar to the new professionals surveyed by ACPA, the job one transition stories written by Carrie, Molly Pierson, Craig, and Kim depict the angst and tension that can arise when expectations for a quick job search process, support from supervisors, the ability to initiate change, and the ease of transitioning to a new community are not met. Fortunately, their learning partnerships helped them recognize the value of their internal voices in navigating and resolving these common job one transition issues. Thus, in addition to helping graduate students cultivate the capacity to effectively respond to their new professional realities (a hallmark of the trusting one's internal voice phase of self-authorship), it is important to encourage emerging professionals to develop realistic expectations of professional roles, responsibilities and environments.

Graduate Students

Explicit in Baxter Magolda's (2009) learning partnerships model is the assumption that you, the student, should work with faculty, peers, and supervisors to cultivate the conditions that promote your own cognitive, intrapersonal, and interpersonal development. One step you can take to cultivate and trust your internal voice is to enact the assumption that knowledge is complex and socially constructed. This necessitates seeking out opportunities to move beyond comfortable and familiar learning environments in the interest of exploring diverse perspectives and contexts that are likely to foster a productive sense of disequilibrium and cognitive dissonance. Rather than quickly resolving this cognitive tension by soliciting the expertise and guidance of external authorities, you must grapple with the ambiguity inherent in new experiences and take responsibility for making meaning, thoughtfully reflecting on, questioning, and integrating new perspectives and bodies of knowledge you encounter. Although intentionally pursuing disequilibrium via study abroad opportunities, off-campus internships, new assistantship responsibilities, or volunteer efforts will no doubt increase your sense of vulnerability and foster self-doubt, productively navigating these challenges will strengthen your capacity to draw upon internal sources of knowledge in the development of cognitively complex and contextually relevant solutions to professional challenges. Shiloh's thoughtful reflections on the powerful insights she gleaned from her east coast summer internship and the intentionality with which she pursued new professional challenges as a second year master's student are wonderful examples of translating into action the assumption that knowledge is complex and socially constructed in the interest of assuming greater responsibility for one's own learning and development.

Shiloh, Shamika, Sarah, Kim, and Carrie discussed the value they derived in graduate school from placing their identities, values, interests, and experiences at the center of structured learning activities (enacting the assumption that self is central to knowledge construction). These new professionals found guided reflection on experiential learning endeavors, course papers that invited them to demonstrate knowledge of student development and identity theories through analysis of their own developmental journeys, and student-centered advising relationships to be powerful vehicles for helping them listen to, cultivate, and trust their internal voices. From your graduate student perspective, the goal is to engage in authentic and learning-oriented forms of self-reflection that facilitate reliance on insights gleaned from candid examinations of your values, beliefs, and behaviors to inform future decisions. Craig's job search blog and graduate school academic assignments helped him identify his professional passions, strengths, and goals, and critically examine the limitations of his past job search strategies. Progressing beyond superficial forms of reflection requires honesty and a willingness to work on those areas in need of further growth and development.

Student affairs professional preparation programs often exhibit a strong commitment to enacting the third learning partnerships assumption—authority and expertise are shared in the mutual construction of knowledge among peers—through group project assignments and shared responsibility for leading seminar discussions. Although we recognize that group projects can be time-consuming and frustrating when teammates fail to meet expectations, they are also an important means of developing the ability to work interdependently and provide wonderful opportunities to cultivate good company on the journey to self-authorship. Accordingly, our graduate student recommendations for enacting this dimension of the learning partnership framework center on making the most of collaborative learning opportunities. Specifically, we encourage you, the student, to recognize the powerful learning potential of team projects and use them as safe spaces to practice and sharpen competencies you will be called upon to exhibit as a full-time professional (e.g., negotiation, compromise, providing feedback). Guided by the heightened self-awareness generated as a result of authentically reflecting on your behavior in groups, we urge you to practice, not avoid, negotiating the tensions often encountered in efforts to mutually construct meaning (e.g., addressing differences of opinion and holding classmates accountable).

Enacting a commitment to the mutual construction of knowledge also necessitates that you identify individuals who can offer you good company on the journey toward the world of full-time work. DuJuan, Molly Pierson, Carrie, Shiloh, and Shamika discussed the powerful role faculty, supervisors, family members, peers, and mentors played in helping them cultivate and trust their internal voice as they formulated professional goals, embarked upon the job search process, and forged new professional identities. Although we certainly hope that faculty, peers, and graduate assistantship supervisors are sources of support, we encourage you to cultivate a diverse and broad network who can offer new perspectives. Transitioning from the role of full-time student to full-time professional is an exciting and anxiety-producing journey—one that you should not travel alone.

New Professionals

Our recommendations for you, the new professional, begin with a reminder about the responsibility that you have for your own experience. We have made a case for graduate preparation faculty and seasoned student affairs professionals to be intentional about fostering the self-authorship development of new professionals; however, the fact remains you are primarily responsible for the ongoing process of defining your belief system, your identity, and your social relationships in a way that is coherent with the commitments you have embraced for yourself (Baxter Magolda, 2009).

Shifting away from a formal student role leaves you, the new professional, with the responsibility for processing your own learning experiences. If you know that you learn best in conversation with others, as Molly Pierson described, it is essential that you identify people with whom you can share insights and gain perspective. If solitary reflection is your preference, we recommend that you determine how to build that practice into your professional life. Blogging, journaling, or even writing an article for publication could be useful methods to monitor your experiences as a learner. The narratives from Carrie, David, and Sarah as well as the findings of Renn and Jessup-Anger (2008) underscore the value of building on the learning identity that you have keenly honed over the many years of being a student.

In the early days of job one, it may be wise for you to listen more and seek the answers that more experienced professionals can provide while taking care to balance those answers with your own insights. In doing so, you acknowledge that knowledge is complex and socially constructed. Frame consultations with a supervisor or other supporters as an invitation to exchange ideas rather than a request for their version of the "right answer." Recall the examples of Carrie, Sarah, and Shamika, who worked through opinions and perspectives of others to reach the best conclusions for themselves.

Are there elements of identity that will shape or heavily influence your work? Monitor the values that guide your choices. Reflection and awareness of your inner dialogue are critically important to actively placing yourself at the center of knowledge construction. Craig, Matt, and Shiloh provided diverse examples of how intentional reflection on identities and values guided them to work environments that truly fit.

Working to get to know your new supervisor and colleagues as you begin job one is sage advice. Identify your expectations for these new relationships and share them to determine how your expectations intersect with the needs and wants of your colleagues. Reflect on the relationships and structures that have been particularly helpful and consider how to incorporate any elements of those relationships or structures in your new setting. We encourage you to intentionally maintain relationships you have already cultivated, as you will undoubtedly need support and perspective outside of your new environment. Stories written by Kim and Molly Pierson are particularly good examples of the value of building and maintaining relationships in and out of the workplace.

As you settle into your new position, it is prudent to pay attention to how decisions are made and how new initiatives are successfully implemented. Who participates in strategizing and problem solving? If your organization has not made the commitment of sharing authority and expertise with new professionals, you are not necessarily left without the opportunity to mutually construct meaning. One strategy is to develop mechanisms by which to share authority and expertise within your own sphere of influence, which can further your development as well as the development of other professionals you include in your work. When authority and expertise are shared in the mutual construction of knowledge among peers, individuals and organizations become more capable of facilitating student development. DuJuan and David both illuminated the powerful results for students when new professionals engage in dynamic collaborations with co-workers.

Supervisors, Mentors, and Seasoned Professionals

The opportunity supervisors, mentors, and seasoned professionals have to effect positive change via interactions with new professionals cannot be overstated. New professionals bring a number of assumptions, fears, and hopes to job one. You can validate their capacity to know by discussing with them their beliefs and concerns and sharing insights about transitions into job one and the profession. You, the seasoned professional, can offer multiple perspectives on campus culture, functional areas, and student affairs practice and invite new professionals to talk about how they are making sense of this information and what conclusions and questions are emerging from the process. We encourage you to incorporate reflective activities during training and at regular intervals thereafter. The example of Shiloh's summer internship supervisor demonstrates how one can engage someone new to the profession in the onboarding process.

In your role as a supervisor, mentor, or supportive seasoned professional, you can situate learning by inviting new professionals to actively engage in reflection on how who they are affects and is affected by what they do. Consider sharing how you balance your own dimensions of self to create a safe space and inviting new professionals to do the same.

Perhaps the most obvious way to demonstrate the value you place on new professionals' perspectives is to include them in complex decision-making. When you include new professionals in planning committees and task forces, discuss with them the implications of a new trend in the field, or talk with them about the relationships that are influencing their transitions, you mutually construct meaning with them. In David's story, we learned how his supervisor supported David's observation and proposal for further research and how David and other colleagues together reached new conclusions about their students' knowledge gaps that improved their practice and that bolstered David's self-authorship development.

New professionals often have very particular expectations for their supervisory relationships (Renn & Jessup-Anger, 2008). We invite you—whether a supervisor, mentor, or supportive seasoned professional—to have conversations about expectations and relationships. Be frank about your own limitations regarding mentorship and consider helping the new professional identify someone who can offer the desired support (e.g., a former supervisor or instructor, another seasoned professional on campus, a connection made through a professional association). Most new professionals encounter sufficient challenge to spur development. The goal for you is to identify the support that is in place for them. Individuals and organizations must commit to being good company.

EPILOGUE

Rozana: Congratulations on your new job, Diana! I am sure you are relieved to bring your job four search (and this writing project) to a close. To what extent or in what ways do you think the themes and lessons we explored in this chapter influenced the latest phase of your professional journey?

Diana: It was a relief not only to close my job search but also to discover an unexpected environment with which I am delighted. Perhaps you remember what I said back in our graduate school days that residence life was fine as a graduate assistantship, but that I would never do it professionally. I am working at a small art school here in Portland, significantly expanding the residence life program with our first dedicated student housing facility opening in less than a year.

Rozana: Residence life! I can't believe it.

Diana: How I ended up here is a story in itself, but I will give you the highlights. As I considered applying for this opportunity, I had reached the stage in my job search where I felt the need to reevaluate my self-imposed job parameters. When I reflected upon what had brought me the most satisfaction at work, I realized that what mattered most to me were the people with whom I would work, the opportunity to grow my skillset, and the ability to take ownership over my work. I knew that I would not be able to truly assess those things by merely reading job titles and position descriptions, so I applied to this position and a few others that did not appear on the surface to be a "logical" next step for my career but that I determined had potential to meet my new list of "must haves."

Much like the new professionals featured in this book, I sought a great fit and reflected upon my values to find it. I also fortified myself for what could be a big risk by leaning on my partner and the perspectives of trusted friends. Less money, a less prestigious title, and fewer resources do not look like the equation for career satisfaction, but I used the interview process to see if I would get what most matters to me. I am pleased to report that I have wise, supportive colleagues, and the students are introspective and creative. I am learning about my new functional area and about myself each day. And talk about ownership—I'm on a really small campus, and I am it for professional residence life staff! A learning orientation has been key in my first few months in job four. It has provided me with a familiar role in my new setting, and it has also helped me to keep at bay any impatience I have with myself. I have a lot to learn, and that is expected and normal even with all of my experience. It is exciting, challenging, and at times overwhelming. Does that sound anything like your experience in your first faculty position?

Rozana: I am so pleased that you found a job that challenges and excites you. Although I did find the process of writing this chapter to be helpful with respect to reminding me I need to attend to my own self-authorship development as I embark upon my relatively new career as a faculty member, I think the most powerful lessons I will take away from this project relate to my role as good company for graduate students preparing to assume their first full-time job.

Diana: What does being good company look like for you?

Rozana: I regularly teach the student affairs administration seminar, a course that provides both a broad introduction to the student affairs profession as well as a more detailed review of key administrative knowledge bases (e.g., professional standards, supervision, crisis management). I try to cover a tremendous amount of content in 15 weeks in the interest of ensuring that students acquire the professional knowledge they need to succeed in entry-level student affairs positions. I have always espoused a commitment to Baxter Magolda's learning partnership principles and described them as the foundation of my teaching philosophy, but reading the *Job One 2.0* new professional narratives and revisiting the literature of self-authorship has made me question whether my preoccupation with curricular content and students' knowledge acquisition is undermining my commitment to the pedagogical process of forming learning partnerships.

In the process of writing this chapter, I frequently found myself asking, "To what extent am I enacting the assumptions and principles that support students' self-authorship development? How am I situating learning in the students' experience? In what way do my class sessions and seminar assignments validate students as knowers and support the mutual construction of knowledge?" Yes I incorporate self-reflective activities and team projects in all my classes, but am I really providing students with the kind of company they need to successfully transition to the world of full-time work?

I need to take my own advice and adopt a more intentional approach to creating classroom conditions and advising relationships that foster self-directed learning, the capacity to negotiate ambiguity, and trust in internal sources of knowledge. I am not saying that I plan to abandon my focus on helping students acquire and apply essential professional knowledge; it is important that new professionals demonstrate the ability to articulate the field's foundational principles and describe the significance of key moments in higher education history. Co-authoring this chapter has helped me realize that I play an important role in supporting the self-authorship development of graduate students, and the fulfillment of this responsibility necessitates that I spend equal, if not more, time attuned to the process as opposed to the content of student learning. I have already begun to reflect on ways I can revise and reimagine the student affairs administration seminar to reflect this renewed commitment to fostering self-authorship. It is a daunting but exciting challenge.

Diana: Your commitment is inspiring! I offer my company to you as you face that challenge. Our journey has already had significant twists and turns since we met a long time ago. I trust that we both will continue to benefit from the support and perspective we offer each other as we continue on our respective paths.

REFERENCES

ACPA–College Student Educators International & NASPA–Student Affairs Administrators in Higher Education. (2010). *Professional competency areas for student affairs practitioners.* Washington, DC: Authors.

Baxter Magolda, M. B. (1992). *Knowing and reasoning in college: Gender-related patterns in students' intellectual development.* San Francisco, CA: Jossey-Bass.

Baxter Magolda, M. B. (2001). *Making their own way: Narratives for transforming higher education to promote self-development.* Sterling, VA: Stylus.

Baxter Magolda, M. B. (2002). Helping students make their way to adulthood. *About Campus, 6*(6), 2-9.

Baxter Magolda, M. B. (2003). Identity and learning: Student affairs' role in transforming higher education. *Journal of College Student Development, 44,* 231-247.

Baxter Magolda, M. B. (2007). Self-authorship: The foundation for twenty-first century education. In P. S. Meszaros (Ed.), *Self-authorship: Advancing students' intellectual growth: New Directions for Teaching and Learning. No. 109* (pp. 69-83). San Francisco, CA: Jossey-Bass.

Baxter Magolda, M. B. (2008). Three elements of self-authorship. *Journal of College Student Development, 49,* 269-284.

Baxter Magolda, M. B. (2009). *Authoring your life: Developing an internal voice to navigate life's challenges.* Sterling, VA: Stylus.

Benjamin, M., & Hamrick, F. A. (2011). Expanding the learning environment. In P. M. Magolda & M. B. Baxter Magolda (Eds.), *Contested issues in student affairs: Diverse perspectives and respectful dialogue* (pp. 23-34). Sterling, VA: Stylus.

Carducci, R. (2011). Tempered radicals: Managing risks in negotiating differences. In P. M. Magolda & M. B. Baxter Magolda (Eds.), *Contested issues in student affairs: Diverse perspectives and respectful dialogue* (pp. 466-471). Sterling, VA: Stylus.

Cilente, K., Henning, G., Skinner, J., Kennedy, D., & Sloane, T. (2007). *Report on the new professional needs study.* Washington, DC: ACPA–College Student Educators International.

Collins, D. (2009). The socialization process for new professionals entering student affairs work. In A. Tull, J. B. Hirt, & S. Saunders (Eds.), *Becoming socialized in student affairs administration: A guide for new professionals and their supervisors* (pp. 3-27). Sterling, VA: Stylus.

Fried, J. (2006). Rethinking learning. In R. P Keeling (Ed.), *Learning reconsidered 2: A practical guide to implementing a campuswide focus on the student experiences* (pp. 3-9). Washington, DC: ACPA, ACUHO-I, ACUI, NACA, NACADA, NASPA, and NIRSA.

Hamrick, F. A., & Benjamin, M. (2009). *Maybe I should . . . Case studies on ethics for student affairs professionals.* Lanham, MD: ACPA/University Press of America.

Jones, S. R. (2009). Constructing identities at the intersections: An autoethnographic exploration of multiple dimensions of identity. *Journal of College Student Development, 50,* 287-304.

Keeling, R. P. (Ed.). (2004). *Learning reconsidered: A campus-wide focus on the student experience.* Washington, DC: NASPA and ACPA.

Keeling, R. P. (Ed.). (2006). *Learning reconsidered 2: A practical guide to implementing a campuswide focus on the student experiences.* Washington, D.C.: ACPA, ACUHO-I, ACUI, NACA, NACADA, NASPA, and NIRSA.

Kolb, D., & Yaganeh, B. (2011, September 13). *Deliberate experiential learning: Mastering the art of learning from experience* (WP-11-02). Cleveland, OH: Case Western Reserve University, Weatherhead School of Management. Retrieved from http://weatherhead.case.edu/departments/organizational-behavior/workingPapers/WP-11-02.pdf.

Magolda P. M., & Baxter Magolda, M. B. (2011). Engaging in dialogues about difference in the workplace. In P. M. Magolda & M. B. Baxter Magolda (Eds.), *Contested issues in student affairs: Diverse perspectives and respectful dialogue* (pp. 453-465). Sterling, VA: Stylus.

Meyerson. D. E. (2008). *Rocking the boat: How to effect change without making trouble.* Boston, MA: Harvard Business Press.

Pizzolato, J. E. (2003). Developing self-authorship: Exploring the experiences of high-risk college students. *Journal of College Student Development, 44,* 797-812.

Pizzolato, J. E. (2004). Coping with conflict: Self-authorship, coping, and adaptation to college in first-year, high-risk students. *Journal of College Student Development, 45,* 425-442.

Pizzolato, J. E. (2005). Creating crossroads for self-authorship: Investigating the provocative moment. *Journal of College Student Development, 46,* 624-641.

Reason, R. D., & Broido, E. M. (2011). Philosophies and values. In J. H. Schuh, S. R. Jones, & S. R. Harper (Eds.). *Student services: A handbook for the profession* (5th ed.; pp. 80-95). San Francisco, CA: Jossey-Bass.

Renn, K. A., & Hodges, J. (2007). The first year on the job: Experiences of new professionals in student affairs. *Journal of Student Affairs Research and Practice, 44,* 604-628.

Renn, K. A. & Jessup-Anger, E. R. (2008). Preparing new professionals: Lessons for graduate preparation programs from the National Study of New Professionals in Student Affairs. *Journal of College Student Development, 49,* 319-335.

Torres, V., & Hernandez, E. (2007). The influence of ethnic identity development on self-authorship: A longitudinal study of Latino/a college students. *Journal of College Student Development, 48,* 558-73.

Tull, A., Hirt, J. B., & Saunders, S. A. (2009). Conclusions and recommendations. In A. Tull, J. B. Hirt, & S. A. Saunders (Eds.), *Becoming socialized in student affairs administration: A guide for new professionals and their supervisors* (pp. 217-232). Sterling, VA: Stylus.

Appendix

Moving into Job One: Resources and Recommendations

Stephanie N. Kurtzman and Jen-Chien Yu

This appendix includes practical online resources compiled by young professionals. For many student affairs professionals, the transition to job one involves a move to a new city, region, and/or institution. Your level of satisfaction and comfort with that transition will influence your performance at work, making it important that you attend to all aspects of your transition and not solely the job search.

Looking Out

Online Resources

Looking out to the "real world," searching for new job opportunities, and anticipating the first real paycheck can be exciting. However, a job title and salary, no matter how compelling they feel to you, should not be your only considerations. Does the institution offer competitive pay? How does the cost of living compare in the state/city/community you are considering? And taxes—how much would you be paying for sales tax, income tax, and possibly personal property tax?

When you evaluate a job opportunity, we recommend you consult some data sources that provide updated, non-biased overviews relevant to the profession, institution, or community you are considering.

College Navigator (http://nces.ed.gov/collegenavigator/) is a free tool that the National Center for Education Statistics developed to help students locate information about colleges and universities. College Navigator summarizes statistics that each college or university reports to the government and provides easy-to-use information to the public. For example, as a student affairs professional, you can find the demographic profile of a university's student body. You can research how an institution's profile has evolved over the years and gain insights about the challenges you might encounter.

American FactFinder (http://factfinder2.census.gov) is a web portal to data compiled by the Census Bureau. You can easily find community facts about a neighborhood and even the specific block where you might live. If you find an ad on Craigslist about someone subletting an apartment, you can determine whether it is in the middle of undergraduate housing complexes. On the American FactFinder website, you can enter an address and find demographic profiles (e.g., age group and education attainment). You also can access socioeconomic characteristics such as housing (e.g., number of home owners vs. renters) and commuting patterns (e.g., percentage of people travel to work by public transportation).

Higher Education Salary (http://www.higheredjobs.com/salary) is a website that provides the average salary for a higher education position (e.g., academic advisor/counselor, residence hall manager) by institution type (e.g., doctoral, master's, baccalaureate, and two-year). The law requires that public institutions make public all institutional information, including salary. Some institutions have salary information available in print, in which case you would need to contact human resources or institutional research to learn how to access it. Some state authorities or non-profit organizations post salary information online. For example, the State Treasurer of Ohio sponsors the Higher Education Salary website (http://www.tos.ohio.gov/higher_education_salary).

Cost of Living Calculator (http://money.cnn.com/calculator/pf/cost-of-living) allows you to compare salary and cost of living in two different cities. It may be helpful to compare the cost of living between your current city and the city you are considering to better prepare for the transition. Look closely at the source of the data to ascertain how frequently the website is updated.

A list of taxes by state is available from the Federation of Tax Administrators—State Comparisons http://www.taxadmin.org/fta/rate/tax_stru.html). In addition to learning about taxes and planning for them, you can use this tool to learn about tax breaks or incentives. For example, some states offer "sales tax holidays."

Occupational Outlook Handbook (http://www.bls.gov/ooh) published by the Bureau of Labor Statistics (BLS) provides historical, current, and future trend data for different occupation groups. This site answers questions such as "How many postsecondary professionals currently work in an area?" and "What is the projected employment growth rate in 10 years?" You can explore BLS data by subject (e.g., employment/unemployment, inflation) or geographic area.

Additional "Looking Out" Resources and Considerations

Local Organizations and Resources to Investigate

- Chamber of Commerce
- Visitors Bureau
- School district office
- Event calendars and guides
- Entertainment newspapers
- Publications for families & children
- City hall (for laws and ordinances)
- Weather & seasonal allergy information

Cost of Living Considerations

- Apartment rental prices
- Real estate prices
- Grocery prices
- Gas prices
- Public transit availability and cost
- Commuting distance
- City and state taxes
- Personal property tax (in some states)
- Child care rates
- Private school tuition

Institutional Considerations

- Financial health of the state and the institution
- Implications for the type of institution (e.g., religious, public, private, small, large)
- Opportunities for career advancement
- Institutional structure, politics, culture
- Number of new employees in the department or division
- Results from institutional surveys

Benefits Considerations

- Time off policies
- Approval for a vacation planned prior to your hire
- Support for moving expenses

- Dual career job search support
- Child care resources
- Health insurance options and what the provider defines as "in network" or "out of network"
- Domestic partner benefits
- Retirement plan options and institutional contribution policies
- Life insurance
- Tuition support for you and/or family members
- Support for professional development (e.g., training/travel funds, time off, institutional programs)
- Access to athletic facilities for personal use
- Staff discounts with local service providers (e.g., cell phone companies)
- Staff discounts on tickets (e.g., athletics, performing arts)
- Meal plans (as a benefit or as an option to purchase)
- Housing options and/or subsidies

Questions to Ask Your Potential Employer During Your Interview

- Will the on-campus interview process include campus and community tours?
- Will the on-campus interview schedule be extended an additional day (at your expense) to explore the local community?
- Is there a guidebook that includes information about local resources such as banks, hair stylists, and doctors?

Questions to Ask Yourself Before and After the Interview

- What are your needs, obligations, or preferences that might influence your decision-making?
- What are your "deal-breakers" that would make you decline a position?
- Who are your "lifeline" mentors with whom you can consult about difficult situations?

Practical Tips

- Seek guidance on negotiation skills and how to ask for what you need from potential employers.
- Pay attention to time zones for phone and Skype interviews.
- Dismiss phone calls if you are not in the right frame of mind to answer.
- Use a landline for phone interviews.
- Communicate regularly with your references.
- Advocate for yourself if you have special needs (e.g., dietary, mobility, lodging).

- Pack a snack in case you are hungry or could not eat enough during an interview over a meal.

MOVING IN

Moving in! Even if you are taking a job in a familiar community, your needs, interests, and questions may be different as you consider life through the lens of a full-time professional.

In a new location, you might not be able to secure Internet access immediately in your new home, so it is a good idea to load some mobile apps on your smartphone. GPS devices can help you navigate. Mobile real estate apps can help you with house/apartment hunting. Wi-Fi finder apps can help you find free Wi-Fi while on the road.

Online Resources

Mobile apps such as *Padmapper* (https://www.padmapper.com/) put rental properties on a map and let you filter for price range and features. Websites such as *Trulia* (http://www.trulia.com) let you create email alerts whenever a property meeting your search criteria becomes available. If you are looking for the perfect place to rent or buy, you might be driving a lot and could benefit from gas price comparison mobile apps such as *GasBuddy* (http://www.gasbuddy.com).

CrimeReports (http://www.crimereports.com) is an important resource to consult before you decide where to live. On CrimeReports, you can see real-time criminal activities and registered sex offenders in the proximity of the location where you are considering moving. Another resource you might want to keep in mind is the *National Sex Offender Public Website* by the U.S. Department of Justice (http://www.nsopw.gov).

In the digital age, everyone can use Google and find information on the web. Nevertheless, how do you search when you do not know what you are looking for? How can you find what is available in a community using only one search? With community-focused web services such as *Craigslist* (http://www.craigslist.com), *Yahoo! Local* (http://local.yahoo.com) and *Patch.com* (http://www.patch.com), you can find information such as news, businesses, events, and classified ads for communities of all sizes, even those so small that they do not have a newspaper.

Additional "Moving In" Resources

Checklist for Moving to a New Community

- Register vehicle.
- Secure local driver's license.
- Notify car insurer about new address or change insurance.

- Explore options for apartment rental insurance or homeowner's insurance.
- Register to vote.
- Select a bank. (Complete this task before you begin work so that you can set up direct deposit.)
- Submit forwarding mail and change of address notifications to post office.
- Secure temporary storage space if needed.
- Notify family, friends and colleagues with your new contact information.

Housing Considerations

- Commuter/traffic patterns
- Public transit
- Biking/walking options
- Parking on campus— availability and cost
- Roommate(s)

Travel Considerations

- Calculate distance to local airports, train stations, or bus stations.
- Identify airlines that serve the local airport.
- Investigate the frequency of flights to locations that matter to you.
- Investigate availability of direct flights.

Questions to Ask Employer Regarding Moving In

- Is there a moving company affiliated with the university? Does the university offer a moving allowance?
- Is there a bank/credit union on campus?
- Does the university provide temporary housing for new employees?

SETTLING IN

"Have you settled in?" You may find yourself routinely answering this question, and asking it of yourself. Unlike the Looking Out and the Moving In phases, it is difficult to define an end date for the Settling In phase. Many dimensions add complexity to this phase. Settling in to your work, personal life and local community are not likely to happen all at once.

Online Resources

One benefit of working at a college or university is that you are part of a vibrant and intellectually stimulating community. Regardless of your religion, ethnic background, sexual orientation, gender identity, gender expression, political affiliation, or lifestyle, a college or university community often has something for everyone. The challenge is discovering meaningful programs and resources. Make sure to take advantage of social media such as blogs, Facebook, and Twitter—not only to stay connected with old friends and family but also to explore the new community. Try searching for hashtags for the community you are moving to such as #CITY NAME (e.g. #Chambana or #stlouis) and find out what is trending in your community. Different organizations such as student affairs professional associations and local political groups maintain Facebook pages or Twitter accounts to share news and events within the community as well. For example, @ACPA tweets about student affairs job openings and professional development opportunities. ACPA also provides a list of various higher education professional associations at (http://www2.myacpa.org/resources3/professional-associations).

To settle into your work, you will need to actively research the culture and climate at your institution. The *Chronicle of Higher Education* website (http://www.chronicle.com) is a great place to start learning about current trends and issues in higher education. In addition, you can find data about students, faculty, and financial situation by state or by institution type in the *Facts & Figures* section (http://chronicle.com/section/Facts-Figures/58/). Your institution might also conduct assessment projects such as online/paper surveys and focus groups to gather data about different aspects of campus life and compile reports to the public. Some institutions administer the *National Survey of Student Engagement* (NSSE; http://nsse.iub.edu) or the *Faculty Survey of Student Engagement* (FSSE; http://fsse.iub.edu) to assess student engagement, and some institutions that are working on improving the first-year experience might conduct surveys such as the *CIRP Freshman Survey* or *Your First College Year* (YFCY) survey (http://www.heri.ucla.edu). Some institutions administer climate surveys they either developed themselves or that were developed by higher education consulting services in order to examine the level of inclusivity and diversity on campus. As a new student affairs professional, these data will help you better understand your students, their perceptions and behaviors, and challenges that may lie ahead.

Additional "Settling In" Resources

Assessing Climate and Resources Available to Identity-based Communities

- Call local organizations and ask for their assessment of the local climate for identity-based communities.
- Identify chambers of commerce that serve specific cultural/ethnic communities.
- Research the local climate on http://www.tolerance.org or http://www.hrc.org/states.

- Explore churches, synagogues, mosques, and other places of worship.
- Visit culturally specific grocery stores.
- Contact Immigration/naturalization services.
- Gather data about local hate crimes and sex offenders.

Social/Cultural/Recreational Resources

- Alumni chapter of your alma mater
- Alumni chapter of Greek-letter organizations
- Young professional groups and boards
- Local non-profit organizations
- Local chapters of national non-profit organizations
- Ethnic/cultural groups
- Religious organizations
- Sports leagues
- Gyms/fitness classes
- Lifelong learning classes

Given the many considerations involved with your transition to job one, it may take some time for all of the pieces to fall into place. Don't give up! Many people at your new institution and in your local community are available to assist and support you; in time, you just may be the one offering wisdom to someone who joins the community after you.

Author Index

Contributors

CRAIG R. BERGER

Craig Berger is Coordinator of Student Life for Campus and Civic Engagement at the University of Maryland, Baltimore County. Craig completed his M.S. in student affairs in higher education at Miami University in 2011. Before his graduate studies, Craig worked as Residence Life Coordinator at Penn State Erie, The Behrend College in Erie, Pennsylvania. He earned his B.A. in political science in 2006 from Allegheny College in Meadville, Pennsylvania. Craig's professional interests include civic engagement, student government, social media in higher education, and campus culture.

ROZANA CARDUCCI

Since the publication of *Job One*, Rozana Carducci left her student affairs administrative position to pursue a doctoral degree in Higher Education and Organizational Change at UCLA. During her graduate studies, she worked as a research assistant in the Community College Studies program and Student Affairs Information and Research Office. Rozana is currently a faculty member in the Higher Education in Student Affairs program at Salem State University.

JILL E. CARNAGHI

Jill Carnaghi has been at Washington University in St. Louis since 1997 and currently serves as an Associate Vice Chancellor for Students and Dean of Campus Life. Prior to Washington University, Jill worked in housing and residence life—from a graduate resident advisor at Michigan State to assistant director at the University of California, Davis, to Director of Residential Life at the University of Vermont. She has degrees from Purdue, Michigan State, and Indiana. Jill has been involved in professional associations, including serving as 203president of the American College Personnel Association (ACPA) and treasurer of the ACPA Educational Leadership Foundation.

KATHLEEN GARDNER

Kathleen Gardner has served as the Associate Director for Residence Life at Southern Illinois University Edwardsville since 2005. She has worked in student affairs for 15 years and previously held positions at Washington University in

St. Louis, the University of Maryland, and the Illinois Institute of Technology. Kathleen's ACPA leadership experience includes Chair of the Commission for Housing and Residential Life, Co-chair of the Presidential Task Force on Sustainability, and faculty member for the Residential Curriculum Institute. She received her M.Ed. in college student personnel and her B.A. in journalism from the University of Maryland, College Park.

MOLLY REAS HALL

Molly Reas Hall is a doctoral candidate in educational research and evaluation at Virginia Tech. Before returning to school, she worked in student affairs positions at Radford University, Tufts University School of Medicine, and Santa Clara University and as a program officer at a statewide education foundation. She holds a master's degree in college student personnel and a bachelor's degree in psychology and sociology.

DIANA JARAMILLO

Diana Jaramillo returned to Los Angeles and her undergraduate alma mater, University of Southern California, for jobs two and three. After four years as a career counselor and eight in academic advising, Diana now works at Pacific Northwest College of Art in Portland, Oregon, managing residence life and student activities.

CHRISTANA J. JOHNSON

Christana J. Johnson is the Assistant Vice President for Student Affairs for Student Success at Shepherd University in West Virginia. Prior to her tenure at Shepherd, she was Assistant Dean of Students/Director of Intercultural Life at Cornell College in Iowa. Chris also is pursuing her doctorate at Colorado State University in college and university leadership. Her dissertation centers on civic engagement, service learning, and multicultural education.

SHAMIKA N. JOHNSON

Shamika (Mika) Johnson is the Assistant Director of New Student Programs at Miami University. She received her M.S. in student affairs in higher education from Miami University and her B.A. in history from Bowling Green State University.

STEPHANIE N. KURTZMAN

Stephanie Kurtzman serves as Director of the Community Service Office and Associate Director of the Gephardt Institute for Public Service at Washington University in St. Louis, where she has been since 1998 and where she built the Community Service Office. She received her M.Ed. in higher education and student affairs administration from the University of Vermont in 1998 and her B.A. in psychology from Occidental College in 1995.

MATTHEW KWIATKOWSKI

Matt Kwiatkowski joined Baylor University as a Residence Hall Director in July 2010. His current work with living-learning communities allows him to intersect with leadership development, civic engagement, and service learning, through instruction of first-year courses. He received his M.S. in student affairs in higher education from Miami University and his B.S. in secondary education-social studies from Slippery Rock University.

PETER M. MAGOLDA

Peter M. Magolda is a professor in Miami University's Student Affairs in Higher Education program. He teaches educational anthropology and research seminars, and his scholarship focuses on ethnographic studies of college students and critical issues in qualitative research. Peter received a B.A. in psychology from LaSalle College, an M.A. in college student personnel from The Ohio State University, and a Ph.D. in higher education administration from Indiana University.

CARRIE MILLER

Carrie Miller is a doctoral student at the University of California, Los Angeles where she is studying higher education and organizational change. Previously, she worked in residential life at Ohio Wesleyan University and student activities at Dean College. Her M.S. in college student development and counseling is from Northeastern University, and her B.A. in political science is from the University of Maryland, Baltimore County.

SARAH O'CONNELL

Sarah O'Connell is an education abroad advisor at Wright State University. Before graduating from Miami University's Student Affairs in Higher Education program. Before beginning her graduate studies, Sarah worked at the Greater Cincinnati World Affairs Council, a non-profit organization focused on international education and citizen diplomacy. She received her bachelor's degree from Kent State University in international relations.

MOLLY PIERSON

Molly Pierson has served as a Residential College Director at Washington University in St. Louis since 2010 and was recently promoted to Assistant Director for Off Campus Students. She previously worked at St. Louis University as the Honors Program Coordinator. She earned her M.A. in college student personnel from Bowling Green State University in 2009 and a B.A. in biology from Washburn University in Topeka, Kansas.

KEVIN PISKADLO

Kevin Piskadlo is currently the Assistant Dean of Academic Services and Advising at Stonehill College in Massachusetts. Before assuming his current position, Kevin spent nine years at Bentley University serving as the Assistant Dean of Academic Services and Director of the Undergraduate Academic Advising Center after starting his career in advising at the University of Notre Dame. In addition to teaching in the Higher Education in Student Affairs program at Salem State University, Kevin is currently working on his dissertation in higher education at the University of Massachusetts, Boston. He has an M.S. in college student personnel and a B.A. in politics.

KIMBERLY RUTLEDGE

Kimberly Rutledge is the Learning Center Director at the University of San Francisco (USF) where she has worked for over four years. After earning a master's degree in college student personnel, Kimberly accepted a position with USF as Program Coordinator Assistant for all of Academic Support Services. Before beginning her graduate studies, Kimberly worked as Coordinator with the college access program GearUp in Cincinnati, Ohio.

KATIE SHOEMAKER

Katie Shoemaker began work as First-Year Adviser at Miami University in July 2011. She previously worked at Capital University as a Residence Hall Coordinator. She earned her M.A. in higher education and student affairs from The Ohio State University and her B.A. in English from Wittenberg University.

WILL SIMPKINS

Will Simpkins is the Director of the Center for Career and Professional Development at John Jay College of Criminal Justice, a college of the City University of New York. He oversees a comprehensive program of career services to almost 15,000 undergraduate and graduate students plus alumni/ae throughout the country. Before coming to John Jay, Will served in a variety of roles in student activities, LGBT student services, service-learning, and career services at Barnard College. Will received his M.Ed. in counseling and personnel services from the University of Maryland, College Park in 2001 and a B.A. from Virginia Tech in English in 1999.

DUJUAN SMITH

DuJuan Smith is the Assistant Dean of Students at the University of Houston. He oversees the student conduct system for 40,000 students. He will be serving as Assistant Dean of Students for the 50th Anniversary spring 2014 voyage of Semester at Sea. Previously, he served as the Coordinator of Judicial Affairs at Moraine Valley Community College in Palos Hill, Illinois. He completed his

B.A. in applied sociology with a minor in Black studies and M.S.Ed. in clinical mental health counseling at Northern Illinois University in DeKalb, Illinois.

DAVID STANFIELD

David Stanfield is a Research Assistant at the Center for International Higher Education and doctoral student in the higher education administration program at Boston College. His research interests include cross-border higher education in the Middle East, North Africa, and East Asia and international student affairs. Previously, David served as the Director of Student Activities and First-Year Programs at Carnegie Mellon's branch campus in Doha, Qatar. David received an M.S. in college student personnel from Miami University and a B.A. in marketing from Texas A&M University.

SARAH STEWARD

Sarah Steward serves as the Career and Community Engagement Coordinator at Naropa University in Boulder, Colorado. She also teaches two career development courses and one internship course. These positions have been Sarah's job one(s) since earning a college student personnel degree in 2008. Prior to her graduate studies, Sarah worked for a year as the interim Internship Coordinator at Luther College where she also completed her B.A. in sociology and management.

SHILOH VENABLE

Shiloh Venable is the Assistant Director in the Leadership Center and Student Activities & Organizations at the University of Texas at Arlington. Prior to relocating, she served as the Assistant Director of the Community Service Office at Washington University in St. Louis for three years. Shiloh received her M.S. in student affairs administration in higher education from Texas A&M University in 2010. Prior to her student affairs career, Shiloh worked in human resources and received her B.S. in human resource development from Texas A&M University in 2005.

CRAIG WOODSMALL

Craig Woodsmall served in the positions of Coordinator for Outreach, Staff Psychologist, and Coordinator of Training for the Student Health Service at Washington University in St. Louis from 2000 to 2011. He graduated from William Jewell College with B.A. degrees in psychology and communication, received his M.A. in counseling and guidance from the University of Missouri at Kansas City, and completed his Psy.D. in clinical psychology from the Illinois School of Professional Psychology–Chicago. He currently works as Psychologist Reviewer at OptumHealth, a leading managed care company and serves as an adjunct faculty member at Washington University in St. Louis, Southern Illinois University Edwardsville, and McKendree University.

JEN-CHIEN YU

Jen-chien Yu is the Coordinator for Library Assessment at the University of Illinois at Urbana-Champaign. Previously she was the Electronic Information Services Librarian/Data Specialist (2001-2012) at Miami University. She received her MLIS from the University of Pittsburgh and B.A. in educational media and library science from the Tamkang University in Taiwan.